THROUGH IT ALL, HE WAS THERE

By
Sharon Libby

AN INSPIRATIONAL STORY OF FAITH

xulon PRESS

THROUGH IT ALL, HE WAS THERE
by Sharon Libby

Printed in the United States of America

ISBN 9781615792986

www.xulonpress.com

Foremost, I dedicate my book to my Lord and Savior,
Jesus Christ. Without Him, I would have never survived the
many challenges I have had to face throughout my life.

Secondly, I dedicate my book to Rick, my husband.
Rick showed me the true
meaning of unconditional love.

To my sons, David and Neil,
without whom, my life would not be complete.

ACKNOWLEDGEMENTS

I want to thank my husband, Rick, for his tireless support and encouragement during the writing of my book. Rick has been with me through every tear, heartache, and joy that I have gone through over the past 39 years. He is my gift from God.

I want to thank my two sons, David and Neil. They have taught me so much. Their love has sustained me through the good and the bad times. I cannot imagine my life without them. To the rest of my family, I say thank you for your encouragement to keep pushing me forward.

Bless you, Marie Chapian, Ph.D., for your inspiratioin in fulfilling my dream.

I give humble praise to Pastor Orval C. Butcher for his willingness to read and comment on my story and for his wonderful ministry to his "flock" at Skyline Wesleyan Church in Lemon Grove, California. Pastor Butcher has been a great source of support for me during the valleys that I have gone through. After leaving Skyline Wesleyan Church, Pastor Butcher and his wife ministered together at a retreat run by Wycliffe Bible Translators in Idyllwild, California for ministers and missionaries. Pastor Butcher still continues his ministry of compassion and caring through correspondence and e-mail to those in ministry or missions and others in need through his organization under Orval Butcher Ministries in Lemon Grove, California. He is now 91 years young. We still correspond by e-mail and talk on the phone. He also is my prayer partner. Pastor Butcher continues to give me great comfort when my heart is heavy.

A special thank you to Charlie and Sandy Chandler, leaders of my Young at Heart Life Group at Central United Protestant Church in Richland, Washington. Their prayers, their love, their compassion, and their encouragement have helped me bring my book to its fulfillment.

To my friend, Linda Neu, who spent countless hours editing my book: "Friends are kisses, blown to us from angels."

CONTENTS

FORWARD

"THROUGH IT ALL, HE WAS THERE"

"It is my conviction that this book should be read by everyone to help them understand the emotional testing of a person who experiences the trauma of being stricken with a disability as a child. Imagine the FRIGHT of a six-year-old paralyzed and unable to walk due to polio... the indescribable value of FAMILY, parents and grandparents, unfailing support... then a lonely 15-year-old with FAULTY discernment in making marriage decisions... at that time FAVORED with two precious boys... then experienced the sense of absolute FRUSTRATION when neglected by the church and Christian friends... but had constant hope of FAITH in the Word of God... then divine FULFILLMENT of marital happiness. The reading of this book will give you a new focus on the power and enabling of our Lord."

Dr. Orval C. Butcher,
Founding minister Skyline Wesleyan Church, Lemon Grove, CA

PREFACE

Have you ever faced adversity? Have you ever wondered if you would survive the various challenges that came your way? Have you ever wondered if the Lord was there? If you answered yes to any of these questions, then this is the book for you.

I invite you to witness the power of God's Holy Spirit as He took me out of despair repeatedly. After many years of searching for answers, I can attest that Jesus Christ was with me through every challenge that I faced as a handicapped woman living in an able-bodied world. Disabled or handicapped are words that have defined me since the age of six, when I contracted polio. As far as society is concerned, I am not normal; I am different. Many times, I tried to fit in; many times, I did not. I tried to take care of my own problems instead of giving them to the Lord. There were times I turned away from God's Spirit and made some poor choices. Sometimes I had wondered if there was a God when I went through some deep valleys, not knowing if I would ever be back on that mountaintop again. For years, my faith was tested.

One day I felt God tugging at my heart, encouraging me to tell my story. I had no idea why, except to tell others that when you go through challenges you can come out on the other side a much stronger person. Through every challenge, there is a reason why things happen. We do not always understand the "whys and how comes," so we endure what is transpiring and do the best we can on any given day. At times, we fall down, pick ourselves up, and hope we do not make the same mistakes again. During these times, if we have a strong belief system in the Holy Trinity, we grab onto God and hang on for dear life, face the challenges, and pray that we will eventually see the light at the end of the tunnel. On the other hand, if we turn away from Him and try to fix our own problems, we will make poor choices. Because of those choices, we can suffer guilt and go into a deep valley of despair.

As you take this journey with me, I pray if you are disabled, you will find help in dealing with your disability. On the other hand, if you are not disabled, you might better understand and appreciate what difficulties disabled persons face every day. While writing this book, there were days when tears streamed down my face one minute and I laughed aloud the next. The more I wrote, the more I saw and felt God's presence, His compassion, and His unfailing love. God used this writing as an instrument to heal me. Through each circumstance, the Triune God was molding me into what He wanted me to be. I am still a work in progress. I continue to believe that THROUGH IT ALL, HE WAS THERE, and He always will be.

And so, my story begins...

By Sharon Libby

1

A LIFE CHANGING EXPERIENCE

It was one of those hot, humid mornings in September of 1949. I was lying in bed looking around my bedroom that Mother and Daddy had just finished decorating. Beautiful wallpaper covered the walls with women's fluffy powder puffs, lipstick, rouge, and eyelashes all over it. For some reason my room felt very stuffy this morning. Maybe it was the weather. We were used to muggy days in the summer and early fall in New Jersey. My Sunday school teacher often said how wonderful it was that God made the four seasons. "Fine," I thought, "but why did God have to make some months this hot and sticky?" When I heard my parents' alarm go off, my daydreaming stopped.

Within minutes, Mother was next to my bed, leaning over me, and instructing me to get up. Then she went into my brother's room to wake him up too. Neil, my twin brother and I were only six years old, almost seven. It was Sunday morning and our usual "plan of attack" would begin. Daddy would go downstairs and prepare breakfast while Mother helped Neil and me get dressed and make our beds. My parents showed their love towards us in everything they did.

After we had finished upstairs, we raced down to the kitchen to spend time with Daddy. We did not get to see him much during the week; Daddy had to work ten-hour days, six days a week because of the war. The aroma in the kitchen was heavenly. The bacon was cooking and Daddy was tossing pancakes up in the air to entertain us. It was fun watching him cook. While we were eating, we talked about our plans for the day. After church, we would visit my grandparents. Daddy's parents, Grandma and Grandpa, lived in Clifton, New Jersey in the same town where we lived. Mother's parents, Nana and Granddad, lived nearby in Garfield.

After breakfast, we put on our hats, grabbed our Bibles, and went off to church. When we arrived, Reverend Ammerman greeted us with a big smile and friendly handshake. As soon as we entered the church, I started running down the aisle. Mother quickly caught up with me, grabbed my arm, and stated very sternly, "You are not to run in church young lady! One of these days I'm going to tie your legs together so you can't run!" I always got into more trouble than my brother did. I loved going to church. I hoped that one day I would be able to sing in the choir just like Daddy.

When we left church, we headed to Grandma and Grandpa's house. We stayed there for a while before going over to Nana and Granddad's for dinner. My parents always reminded Neil and me how important family was. We had many aunts, uncles, nieces, and nephews all living in New Jersey. Daddy had four brothers, but Mother was an only child. Nana had five siblings; Granddad had 16! Grandma had five siblings; Grandpa had three.

While we were visiting at Nana and Granddad's, I started getting a headache and felt hot. I told Mother I was not feeling well, so we left right after dinner, earlier than we usually would leave. When we arrived home, Mother took my temperature immediately. Sure enough, I was running a fever. Mother helped me get ready for bed, tucked me in, and gave me an aspirin.

In the middle of the night, I had to go to the bathroom and started to get out of bed. I took a few steps and fell, crashing to the floor. In my panic, I screamed for my parents. Mother came rushing into my room to find out what was wrong. "I don't know. I can't walk! I have to go to the bathroom." I cried out, "Please help me!" Mother could hear the terror in my voice.

Soon Daddy and Neil were in my room wondering what was going on. Daddy picked me up and carried me to the bathroom, but nothing happened. I was burning up with fever and in a lot of pain. Mother stayed with me while Daddy called the doctor. He told Daddy to take me to Bergen Pines Hospital. Daddy questioned him because we did not live in the right district, but the doctor said it was closer and time was of the essence. Mother called Nana and Granddad to tell them what was going on and asked them to come over and stay with Neil while we were gone. As soon as Nana and Granddad arrived, we left.

Mother and Daddy went with me to the examining room to meet with our doctor. I was scared to death! My stomach was huge, and I still could not urinate. Soon there were five doctors examining me from head to toe, and then a specialist came in the room. He took one look at my stomach and yelled, "Catheterize that girl immediately!" I was in so much pain while many hands probed my small body trying to figure out what was wrong. After many hours of tests, my doctor came back and told my parents that he was sure I had contracted polio. Poliomyelitis, a more technical term, is a viral disease that can affect nerves and lead to paralysis. Polio destroys the spinal cord's motor nerve cells. It was highly probable that I would never walk again. I had all the symptoms: fever, headache, stiff neck and back, and muscle pain and tenderness. The doctor left the catheter in because the involuntary muscles were still not working and I could not move my legs.

In 1949, there was no Salk vaccine. For many years, each person that had contracted polio suffered a different prognosis, so the doctors had to treat each patient differently. "Polio is an acute viral infection, also known as Infantile Paralysis. Mostly children were affected. The virus entered the body by mouth and then went to the blood stream. In some cases, the virus was carried to the gray matter of the spinal cord and brain. Approximately 25% of all those affected had severe permanent disability; 25% had mild disabilities and 50% recovered fully." [1] Polio affected my lower back and both legs. Much later, I found out how I had contracted polio. I had taken gum out of my girlfriend Sandy's mouth and chewed it.

The following day, the doctor sat my parents down, and said, "I am pleased to tell you we removed Sharon's catheter. This means that all her internal plumbing is working. I am very encouraged. Sharon's muscles are not working right now, but there is a good chance that some movement in her legs will come back. The paralysis could be temporary or permanent. We're just not sure at this time."

"This is hard to comprehend," Mother said, expressing shock and disbelief.

"Helene, I know this is a lot for you and Bill to take in, but I must be honest with you. It could be worse. At least Sharon has feeling in her entire body, which is different from a spinal cord injury. However, I am sorry to say that there is a good chance that she will never be able to walk again without the aid of crutches. The hardest thing is that she will never have what we refer to as a normal life again."

"Oh Bill, this can't be happening to our little girl," Mother said, crying hysterically, as she collapsed into Daddy's arms. Daddy tried to console her, but it was useless.

Mother and Daddy were in a state of panic that dreadful day. Rightfully so, as polio was a word that made people panic because death was often associated with it. The sudden presence of polio can be very frightening and confusing to those affected and their families as well. "In the first polio epidemic in 1916, the figures were almost inconceivable; out of 28,767 cases there were 6,000 deaths. In New York City alone 2,407 people died. In 1949, there were 42,033 cases of polio reported. Epidemics dominated the news and newspapers and radio stations reported daily polio totals as they did baseball scores." [2] "This 'polio panic' went on for many, many years on into the future. Even as late as 1954 when Dr. Howard Rusk in the NEW YORK TIMES found polio's story, "one of the most feared of diseases...capricious, unpredictable," and a SATURDAY EVENING POST article read, "Polio - a word that strikes more terror in the hearts of parents than the atom bomb." [3]

To see their little girl, who was so active, lying motionless in a hospital bed was almost more than my parents could bear. They were afraid that I might die because every day children were dying all around me in the hospital. I had a small problem with my breathing, but was fortunate not to have to go into an iron lung. Many patients that used an iron lung still died.

Being only six years old, I did not fully comprehend what was happening to me. Maybe, in that sense, it was a blessing. Mother and Daddy contacted Reverend Ammerman to ask the church to pray for me. I was highly contagious and could not have visitors, except my parents. When they came to visit me, they had to wear hospital gowns, booties, facemasks, and gloves.

The question that haunted my parents the most was what would my future hold. The doctor told them I would have to learn to accept my disability and make the necessary adjustments. This, of course, would not happen overnight and could take years.

A few days later, the doctor sat my parents down and said, "As the months and years go by there will be barriers regarding Sharon's disability that will hurt her both physically and emotionally depending on how she handles each problem. You must be careful not to suffocate her or be too protective. Parents can either help or hinder their child as he or she grows up with a permanent disability." He went onto say, "You have to be careful how you perceive your daughter now that she can't walk. The message you convey to her daily will be very important during her growing up years. This is going to be a challenge for both of you and your entire family. It will also be a challenge for Sharon; and, be ever so mindful that you have another child in the mix that is not disabled. You will be playing a balancing act trying to keep your family running smoothly." With those words, the doctor wished Mother and Daddy the best and left the room.

Over the next few weeks, I experienced a lot of pain and discomfort in my legs because the muscles would tighten. The only way to relax them was to go in whirlpool hot tubs. These hot tubs were set at 105 degrees Fahrenheit. When they lowered me into the water, I would scream because my legs were so sensitive. I was not the only one crying. You could hear children throughout the hospital crying because of this water therapy and the pulling of tender muscles during hours of physical therapy.

I was going to be celebrating my seventh birthday soon. Mrs. Iozzio, my nurse, and I were working diligently so that I could sit up unassisted in my wheelchair. It was hard to keep trying and getting such slow results. Mrs. Iozzio always encouraged me and kept repeating the words, "You must keep trying! Look how far you have come. You must never give up!" Being so young, I did not realize how profound those words would be now and in the future.

When my parents came to visit, they looked tired. With Daddy having to work such long hours and be there for my mother and brother, I often wondered where he got his strength. Mother looked drained. She was the most beautiful mother in the world, not just for all the motherly things she did, but because she had been a John Power's model in New York City prior to marrying Daddy. Running back and forth to the hospital, she was losing a lot of weight. She looked terribly thin because she was 5'8" tall and only weighed 97. I felt it was my fault for everything that was happening. I was the one who took the gum out of my friend's mouth and got polio. I was the one that was causing my parents to be tired because of their daily trips to the hospital. I did not know how to cope. Many nights I cried myself to sleep.

My brother was getting the brunt of things too because our parents were spending so much time with me at the hospital. Neil spent a lot of time at Nana and Granddad's house after school and on weekends. Every year we had a big family birthday party for the two of us. This year we would have to celebrate our seventh birthday apart.

On October 18, 1949, all my hard work paid off. As we anxiously awaited my parents' arrival, Mrs. Iozzio fixed my hair and dressed me in a pink hospital gown. When she heard that my parents were in the hospital, she quickly, but gently placed me into my wheelchair. As my parents entered the room, I was sitting up, unaided by my nurse. They were amazed, shocked, and thrilled all at the same time! Tears filled their eyes. They ran over to me, put their arms around me, and kissed me. "I told you I would be all right!" I said, trying to reassure them. My parents looked at me and then at each other. I had this feeling that they were not telling me something. There was no way I dared question them on this special day. I did not understand why they seemed both happy and sad at the same time. Maybe it was because my brother could not be with us. After the initial excitement, we celebrated my birthday. Mother and Daddy brought in a big sheet cake to share with the staff and the other children. Considering the atmosphere, we had a good time.

Later that evening, after my parents left, I wondered why my parents seemed different. They seemed happy that I was able to sit up by myself, but there were glances between them that I did not understand. This happened quite a bit. When it did, I started asking myself questions. Did I do something to hurt them? Did I do something wrong? Were my parents keeping something from me? I started to cry. All of a sudden, I felt a hand on my shoulder. It was Mrs. Iozzio. I grabbed her around the neck and hugged her as tightly as I could while sharing my thoughts with her.

She tried to reassure me by saying, "Go to sleep, my dear. Everything will be okay. You must put those troubled thoughts to rest."

"I will," I said, "and please don't tell Mother and Daddy I was crying. I want them to think that I am a big girl. Okay?"

Mrs. Iozzio nodded, turned out the light, and left my room.

A few days after my birthday, the hospital administrator told my parents I would have to move to another hospital about 100 miles farther away. They knew this day would come eventually because Bergen Pines was out of our district. Because I was already a patient, they were hoping I could stay until I was able to go home. Mother raised her voice at the hospital administrator saying, "Absolutely not! I will take my little girl home before you transfer her that far away." Daddy tried to calm Mother down, but that was impossible.

The administrator told my parents they did not have the proper facilities to care for me at home, but Mother did not care. She pleaded with him to give her and Daddy time to check things out before making a final decision. He agreed to let me stay awhile longer.

Daddy took time off from Curtis-Wright Corporation where he worked, and he and Mother left immediately for New York City to visit the Sister Kenny Foundation. While there, they learned all about the Sister Kenny Method of treatment that was in practice at some hospitals and how they could incorporate this method into their home environment. In the book, SISTER KENNY — THE WOMAN WHO CHALLENGED THE DOCTORS, Sister Kenny spoke of times when she visited hospitals and saw children "lying stiff and rigid, crying with pain, even though - as she saw - they were not necessarily paralyzed."[4] Sister Kenny was a mighty woman because she had the determination to "fight city hall." It was because of her determination and belief in the "hot pack" method of therapy that many children were free from excessive amounts of pain. In the same book she states, "Maybe moist heat was the answer. There was a blanket on the bed - a heavy one of soft Australian wool and, almost in desperation, I seized it and tore it into strips of wool in a basin and poured boiling water over them and wrung every drop of water out. Gently I wrapped the hot, damp cloth around the tortured limbs and in a matter of moments the child stopped whimpering."[5]

My parents learned the Sister Kenny Method of Rehabilitation consisted of whirlpool hot baths of 100 degrees Fahrenheit, followed by hot packs, eight to ten times per day, weight exercises, treadle sewing machine exercises, walking up stationary steps, hot lamps for circulation, riding an exercise bike and plenty of water therapy in a heated pool. They collected all the information they could and headed home. They knew there was a lot of work to do. Time was of the essence.

After returning home, Daddy showed a diagram to Granddad to get his input on changing our basement into an exercise room. Daddy asked Granddad if he could take time off work to help him. "I hate to ask you for help all the time, but my parents aren't well. There is no way they can do physical labor," he explained.

"No need to bother them. I can take time off work and we can get your basement done in no time at all. The sooner we get started, the sooner Sharon can come home. That will be a glorious day!"

"You can say that again. I am deeply concerned about Helene. She is wearing herself out running to the hospital every day."

"Well then, let's plan on starting Monday," Granddad said.

"That sounds great. Words can't express how grateful I am for all your help," Daddy said.

"No need for thanks, Bill. That is what families do. They help each other. I'll see you Monday, if not before."

A few days later, Daddy and Granddad went to work. First, they emptied the basement and paneled all the walls with knotty pine wood. Next, they refinished the cement floor, and Daddy built stationary steps for me to walk up and down. The biggest job was installing an indoor swimming pool with removable handrails. By using the handrails, I could learn to walk in the water. When the handrails were removed, I had room to swim and do water therapy. These two men worked day and night to get everything ready, so I could come home.

My parents were going to need help when they brought me home, so they contacted the March of Dimes. The secretary did some research and said that Mrs. Iozzio could remain my private duty nurse at home for a while to help train my parents. In addition, they would provide a special nurse to help with my physical therapy three times a week for one year. This therapy was vitally important because the counselors at the Sister Kenny Foundation told my parents that the muscles were constantly going to be pulling against each other, and this would be very painful. To keep my muscles limber, my mother would have to stretch and work my muscles on a daily basis. This was going to take a lot of hard work, but she was willing to do whatever it took to help me walk again.

After what seemed an eternity, the day came for me to go home. Mrs. Iozzio helped me get dressed and packed my suitcase. Leaving the confines of the hospital was a little frightening. There were so many questions that I asked Mrs. Iozzio while we were getting ready to leave. "How am I going to manage at home? Our home has two stories, plus a basement. How am I going to get upstairs to my bedroom? How am I going to get downstairs to the basement to do my exercises? Winter is coming. How will I be able to go outside in the snow?"

Mrs. Iozzio responded by saying, "You're way too young to be worrying so much. Things will work out. Do not forget, there will be plenty of people around to help you any way they can."

I had to clear my mind of these thoughts and enjoy the day.

When Mother and Daddy arrived at the hospital, I was so excited. In a short time, I would see the rest of my family and friends. This meant a lot to a seven year old who was not able to have any visitors in the hospital. It was hard to say good-bye to everyone, but the joy of going home was much more overpowering.

When Daddy pulled the car into our driveway, I started to cry. I realized I was finally home! I was so happy! Family, friends, and neighbors were all out in front to welcome me home. My brother was the first one to greet me. I was so glad to see him. He had this happy grin on his face and gave me a big hug. It was good to see everyone again and finally be home. Reverend Ammerman was also there. "It sure is good seeing you again, Sharon," he said, "I, along with your entire church family, have been praying for you to come home, and here you are. Once this celebration is over you will have a lot of work ahead of you so you can walk again. Just remember not to give your parents a hard time."

"I'll do my best," I told him. "Now can we go inside?"

Everyone started laughing as we all went inside to enjoy my homecoming. Nana and Granddad set up a large table with food, drinks, and a large sheet cake for everyone to enjoy. I was not interested in eating; I wanted to see my exercise room that Daddy and Granddad worked so hard on. More than that, I wanted to see the pool. With Mother by his side, Daddy picked me up out of my wheelchair and ever so gently carried me downstairs. Family and friends followed behind us because they wanted to see too. I could not believe my eyes! There was so much love expressed in that room. Everything was beautiful! I could smell the aroma of fresh wood. Nana had crocheted "Dolls of the World" and they were sitting on small ledges all around the room. There were exercise mats on the floor, stationary steps for me to learn to walk up and down with my crutches, and a pool. Everything that my family did to our basement made it a show place for everyone to admire.

"Can I go swimming now?" I pleaded.

"Not so fast, my dear," Mother said, chuckling. "This is a day off for everybody. First, we will get you and Mrs. Iozzio settled. There will be plenty of time to start your exercise routine tomorrow. We have waited a long time for you to come home. Today we're all going to relax and celebrate." I nodded with a big smile.

A few hours after we ate, I felt sleepy. It was a long, tiring day visiting with friends and family. Daddy carried me up the long flight of stairs to my bedroom and placed me in bed, gave me a hug, and kissed me gently on the cheek. "It sure is good having you home," he said, holding me tenderly. A few minutes later, Mother and Mrs. Iozzio came in my room to help me get ready for bed. The only pain I felt that day was when Mrs. Iozzio placed me on my back and tied my feet to a board in order to keep my legs straight so that the muscles would not tighten while I was sleeping. This was quite painful and very uncomfortable because I had to sleep on my back all night.

Mother knew I was hurting because I started to cry. She immediately sat down beside me and held me in her arms, and said, "I know this hurts, but it must be done. Please try not to cry. Everything will be okay. It sure is good having you home."

"I am so glad to be home," I said, as she wiped my tears away, and we kissed each other goodnight.

I could not believe I was sleeping in my own bed again. My life outside the hospital, as a handicapped person, was just starting. To be in my own room again made me smile as I looked around and saw the makeup on the wallpaper. To hear familiar sounds of laughter coming from my home was reassuring. I felt I had come a long way from the sounds of children screaming and crying with pain and the terrible smells in the hospital. I was feeling very fortunate. I thought to myself how lucky I was to have such a loving family. I closed my eyes and fell asleep with a sense of peace that I had not felt in a long time.

2

ANOTHER STEP FURTHER

Reality was about to set in as Mother and I started exercising eight hours a day; day after day. Mrs. Iozzio worked with the two of us for a few weeks and then she had to leave. We were sad to see her go, but other patients needed her more. Once Mrs. Iozzio left, Nana came over every day to help Mother with housework, so she could spend her days with me doing physical therapy. I was mostly around Mother and Nana because Daddy and Granddad were at work and my brother was in school for most of the day.

Next, the March of Dimes sent over Miss Jones, a physical therapist. She started coming three days a week to help Mother and check my progress. My parents were thankful to the March of Dimes for the help they provided.

My parents were hoping that I could attend regular school with my brother, but the State of New Jersey would not allow me to because of my disability. Instead, they provided me with a tutor, Miss VondenDeale. She tutored me at home two hours a day, so I could continue my studies. It was a welcome change. I enjoyed learning. It also gave me time to think about something besides exercising. Even with my tutoring, I still spent eight hours a day in the basement exercising. The only part of my exercises that I really enjoyed was swimming. Mother and Daddy used to call me their "little mermaid" because I loved being in the water and I hated to get out. At times, I was angry with Mother, as this daily ritual was getting very old to a seven year old who wanted to play and have fun. Mother said all that would have to wait. I did not like it, but she was the boss.

According to my mother, being around adults so much made me more mature for my age. The only friends I had were the friends that my brother brought home. I do not know what I would have done without his friends because I could not make friends of my own anymore.

One late afternoon, while I was exercising with Mother, I started thinking about my girlfriend, Sandy.

"Why doesn't Sandy come over to visit me?"

Mother got this troubled look on her face, paused for a moment, and said, "I wondered when you would ask me about her."

"Why? Is something wrong? Is she all right?"

Mother came closer to me, put her arm around my shoulder, and said, "Sandy went to be with God in heaven. When she got polio, it hit her harder than it did you."

I started crying; the tears would not stop. I knew it had been awhile since I had seen Sandy, but I never dreamed anything happened to her.

With tears still streaming down my cheeks, I asked, "Why didn't God take me to heaven? I had polio too. It's not fair!" I was gasping for breath because I was crying so hard. Mother tried to comfort me, but the tears would not stop.

"Sharon, there are going to be many things that happen in your life and in ours that are not fair. We have to learn to accept whatever life dishes out, take one day at a time, and do the best we can on any given day. For whatever reason, God wasn't ready for you to be with Him yet."

We sat there for the longest time with my head resting in her lap. Mother just sat there stroking my back.

"We'd better get done with these exercises. Better yet, why don't we stop and we can get back at it tomorrow," Mother said.

"Don't I have to exercise after dinner?" I asked her.

"No. You have had quite a shock hearing about Sandy and need time to relax." Mother had this instinct about knowing what I needed and she knew losing Sandy was hard on me.

"That's fine. I feel tired. I'll see Sandy again in heaven, right?" I asked.

"Yes, Sharon, you will see Sandy again and you won't have any more pain or suffering in heaven either. God made that promise to all of us."

After months of physical therapy, I finally was able to give up my wheelchair, advance to a walker, and start using crutches once in awhile. Mother decided that we could now take Sundays off from our exercise routine, except for my water therapy and stretching my leg muscles. Mother continued working my muscles by massaging them with cocoa butter three times a day. Many polio victims have very thin legs. Mother was hoping that this would not happen to me. My physical therapist was pleased with my progress and told Mother that my legs appeared normal in size. When we went out in public, people could not tell I had polio. I looked normal until I stood up. The curvature in my spine, known as scoliosis, made my butt stick out. The doctor told my parents I was too young to have surgery to straighten my spine.

As a child, I felt guilty for contracting polio because it put such a strain on my entire family. Mother still looked thin. On some days, you could cut the tension between us with a knife; on other days, we were the best of friends. Once my physical therapist left, Nana and Granddad put their house up for sale and moved in with us to help lighten the load on my mother. They were concerned for her well-being. Daddy also seemed overworked. Building my exercise room cost a lot of money and put a financial strain on the family. My daddy's parents still could not help due to their physical problems that seemed to get worse. I never understood all that was wrong with them, but they were never as active as Nana and Granddad.

One night while lying in bed, I could hear Mother crying in the next room. My ears perked up.

"Bill, what did we do to deserve this? Why did Sharon get polio? Is God punishing us?" Mother asked Daddy.

"We did nothing, and God is not punishing us! We have to learn to deal with the problem and do the best we can."

Daddy tried to console Mother. He gave her so much strength, but that night I felt guilty and started crying. Everyone made so many sacrifices for me. I was making people hurt and I did not know what to do.

Mother continued talking to Daddy. "Remember that Sunday morning, prior to Sharon getting polio, when she was running in the church and I grabbed her and told her I was going to tie her legs together if she didn't stop running?"

"Yes," Daddy replied. "Do you really think just because you said that she got polio?" Daddy asked, his emotions rising to the surface.

"Not really, but I feel guilty for saying those words," she said, continuing to cry even louder.

"I can only imagine how you feel, Helene, but you can't start thinking about that now. That is in the past. We have to accept the fact that our little girl will never walk again without the aid of her crutches," Daddy told her.

"No!" Mother yelled. "She will walk again! She has to!"

"This cannot go on. You are going to drive a wedge between you and Sharon that you will never be able to repair. Be thankful that our little girl didn't die like so many others," Daddy said, trying to comfort her.

"I don't know what to do, Bill. I definitely do not want to go to church anymore. If there were a God, He would not have allowed this to happen to our little girl," Mother said, raising her voice.

"Helene, what can I do to help you? I know you are hurting. I am as well, but we have to accept what has happened and trust God that everything will work out. It is not God's fault!" With those words, the house went silent.

As I lay there, I felt terrible because my parents were fighting over me. Mother knew in her heart that I had to walk again. Fear gripped my soul. I was so confused. I wondered what would happen if I never walked again without the aid of crutches. I made up my mind that I would have to work extra hard so that I would walk one day, or else my parents would stop loving me.

At 8-1/2 years old I started to be able to move the toes in my right foot and had some movement in my right leg. The left leg still did not move. My parents were thrilled with my progress. Mother lightened my exercise routine even more by taking Saturdays off. Now I would have two whole days to enjoy life. The only question that went through my mind was "How would I ever be able to walk if I exercised less? On the other hand, if I did not have to exercise as much, then Mother and I would be able to have more free time. That sounded good to a kid like me."

We started going to church again even though Mother did not really want to. As head of the family, Daddy said that we should go, but we went less often. When we went that first Sunday, people were amazed at the progress I had made. They were impressed with my using crutches called Canadian walking sticks. They came up just below the elbow and were much more comfortable for me than underarm crutches.

One Sunday I actually sang at church. I could not understand why so many people were crying. Later, Mother told me that they were tears of joy for many answered prayers. When so many adults and children were still dying from polio, it was good for the people at church to see the progress I had made.

On the weekends, in the summer, the entire family went to the beach. Daddy would carry me into the ocean and I would swim for hours. I loved the water and was a good swimmer. Nobody understood how I could swim so well, but not be able to walk. I cherished the times we went to the beach with my parents, my brother, and my grandparents. I was getting a lot of exercise swimming in the ocean. Not having to exercise at home was great, especially for a young girl who just wanted to have some fun.

Another one of my favorite things to do occurred in the winter. A few months after our ninth birthday, my brother and I went outside with Mother to ride on our sleds. Mother loaded me onto my sleigh and pulled me all over the snow. We all romped, played, and laughed. It was so much fun to be able to have this special time together.

"Mother, it's good to hear you laugh again," I told her.

"Each day that you improve physically makes me very happy," she said, smiling from ear to ear.

"I really need to ask you a question," I said, sheepishly.

"Sure. What is it?" Mother inquired.

"If I never walk without crutches will you stop loving me?"

"No!" She said. "Why would you ask me such a thing?" She responded.

"I overheard you talking to Daddy a long time ago; and, I felt that if I didn't walk without crutches, you both would stop loving me."

"Don't ever think that! Daddy and I love you and always will whether you use crutches or not. I probably said that when I was feeling very sad. You are the best daughter a mother or father could ever have, and we will love you forever," Mother said, giving me a big hug and kiss.

It felt so good to be close with Mother. These times I shared with my brother were great too. Playing in the snow with him and his friends was so much fun. I wished Daddy could have been with us more, but he had to work. At least now, he had Saturdays off, which allowed us those weekend jaunts to the beach in the summer. Everyone seemed more relaxed. I was hoping that things would keep getting better. Being so young, I could not understand all the answers to the questions that kept running through my mind. As I got older, maybe I would.

Granddad decided to retire from the Garfield Police Department after 25 years. This allowed him to be at home more to help Daddy around the house and help Mother with my exercises. He always loved to give me hot pack treatments and rub my legs with cocoa butter. His hands were rougher than Mother's were, but I did not dare complain. Mother now had time to relax and spend more time with Nana and my brother. Having three generations in one house was a godsend. We had a closeness that would stay with me forever.

My paralysis had improved, but I still had many challenges ahead. I could walk pretty well now using my crutches. Through more physical therapy, I was able to move my right leg even more; but my left leg was not improving. Why one leg was able to move some and the other did not seemed weird. I wondered how I could walk using crutches and not be able to move my left leg when I sat down or was lying in bed. The doctor said that I was using my hip muscles to compensate for the lack of muscle use in my legs.

One night, while the six of us were eating dinner, my parents announced that they decided we should move to California. They had discussed this for quite some time and shared their thoughts with us. They explained that it was a hard decision, but they felt because of the cold winters it made it difficult for me to maneuver outside on my crutches. During this time of the year my circulation was worse and my feet would turn blue. In the summer, my feet swelled. They wanted me to have as much of a normal life as possible and felt living in the East was making it very difficult. This move would also help my brother because he had started suffering from severe allergy attacks. His eyes and nostrils would swell so badly he could hardly see or breathe. My parents felt they had no other choice, but to move.

While still sitting at the dining room table, Mother asked Nana and Granddad if they would consider moving to California. "Bill and I know this is a big decision, but we would be thrilled if you would join us," she said.

Nana quickly replied, "No way are you leaving us behind! We could never stay in New Jersey without you and our grandchildren."

"If you're going, so are we," Granddad added. "You are not moving to California without us! We will all go together!"

"My goodness gracious," Nana said, "that is more than 3,000 miles away! Wait until the family hears this! They're going to think we have lost our minds."

"How do you feel, Neil?" Granddad asked my brother.

"I hate to leave my friends, but I'm sick of being sick. It will be better if you and Nana come too."

"And you, Sharon, how do you feel?" Nana asked me.

"I don't have anything here that I would be leaving, unless you and Granddad decided not to come. If you come, then that is all I need."

After talking for a while, Granddad told Daddy he could use the money they received from the sale of their house for a down payment on a house in California. "Just make sure the house is big enough for all of us," Granddad said, enthusiastically.

"I will. You do not have to worry about that! Thank you so much for your generosity," Daddy replied.

"I agree with Bill. We are very grateful," Mother said. "I don't know what we would have done all these years without you. Ever since the children were born you have always been there for us."

All of us were starting to choke up, when Daddy suddenly said, "Ah gee," which made us all start laughing. Happiness filled the room.

I will forever be indebted to my parents and grandparents for the love that they showed me. It took a lot of love for my father to give up his long-standing job. It took a lot of love for my mother to have the determination to keep me going. Moving to a strange place so far away would be a big adjustment for all of us.

Unknown to everyone, my parents had written a letter to Sacramento, the capital of California, and explained their family's situation. They wanted to move to California, but did not know where to relocate. Sacramento wrote back suggesting the area of Lemon Grove. Mother and Daddy were excited because Lemon Grove was close to San Diego, and they had heard from friends who had vacationed there that it was a nice area.

Within two weeks, Daddy quit his job and left for California to find a job and adequate housing for both of our families. He had his work cut out for him. In a short time, Daddy found a job at Convair and a home in La Mesa, which bordered on the city of Lemon Grove.

Daddy sent for Mother, Neil, and me once the house closed escrow. As agreed, Nana and Granddad stayed behind until our house in New Jersey sold. The next few weeks we spent packing our things, so the moving van could start the long 3,000-mile drive with all of our belongings. Nana and Granddad decided to move in with her sister so their things could go on ahead of them.

When the time came to say our farewells to family and friends, it was sad, but joyous too. I can only imagine how my parents and grandparents felt. They had lived in New Jersey all their lives and had many friends and family there. I told myself not to feel guilty about this move; it was a family decision.

We arrived in California on February 22, 1952. As I exited the plane on my crutches, I wondered where I was or where I came from. I knew Mother, Daddy, my brother Neil, Nana, and Granddad, but I could not remember anyone or anything else! As we left the airport, I remember feeling weird when Mother and Daddy asked me some questions. I realized, at that time, that I could not remember getting polio, being in the hospital or where we lived, or anything about our home in New Jersey. At first, my parents were alarmed, but with all the excitement, they passed it off as a slight memory loss due to all the recent changes. They felt that maybe this was God's way of healing me from all the pain I had endured. Little did I know at the time, that even then, God was watching over me as He blacked out parts of my memory.

This was our new beginning in California. Daddy had found the perfect home for all of us. Our new home was a two-story dwelling built into the side of a hill. We would be living on the upper level, on the same elevation as the street. Nana and Granddad would be living on the lower level. Everybody would have to walk down a long flight of stairs located on the outside of the garage to visit Nana and Granddad. I would get a lot of exercise going up and down those stairs on my crutches to visit them. As soon as Nana and Granddad arrived, we would have three generations living in one house again. I could hardly wait. While waiting for all of our furniture and personal things, Daddy purchased camping equipment for us to use during the interim. It was like camping inside. My brother and I loved it! We had a Coleman stove, cots, sleeping bags, and the like. I never remembered camping before, but this was a blast!

God was looking out for my family and me. There was no doubt about it. God knew, even then, that I was going to go through a lot as a handicapped person living in an able-bodied world. With the love and support of my family, I knew I would be able to face anything. In the Bible, it states, in I Corinthians 13:13, "And now abideth faith, hope, love, these three; but the greatest of these is love." That love was going to be the only thing to get me through what lay ahead in the years to come. God had His arms wrapped around all of us.

3

A NEW BEGINNING

Our new house was the only one on the block. I hated not having neighbors. I felt like we were out in the boondocks. My brother loved to explore the large open fields around our home. Because of using crutches, I could not go exploring with Neil. Mother and Daddy thought it would be too dangerous for me because of the rough and uneven terrain. During my brother's many excursions, he would get a kick out of bringing "critters" home and putting them down my blouse. Neil would laugh while I screamed bloody murder. If there were ever a time for me to get up and walk that would have been it!

I wondered if moving to California was such a good idea after all. "Here I am alone again," I thought. "I have no friends and nothing to do." I could not understand why Daddy had picked this house. Mother seemed to be as lonely as I was. We all missed Nana and Granddad, but Daddy and Neil had other things to keep them busy. We were still waiting for all our things to arrive from New Jersey. Our new house just did not seem like home.

To help pass the time when Daddy and Neil were gone, Mother talked to me for hours about our life in New Jersey and what she referred to as my polio years. She and Daddy were still amazed that my memory had not returned.

"After the movers get here, I'll find the photo album I have from when you were in the hospital and after you came home," Mother said. "I kept all my journals and your progress reports from your various nurses and doctors. One of these days, I'll show you everything I have and maybe you will remember something."

"That should be fun," I replied.

"The next time we go shopping I'll get you a notebook. I think it would do you good to write down your thoughts and feelings too."

After a couple of days, Daddy took us out driving so we could familiarize ourselves with the area. First, we drove around close to our house. Then Daddy drove us to see where he worked. Next, we ventured out to the different beaches in the San Diego area about 30 minutes from our home. The beaches were beautiful. The water was vibrant with colors of blue and green with white caps on the waves as they broke along the shoreline. A little further north was a place called La Jolla Coves that had huge cliffs. People walking along the rocks were looking for something. Later I found out they were looking for crabs. We also noticed people snorkeling. It was starting to turn dusk. The sunset on the water's edge reflected rich shades of red and orange.

"I never saw such a beautiful sunset," Mother said. "It's breathtaking!"

"It sure is pretty, Helene," Daddy said. "Remember, in New Jersey, we never saw this many rocks and cliffs where we used to go to the beach. This will be an adventure for all of us."

"Am I going to be able to swim in the ocean?" I asked.

"Sure, and we can pack a picnic lunch and spend the day. I know you can't remember, Sharon, but Daddy can carry you into the water like he did when we lived back East," Mother explained.

"This is going to be so much fun," I told my parents. Then I asked Neil, "Are you excited about swimming here?"

"I'm like you. I'll be glad when summer gets here," he replied.

"I'm surprised to see so many people in the water," Daddy said. "We would never swim in the ocean in New Jersey during this time of year. The water was way too cold."

"When will we be able to go swimming?" I asked.

"We have to get settled in our home first," Daddy replied.

"Don't worry. We will be down here plenty," Mother said. "Just have patience. Remember, all good things come to those who wait."

"Are you really going to be able to get me into the water, Daddy?" I asked.

"Yes, Sharon," Daddy said, trying to reassure me. "You worry too much. We can also try our hand at snorkeling. How does that sound?"

"Me too?" Neil asked, making sure he was included too.

"For sure," Daddy answered.

"I can't wait!" I said, with excitement and anticipation in my voice.

Checking out those beaches made my day. To anticipate family fun times at the beach would be wonderful. When Nana and Granddad arrive, they will be able to go with us too.

On the way back home, Daddy stopped at a school and said, "Here is La Mesa Elementary School. This is where you and Neil will start school tomorrow."

"You mean I'll be able to go to a regular school?" I asked.

"Yes," Mother said.

Then Daddy added, "We wanted to surprise you. Mother and I wrote a letter to the La Mesa Spring Valley School District, and they responded by saying they had no objection to you attending school here."

"I can't wait. I'll be able to make friends!" I said, enthusiastically.

"The school district said that you are handicapped physically, not mentally, so they were willing to give it a try," Mother explained.

"I'm really excited," I responded.

"The school is only about one mile from our house. I'll drive you and Neil to school at first; and, of course, pick you up," Mother said. "Maybe later you both can ride the bus."

"I can't wait!" I said again.

"Tomorrow I'll register you and Neil in school."

"Oh boy!" I said, jumping up and down in the back seat of the car.

Neil was looking at me as if I were crazy and said, "What's the big deal?"

"It is a big deal to me," I told him. "Can I call Nana and Granddad when we get home to tell them?" I asked my parents.

"Call them if you want to, but they already know," Mother said. "We told them as soon as we heard the good news when we were still living in New Jersey. We did not say anything to you because we wanted you to be surprised. We know how much you wanted to go to regular school with your brother."

The next day I was so excited about going to school. I put on my best dress. Anxiously I waited for my first day at school to begin. Just before we were ready to leave, the phone rang; it was the moving company. They were due at our house later that afternoon. What a glorious day! I was starting school; and, within a few days, our new house would look like a real home.

On the way to school, Mother told me that this was going to be a new experience for me because I had not attended school since I had contracted polio. I did not care. I was more interested in making friends than anything else.

"Mother, don't worry about Sharon," Neil said. "I'll take care of her."

"You are such a good brother. I am so proud of you," Mother replied.

As we got out of the car, that first day at school, I was in awe to see so many kids walking the hallways as we went to the principal's office to register. I was so nervous; my heart was pounding. Mother told me to calm down and tried to reassure me that everything would be okay. Some of the kids were staring at me. They probably had never been around somebody on crutches before.

The three of us met with the principal in his office. He explained the rules that we had to go by. After filling out the necessary paperwork, he took us to our classrooms so that we could meet our teachers. My teacher, Miss Silvernail, welcomed me and assured my mother that I would be fine before Mother left to take Neil to meet his teacher. Miss

Silvernail introduced me to my classmates, gave them a little history about my disability, and instructed us to open our books. My first day at school was underway.

Attending school on crutches was a challenge and a heart breaker too. It did not take me long to notice that I was the only kid at school with a disability. That was hard because I stuck out like a sore thumb. Some days the kids were nice to me; other days they were very cruel. I could not understand it. At times, I felt so inadequate and did not even want to go to school anymore because I was different from everybody else. That was most apparent during physical education. All the kids would go out on the playground while I would sit on a bench and watch them. Mother told me to "keep a stiff upper lip," but it was hard being reminded daily that I did not quite fit in.

One day when I went to get up from my desk, I could not find my crutches. I always laid them on the floor by my desk. Come to find out, one of the kids had taken them and hid them. I was so upset. I was in tears. Miss Silvernail was furious! The boy that had taken them got into a lot of trouble. After I got home, I told Mother what had happened. She was not pleased.

Another time, when I opened the lid of my desk to get something out, I discovered a snake in my desk. I was scared to death and screamed bloody murder! While trying to get up and away from the snake, I neglected to grab my crutches, and fell to the floor. I was so embarrassed and very angry.

When Mother picked us up from school, she knew right away that something was wrong. I told her what had happened, and I wanted her to do something about it.

"We will talk about it later," Mother said. "Right now I have to get you home and then take Neil to the doctor."

Later that night, after dinner, Mother asked me to tell Daddy about the snake. I started crying and told him what happened.

"Things like that are expected from young children, Sharon. That is what kids do. They think they are funny. I know it is not. It's very cruel, but we can't go to school every time the kids play a joke on you," Daddy explained. "We are not going to get involved in all your problems."

"Does your teacher know about the snake?" Mother inquired.

"Yes, she does, and I think she told the principal. I do not know what is going to happen to the kid who put the snake in my desk. Anyway, Daddy, don't you care?" I asked.

"We do care," Daddy replied, "but you need to find ways to fight your own battles."

Mother walked over to me and gave me a hug, saying, "Daddy is right. We will not always be there when you face these challenges. I might call the school regarding the snake. That was a mean joke to play on anybody, let alone somebody in your condition. We have to trust that the principal can take care of problems like this. If things get worse, I might go back in and talk to him; but, I'm not promising you anything."

Much later, I realized that my parents were right by not getting involved in all my problems at school. Teaching me to fight my own battles did make me a stronger person. My parents lived with the philosophy of love her, limit her, but let her grow up as normal as possible, as long as she does not get hurt.

Sadly, I wondered what thrill it brought to the kids in my school to do such terrible things to me. At times, I hated them. Their teasing and practical jokes were hard to take. My parents said that the kids were just acting their age and I would have to accept it. Okay, I thought, if this is the way this game is played, then I will play using my own rules. I realized that I had an advantage because I had two crutches that could "ward off" my enemies. I did what most normal kids did, but my crutches became my weapons; and, I had two of them! If kids started giving me a bad time, I would threaten to hit them with my crutches; sometimes I did! They got the message loud and clear. The saying "kids can be cruel" was true. I was starting to act just like them.

My brother witnessed first hand some of the things that happened to me during school and became very protective of me. Many times, he would wind up in the principal's office because he hit somebody that hurt his sister. If he saw anyone treating me badly, he would take matters into his own hands. This, needless to say, did not go over very well with the school officials and the teachers or our parents. As far as I was concerned, he was the greatest brother in the world. I felt safe having him around. He was my big protector.

Overall, my time at school did get better and so did my classmates' attitudes toward me. They became more compassionate than I ever thought possible. I was on crutches, yes, but underneath I was just a kid too.

Using crutches was a challenge in a school environment. If it rained, the hallways became slippery and I would fall. This was embarrassing. Holding crutches and carrying my books at the same time was difficult. The heavy books made me feel off balance. I also had to allow extra time to get to the bathroom.

Whenever I discussed problems with Mother, she would remind me how lucky I was to be able to go to school and be with other children. There were polio victims worse off than I was. They could not attend school. I told Mother that I was glad I did not remember what it was like to walk, ride a bike, run or play on the playground.

I asked my parents if I could use a wheelchair at school but they said, "Absolutely not!" I tried to convince them that using a wheelchair would be easier for me than using crutches. I even added that it would help my back too. I knew I was being sneaky by saying that purposely to pull at their heartstrings. Another reason for using a wheelchair was that I did not like my butt sticking out; it made me look weird!

"You've come too far," Mother said. "We spent many hours doing physical therapy to keep you out of a wheelchair. I know you do not remember all the hard work we did. Using a wheelchair would be going backwards. Going into a wheelchair is out of the question! I won't hear of it!"

"Daddy, what do you think?" I asked him.

"I agree with your mother. She knows best. She is the one that spent all those hours with you doing your exercises while I was at work. To give up your crutches and go into a wheelchair would be taking the easy way out."

"You both just don't understand!" I yelled at them.

"You'd better think twice about talking to us like that, Young Lady!" Daddy said, in a stern voice, pointed his finger at me, and gave me a dirty look.

I could tell Daddy meant what he said. I tried to apologize by saying, "I didn't mean to upset you, but even though I like being at school with the kids, there are times when it's really hard to maneuver on crutches. I have seen people in wheelchairs when we go shopping. They can really go fast. Everything looks easier for them compared to me."

"Maybe they can't walk on crutches. Remember, each person with a disability has his own special needs and each has his own way of doing things. For right now, though, our decision is final. Crutches it will be," Mother said, and Daddy agreed.

The more I fought with my parents about this subject, the more resistance I received. Even though I did not agree with them, I had to accept their decision. In the back of my mind, I knew that one day I would have my wheelchair. I did not know how, but I did know it would happen.

Our home in New Jersey finally sold. Nana and Granddad arrived in the middle of June. What an exciting day! They were very tired after the long drive. To have all of us together again was great! They thought Daddy did a great job finding a home for all of us to live in. Nana and Granddad loved their home and felt that this was a new beginning for them as well. Neil and I were out of school for the summer, so we would be able to spend a lot of time with them.

We had so many great times together at the beach and in our local mountains. Because of where we lived, we could drive a half hour west to the beach or a half hour east to the mountains. According to Mother, this was a lot different from the way it was in New Jersey. One thing my parents loved about living in southern California was being able to drive to the snow, and then drive home, leaving the snow behind.

Most weekends in the spring, summer, and early fall, all of us would drive to the beach. Boy, did we have fun together! We liked La Jolla Coves the best. Daddy carried me down a long flight of stairs leading down to the coves and put me on a blanket on the sandy beach while everybody else brought our stuff down for the day. We would swim for hours. Once I got into the water, I did not want to get out. Daddy and I loved to snorkel and catch crabs that were plentiful around the rocks. Like most kids, I loved to play with their pinchers. They were so cute trying to run away from me. Neil loved to dive off the rocks. These memories will stay with me forever.

In the winter, we would drive to the mountains. We brought our sleds, and Mother and Daddy would drag me on my sleigh up the incline and then let me go. I would scream all the way to the bottom. Our family was unique. I wish every family could be as close as ours was.

One morning, I asked Mother why she and Daddy always checked the newspaper to find out how many polio cases were in the paper. She said that they were interested in seeing how the Salk and Sabin vaccines were coming along. In 1952, there were 57,879 cases of polio reported. That figure, was up 10,000 more than those infected in 1949. There were still so many people getting polio that it was very alarming.

My life was busy with family, friends, and school now. The hardest thing for me to handle still was my being on crutches. I wanted so much to be able to do everything that my friends did, but it was impossible. Being handicapped was the only way I knew. The more I was around able-bodied kids, the more I was reminded that there was so much I could not do. I wanted to blend in and not be the oddball. One day I shared some of my feelings with my mother.

"It's hard out there in an able-bodied world when most people you know are walking and you can't do a lot of the same things that they do," I said.

"I realize that," Mother said, "but as the years go by things will get better. You will adjust, but it will take time."

"I don't like having all these feelings that I don't understand."

"Are you still writing in your journal?" Mother inquired.

"Yes, I am. I write about my good days and my not-so-good days. I also write down questions, but I get no answers."

"You might never get answers to all of your questions. Enjoy being a kid and quit trying to figure out every little detail about your life. You act like a little old lady sometimes," she said, laughing.

"I enjoy being a kid, but sometimes it's not easy," I said.

"Honey, I know it's not easy. I know some days are rough, but just give it time and everything will work out," Mother said.

I looked at her, nodded, and said, "Okay."

"Would you now like to look at your polio book and all the stuff I saved? Who knows, it might jog your memory!"

I followed Mother into her bedroom. She brought out a big box. We spent quite awhile going through my polio photo album. She showed me pictures of my nurses, the teacher that tutored me, and my exercise room in the basement. We read doctors and nurse's reports. She even read some pages to me out of her journals. I could tell that reliving this time in my life made her sad.

A few weeks later, Mother saw an article in our local newspaper about different doctors that advertised all types of cures and miracle drugs for post polio victims. Mother was encouraged by what she read because she wanted me to walk so badly without my crutches. Daddy seemed to accept my using crutches better than she did. Mother eventually talked

Daddy into looking into one of these instant cures. I think Daddy did this more to appease her. Daddy used to say, "Keep Mother happy and everybody will be happy." Down deep, I wanted to please my parents and would do anything to achieve that goal.

Because Daddy was working, Mother, Granddad, and I would be driving to see a doctor in Los Angeles, about a two-hour drive north from our home. Nana agreed to watch Neil when he got out of school while we were gone.

On my first visit to see the doctor, I was scared to death! I did not understand why I was so afraid. I never remembered any doctor hurting me, but the fear I felt was very real. The doctor ran all kinds of tests; putting needles in my legs with wires attached to a machine to measure the nerve and muscle responses while I exercised. Then he gave Mother a special "potion" that I had to drink every morning. Every week we would drive to Los Angeles. This went on for months and I hated it! This just reinforced my fear of doctors. The daily drink tasted awful and it was so painful to do exercises weekly with needles sticking in my legs. I wanted to become normal, but this had to stop! I pleaded with Mother and Daddy to stop taking me. On many occasions, I wondered why they did not accept me the way I was. If they could not accept me, how would I ever be able to accept myself?

One evening Mother and Daddy went out and Nana came upstairs to watch Neil and me, while Granddad stayed downstairs. While Neil finished his homework and watched TV, Nana and I had time to talk.

"Nana, why are Mother and Daddy still taking me to Los Angeles? I have been going for so long and there is no improvement. I am still using crutches. I am still not walking and I never will. If they keep taking me to all these doctors what good is it going to do?"

"I don't know, Sharon. I cannot tell them what to do or not to do. Just hang in there and know that they love you very much."

"I think Mother just wants me to walk. She does not love me. She will never love me unless I walk again!" I said, throwing my arms up in the air in disgust.

"Sharon, you think way too much. You have to learn to be happy and when you are home and away from the doctors just let it all go and enjoy being a kid. Everything will be okay. What do you say we play a game?"

"That sounds like fun." I knew that Nana was trying to get my mind off everything.

These times I spent with Nana were wonderful. She was older and wiser on so many levels and always made me feel special. Neither she nor Granddad ever treated me any differently than they did my brother. To them I was perfect, just the way I was. I can never remember my grandparents ever saying anything about me walking like a normal person, as Mother and Daddy did.

My spine was another concern for my parents as I had both sclerosis and lordosis now. Lordosis is an abnormal inward curve of the lumbar spine, also known as swayback. Having both meant I had a double curvature in my spine and it was getting worse as I got older. Everything that the doctors had told my parents a long time ago was coming true.

The curve between my shoulders was not causing any immediate problems, but the curve at my waist was causing my spine to push inward, making my butt protrude outward even more. Mother had to keep adjusting the hemline of my clothes.

Now, because of my spine we went to two doctors in Los Angeles. Oh, joy! First, there was the doctor who put needles in my legs. Now another doctor, at the Shiner's Hospital, checked my spine. They took x-rays and afterwards advised my parents to have my spine straightened. This meant that I would have to have my spine fused and be placed in a body cast from my neck down to my thighs for a full year! I also would have to stay in the hospital in Los Angeles the entire time. The doctor explained to my parents that there was no guarantee regarding this surgery. One slip of the knife and I could lose sensation in my legs or my arms or both, making me a paraplegic or quadriplegic. As I sat there and listened, I was petrified! Polio was bad enough, I thought, but at least I had feeling in my legs. To be gone from home and school for that long bothered me. How could they even think of doing this to me?

My parents told the doctor that they would think about it and get back to him. With that, we left, got in the car, and headed home. As I lay on the back seat, I started crying. I was so scared. I felt like I could take no more doctors, tests, medicine, or possible surgery.

After what seemed like forever, I stopped crying, sat up, and pleaded with my parents saying, "Please don't let the doctors do anymore to me! I want to be just the way I am!"

"You have to stop yelling at your mother and me," Daddy said. "We're just trying to do our best for you."

"I don't think so!" I replied. "You are doing what is best for you! Your only concern is that I walk without crutches!"

"You better quit talking to us in that tone, Young Lady," Daddy said.

"You and Mother would fly me to Japan if there were another doctor advertising some miracle drug over there!" I yelled.

My parents did not say much after that outburst. They knew I was upset. I lay back down and started crying again while thinking to myself. "Why are they doing this to me? Why can't they just love me the way I am? I am doing so much better now. I even attend regular school. I do chores around the house and never complain. I get good grades in school. What more could they possibly want from me? My only desire was to be happy." Finally, I fell asleep.

Mother woke me up when we arrived home. After we got into the house, my parents instructed me to sit on the couch. I thought to myself, "What are they going to ask me to do now?"

"We have something to tell you," Mother said.

"What's going on?" I asked her.

"This is our last trip to Los Angeles. We have both decided that we cannot and will not put you through anymore," Mother said.

"Great! You do not know how much I have hated these trips," I said.

"Yes, we do. A lot of this has been my fault," Mother said, "but I had to try to do the very best I could for my little girl." Then she started crying. "I hope you're not too mad at me, and not upset with your daddy. He did a lot of this because I asked him to."

"I'm not mad at you or Daddy. You know I am scared to death of doctors. Then we make all these trips and nothing has changed. We seem to fight more and I don't like that at all." I got up, gave them each a hug and kiss, and went to my room to get ready for bed.

This had been an exhausting day. As I lay in bed, I still could not believe that I did not have to go to Los Angeles again. I felt like I had been through the war and the war was finally over. I think Mother, even more so than Daddy, was finally coming to terms with my contracting polio and not being able to walk without the aid of my crutches. My biggest problem lately was fighting bad feelings that had been building up towards my parents, and I did not know how to handle that. I felt different feelings of love and hate, and I was having a difficult time coping.

I tried so hard to accept my disability and that too was difficult, especially after seeing how much my parents wanted me to walk again. There was this deep desire inside of me for some type of normalcy in my life. I tried in my own way to make some areas in my life perfect to make up for the imperfections in my physical being. Even that did not seem to work. Time would have to heal this situation because I did not know what else I could do. I had to trust in the words that my family kept telling me, and that was, "Do the very best you can on any given day." I will make mistakes along the way, but I also knew that I had a strong family support system that would always be there for me.

4

FINDING MY NICHE

One day, Mother came into my bedroom and said, "I want to talk to you about something that Daddy and I discussed last night."

"Okay," I responded leaning back against my pillows.

"I saw an article in the newspaper about a group of handicapped people who square dance in wheelchairs."

"How can they square dance in wheelchairs?" I asked.

"I'm not sure, but Daddy and I thought that because you're getting older maybe you should be around more people with disabilities. It might be good therapy too. You could share things that all of you have in common."

"It sounds like fun," I replied. "Tell me more."

"They not only do square dances, but also novelty acts. Some dances are done while the person is balancing on the rear wheels of the wheelchair."

"That sounds cool," I said. "I cannot imagine doing that."

"And, listen to this. The group performs all over southern California and in Arizona. They even perform on TV."

"When we go, will you stay with me?"

"I sure will."

I was eager to learn more about this group, and excited to use a wheelchair. I dreamed about using a wheelchair for so long. Finally, Mother and Daddy were encouraging me to do so. I could not believe my good fortune.

The first night that Mother and I went to the meeting, there were about 25 handicapped people there. The founders, Red and Marene Aulger, were both confined to wheelchairs.

Red was paraplegic from a spinal cord injury he sustained during World War II. Marene was a post polio victim like me. They had been married for many years and were dedicated to helping disabled people through this dance organization.

They greeted us and introduced us to the rest of the group. Most of the people were post polio victims. Depending on their disability, some used crutches and some used wheelchairs. Most contracted polio during the polio epidemic of 1952. Everyone got along with one another because they had so much in common. I was the youngest person there. Most were already in high school or working. I had a lot of fun that first night. They made me feel like part of the group. I had been trying to find my place in this world, but I never quite felt like I fit in; maybe, I finally found my niche.

On the way home, Mother and I talked. I started by saying, "I'm glad you and Daddy found this group for me to join."

"I'm glad we did too. You seemed to have a good time, and it looked like fun learning how to control the wheelchair to do some of those tricky dances."

"It was fun and everybody seemed to like me."

"After you learn all those tricky moves with the wheelchair, I'm sure Neil, Nana, Granddad, and Daddy would like to see you dance too," Mother said.

"I would love for them to watch me dance at a show someday," I said. "I could not believe my eyes watching those specialty dances done on the rear wheels. That looked scary. If I tried that, I would probably fall over backwards."

"You will do just fine," Mother responded.

When I went to bed that night, I realized that nobody teased me or called me names. To a young girl that meant a lot. I was looking forward to our practices and performing at shows.

One time we took a bus trip to Arizona to perform. To watch people get onto the bus was a remarkable sight. Those using crutches could walk up the steps and enter. Those that could not walk had to sit on the steps of the bus and go up one step at a time on their butts. I saw a lot of determination watching these people with disabilities. They were all very strong-willed, a trait I wanted to copy.

Every Wednesday and whenever we put on a show, Mother was with me. She loved to watch our practices, and sometimes Neil would come too. Daddy was usually tired in the evenings because of work, so he did not go as often. Nana and Granddad came occasionally. Red and Marene really liked Mother going to the practices and helping with the shows. Mother knew a lot about applying makeup from when she was a John Power's model. She would put on our theatrical makeup when we were on TV. She also helped people change into costumes in between performances.

Our group motto was, "You can still have fun even though you have a disability." Sometimes I felt this was an understatement because I was not just having fun, I was having the time of my life. When Red and Marene found out I could sing and play the accordion, they immediately put my talents to work. I was so excited. They would use my performance to allow people backstage time to change costumes. Mother and I were getting along really well now. We did not seem to have as much friction between us.

One evening I told Mother, "I really feel good around other disabled people. We have so much fun and they do not look down on me."

"I've said to you many times to keep the faith. What is the other thing I always say?" Mother asked.

"All good things come to those that wait," I replied.

"Right," Mother said.

"Mother, what is faith?" I inquired.

"Faith is a feeling that you feel down deep inside of your soul."

Mother reached for her Bible and said to me, "Right here, in Hebrews 11:1 it states, 'Now faith is the substance of things hoped for, the evidence of things not seen.'"

"Wow!" I said.

"In order to go through each and every day of your life you must have faith that God is watching over you. Know in your heart that He is in control of everything. I must admit there were many times that I did not think God was there for your daddy and me. I blamed God for what happened when you got polio, but I'm starting to accept things better now."

"Does that mean God sometimes allows things to happen that are sad?"

"Yes, but only if He thinks you are strong enough to handle it. God will never give you more than He knows you can handle. Always remember that. When you first got polio, I did not think I was strong enough to handle everything that was happening to you, but things worked out. When you were in the hospital, Neil, Daddy, and I would go to church when we could, and people were praying for all of us during that difficult time."

"I will try to have faith that things will work out for me too," I told her.

"That's my girl!" Mother said.

"Why don't we all go to church as a family?" I questioned her.

"We haven't found a church yet, and your daddy and I aren't quite ready to go back right now. When the time is right, we will. You need to get ready for bed, and I need to spend some time with your brother."

To have Mother's assurance about God being there and being in control was reassuring to me. I would have to take one day at a time and trust that God would get me through. One thing I knew for sure, I was very thankful for my family. As a young girl, I did not understand God because I could not visibly see Him, but I could see my family. God had blessed me with all of them.

Some of the same kids that had attended La Mesa Elementary School were with me again at La Mesa Junior High School. I was still the only person there with a disability, but my peers seemed to be more understanding. They saw that even though I could not do everything like them, I could do a lot. My mind wanted to do what my physical disability prevented me from doing.

Occasionally, I brought a friend with me to the Wheelacade. They got a kick out of my being able to dance in a wheelchair. It was hard for them to understand how I could do it because they never experienced it for themselves. For the first time they understood more what I had to go through when I watched them walk or run or play. My friends were amazed when I balanced my wheelchair on the two back wheels. I never thought the day would come when I would actually be able to do something they could not do. Life was so much better than it had been in a very long time.

I had two close girlfriends, Susan and Marjorie. They never judged me. They accepted me the way I was, physically handicapped. They knew my challenges and helped me whenever they could at school. They liked carrying my books for me because the teachers allowed us to leave each of our classes five minutes early to avoid crowded hallways.

One day Marjorie asked me to go to Sunday school and church with her. She told me that in order for me to get to the Sunday school classroom there was a long staircase on the outside of the church building with a hand rail and a few steps to enter the sanctuary. She felt I could manage. I told her I would check with my parents and let her know.

I did not know if I should even discuss this with Mother and Daddy. I did not know if they would allow me to go. They tried different churches, but they never could find the right one. During the summer it would not be too difficult for me to go up a long flight of stairs at Marjorie's church; but, in the winter, especially when it rained, it would be hard because my crutches would tend to slip. In the length of time it took me to walk up 20 steps, I would look like a drenched rat.

I waited a week or so and finally approached Mother to see what kind of a reaction I would get from her before discussing this topic with Daddy.

I started by asking, "Mother, remember awhile back when we talked about church?"

"Yes. Why? Is something wrong?" She asked.

"No, nothing's wrong. Marjorie asked me if I'd like to go to Sunday school and church with her."

"What did you tell her?" Mother asked.

"I told her I'd ask you and Daddy first. What do you think?"

"I have no objections to you attending church with Marjorie, but don't have high expectations. Church is a group of people that come together to learn and worship God, but they are not perfect. I wish we could find a church that the four of us could attend, but we just haven't found one yet," Mother replied.

"I know, but can I go with Marjorie anyway? The church is right by my old elementary school. You could drive me. Marjorie agreed to meet me out front."

"We could give it a try. Go ahead and call Marjorie. Find out when I should have you there this coming Sunday. How is that?"

"Great. I will call her right away. Thanks."

I called Marjorie and gave her the good news. I explained to her that Mother and Daddy had been looking for a church, but could not find one that they liked. I also confided in her that Mother blamed God for my getting polio.

"I don't understand her thinking," Marjorie said. "The main thing is they are letting you go. That is great! We will meet right out front and I will help you up the stairs to my Sunday school classroom. After that, we will go to church. Tell your Mother to have you here at 8:45 a.m. She can pick you up at noon."

"Okay. See you then," I said, hanging up the phone.

After getting off the phone, I was excited about starting another adventure. As I lay across my bed looking up at the ceiling, I started daydreaming. It was as if God were opening another door. My days seemed to be getting fuller and had more meaning. I did not know what was in store for me. All of a sudden, Mother knocked on my bedroom door and came in. "Did you talk to Marjorie?" She asked.

"Yes, I did."

"I hope this works out for you," Mother said. "Our church family was wonderful when we lived in New Jersey. They were like our second family. I hope we can find a church like that."

"Marjorie's church is a First Baptist Church. Is that okay?"

"Yes, that's fine."

On Sunday, my stomach was in knots. At school, my teachers looked after me, but I had nobody to watch over me at church, except Marjorie. The first time doing anything always frightened me unless Mother was there. I had this fear of failure. When Mother was with me, I seemed more relaxed. I could not understand why I had these feelings; but somewhere, rooted down deep inside, I felt that without Mother, nothing was possible.

That first Sunday turned out great. Marjorie and I continued to go to Sunday school and church every Sunday thereafter. I was learning a lot about Jesus. One Sunday the message really hit me hard. I cried almost throughout the entire sermon. At the end, when the pastor asked people to "Come forward and accept Jesus into their lives," I stood up as fast as I could, grabbed my crutches, and headed to the altar. In John 3:16 it states, "For God so loved the world, that He gave His only begotten Son, that whosoever believeth in Him should not perish but have everlasting life." I did believe! I did love God! I could not remember my past upbringing in the church, but I knew Jesus was there. I talked to the pastor and told him about my memory loss. I informed him that my parents told me about the earlier years when I did go to church with my family. He told me that even though I did not remember that, Jesus made a promise to my parents. That promise was, "Train up a child in the way he should go and, when he is old he will not depart from it." Proverbs 22:6. My parents had given me that early training and even though I did not remember, God never left me. He was there waiting to welcome me back. I was coming back to God as He promised my parents I would.

With my going forward in the church, I now had the promise of Eternal Life. The pastor explained that living on earth I would have many struggles to endure. However, when I died, I would be with the Lord; and, at that time, I would leave my crutches behind and walk the streets of gold in heaven. Oh, what a thrill it was for me to hear those words! There would be no more pain or suffering. I had a feeling of warmth and security that I never experienced before. I felt a new independence. As long as I had Jesus, everything would be okay. When I got home, I was excited and shared my feelings with Mother and Daddy.

"Did you know I might not be able to walk here on earth, but when I die I can leave my crutches behind and walk in heaven?" I asked with delight.

"Yes, we knew that. To have no more pain and suffering will be wonderful. We don't want you dying any time soon though," she chuckled. "We almost lost you when you got polio and that was bad enough."

"I'm not going to die, but it's good to know that I won't have these crutches or any pain when I go to heaven."

It was good to see my parents share my joy that day.

Shortly thereafter, my parents found a church. I felt my mother no longer blamed God for my contracting polio because she finally enjoyed going to church again. I was thankful they let me continue to go to my own church. Once in awhile I would go with them and my brother. Sometimes they would go with me.

One Sunday evening, the pastor baptized me at church while Mother, Daddy, Neil, Nana, and Granddad watched. I do not think I will ever forget that night. Mother helped me get into a beautiful white robe. There were three steps going up and then three steps leading down to the baptistery. Then I had to walk forward three steps into the arms of the pastor. Walking in water using crutches was a challenge, but the pastor was right there to help me. He said a beautiful prayer, baptized me, and blessed me with the Father, the Son, and the Holy Spirit signage. The hardest thing was when he lowered me under the water. My legs came up, and I started to float. I did not have enough muscle power to keep my legs down. I thought for sure that I was going to drown right in that baptismal and be on my way to heaven. When it was all over, I felt I had accomplished something splendid for my Lord and Savior, Jesus Christ. Those that witnessed my baptism were in awe that evening.

The days that followed were very special. In the notebook that I still kept, my words were more positive. I seemed happier. My life took on new meaning, and I felt more content. Even though I was not normal, God still loved me. Added to that was a deeper appreciation towards my parents and my grandparents. They were the binding factor in our home. Even though my brother and I had our moments, we still had a unique closeness. Without a doubt, God provided me with a remarkable family. I felt like the luckiest girl in the world.

With school, homework, church, and the Wheelacade, I was experiencing a full life. Summer was just around the corner and we would all be going back to La Jolla Coves. We enjoyed these special times swimming, snorkeling, and being together. Nana and Mother did not like swimming in the ocean because jellyfish came close to the shoreline occasionally. Granddad swam some, but most of the time he liked to sit, read a book, and drink a beer to keep cool.

Riptides were common along the southern California coastline. While snorkeling one day, a riptide pulled me away from my father. I was scared to death and yelled, "Daddy, Daddy! Help Me!" There was no way for him to get to me. I had no choice, but to let the tide carry me. About five minutes later, I started getting really scared. The shoreline was getting farther away, and I had no strength in my legs to fight the hard currents of the ocean. Fear gripped my soul! "What is going to happen to me?" I thought. Then a peace came over me as I remembered a verse in the Bible. I started reciting it. "Yea, though I walk through the valley of the shadow of death, I will fear no evil; For Thou art with me; Thy rod and Thy staff they comfort me." Psalms 23:4.

The riptide carried me more than a mile from shore when finally I hit calm water. I stayed as relaxed as I could and finally caught my breath while I treaded water. I started to swim back towards the shoreline. The closer I got, my legs dragged along the rocks. My legs started to bleed and burn from the salt water. Eventually, I was able to grab onto a rocky ledge and hold on until help arrived. "Thank you for saving me, Jesus," I said, gratefully.

Above the cliffs there were people lined up watching the paramedics lowering themselves down to rescue me. I could see my family up there as well; they were waving and throwing me kisses. It took the paramedics about two hours to rescue me. The paramedics said the only reason I survived was that I could not fight the rip tide with my legs. We continued to go back to the ocean, but my parents always made sure that I did not venture out as far.

As I was maturing, I was beginning to dread Daddy carrying me in public down the stairs and then into the ocean. People would stand and stare at us. I felt angry, and there were times when I would yell at them, "What are you looking at?" Daddy would tell me to hush. I know I embarrassed him.

When I was sunbathing on the beach, people would look at me, and I would appear normal. Those years that Mother and Granddad massaged my legs with cocoa butter paid off. My legs looked normal. There was no deformity whatsoever. If somebody came by and wanted me to go into the water with him or her, they thought I was kidding when I told them I would have to crawl down to the ocean's edge because I could not walk. When I said I could not get up and play, they thought I was kidding. I told them I had polio when I was a young kid, and then they treated me as if I had the plague. Polio was still a fearful word to many people. They did not understand that I was no longer contagious. Someday, maybe people will be more educated about the poliovirus.

One day, while I was at home watching TV with my family, a news bulletin announced the success of the Salk vaccine. This was a real triumph. Oh, what a thrill it was to hear this news. We joined hands and prayed a prayer of thanksgiving to our God for this fabulous accomplishment.

In the book, BREAKTHROUGH — THE SAGA OF JONAS SALK, it states, "On April 12, 1955, the world learned that a vaccine developed by Jonas Edward Salk, M.D. could be relied upon to prevent paralytic poliomyelitis. This news consummated the most extraordinary undertaking in the history of science, a huge research project led by a Wall Street lawyer and financed by the American people through hundreds of millions of small donations. More than a scientific achievement, the vaccine was a folk victory, an occasion for pride and jubilation. A contagion of love swept the world. People observed moments of silence, rang bells, honked horns, and blew factory whistles, fired salutes, kept their traffic lights red in brief periods of tribute, took the rest of the day off, closed their schools or convoked fervid assemblies therein, drank toasts, hugged children, attended church, smiled at strangers, forgave enemies." [6]

Parents could now have their children vaccinated against this terrible virus. There was relief expressed in our home too regarding the future. When the time came for me to get married and bear children, I would have them vaccinated. I would never have to go through what my parents did. Shortly before my 13th birthday, the number of polio cases was less than 29,000 that year. Compared to the figures of 1952 that was about half. This was a real victory. The future looked bright.

These were years of more triumph than tears. Trying to find my place in the world was very important to me. I had areas in my life now that seemed to help fill other voids that I had no control over. I had the reassurance that I did have a purpose in life. God was by my side every minute of every day. In Romans 8:28 it states, "And we know that all things work together for good to them that love God, to them who are the called according to His purpose." God had a perfect plan for my life in the past and He has a perfect plan for my future. He knew everything I went through and everything I will go through. I did not realize that Romans 8:28 would be my crutch, no pun intended.

5

WHAT WERE YOU THINKING?

After we graduated from junior high school, Mother and Daddy wanted to give my brother and me a surprise party. Mother asked Red and Marene if they could have our party at their house because it was bigger and there were no steps. Red and Marene graciously agreed. My parents wanted the entire Wheelacade to attend, along with some of our school friends. When Neil and I arrived, everybody yelled, "Surprise." There was music, games, food, and lots of laughter that evening. Our party was the best ever!

Between junior high and high school, I stopped going to church. Marjorie was unhappy that I did not want to go anymore, but she understood. I attended a Baptist church and they frowned on dancing. They thought only sinners danced. The Wheelacade was a dance club, so I felt torn. I needed this dance group because I felt accepted there. On the other hand, I felt I was not a good Christian because I danced. People judging me, especially at church, killed me. I spent too many years with kids teasing me and treating me badly. Now I had people at church, including the pastor, thinking I was bad because I danced. I did not understand any of this, but I knew I could not give up my dance group.

One Sunday morning, I was alone because my parents and brother were at church. I still had mixed feelings about quitting church. Mother and Daddy knew I did not want to go, so they did not force me. Mother said if they forced me, I might never go back. Added to my confusion, my family seemed divided on the subject, and they were sending me mixed messages. Mother blamed God for my getting polio and it took her years to come to terms with that. Daddy went to church now, only if Mother wanted to. Neil went to church with Mother and Daddy occasionally. Once when Neil gave a sermon, I did go to hear him. I was so proud of my brother. Nana and Granddad did not believe in God. Nana told me that when her mother was dying, her children were all there and her mother promised to write all of them a letter when she got to heaven. Nana was still waiting for that letter. Granddad believed in a "higher power," but he was skeptical about who God was. We were a close family, yet we had so many differences regarding religion. In my own heart, I knew God loved me and my family loved me and that was all I needed to know.

My first day at Helix High School was another new experience. Everybody seemed older and acted more grown up. On crutches, I faced many of the same problems I had before in junior high school. I had six classes, so the school counselor assigned me helpers to carry my books from class to class. We left early so that I would not have to deal with crowded hallways. Having a helper was nice, but made me feel like the odd ball again. My mind went back to wanting that wheelchair to make things easier.

I pleaded with Mother and Daddy repeatedly to let me use a wheelchair at school, but they refused. I hoped that one day my dream would come true. I wanted to wear normal clothes and shoes and carry my own books. I saw myself as the girl who would fall in the hallways when the kids would accidentally hit her crutches. They would stand there staring, not knowing what to say or do. I wore stupid-looking shoes that looked like nurses' shoes. All the other girls wore cute shoes, and their butts did not stick out like mine. Having a wheelchair meant I would be more normal. I would still be handicapped; that would never change, but I felt I would look better and life would be easier. Why my parents did not allow me to use a wheelchair at school was upsetting. After all, they let me use one at the Wheelacade.

High school consisted of being with my friends, going out on double dates, and going to football games. Football was especially fun because my brother was the star quarterback. Neil and I kept our relationship high on our priority list. It was great having a twin because we were in the same grade at school. After all these years, he still was my big protector, and I loved it!

In my first year, I met Karen, and our friendship continued throughout high school. We hit it off right away and became very close. We did everything together! We went out on double dates, and she went with me to my dance practices. We talked for hours on the phone and went shopping. We shared our deepest thoughts in total confidence. I told Mother, "Karen is like a sister, and we have so much fun together. She treats me as if I were normal."

Mother said, "That kind of friendship is hard to find. Remember one of my favorite sayings: 'True friends are like diamonds, scarce and rare. False friends are like autumn leaves, found everywhere,' so do not ever take her for granted. Cherish your friendship with her."

"I will. I know a lot of people, but Karen is my only true friend."

One day when the Wheelacade was putting on a show in San Diego, I met an able-bodied man. He was in the military and came to one of our shows. He paid a lot of attention to me most of the evening. Mother took quite a liking to him and so did I. Tom was sweet and very good looking. After that first evening, we started talking on the phone, and he started coming over to our house quite a bit. Even more pleasing to me, he took an active part in my dance group. This went on for months.

One evening after Tom and I went to my dance practice, my one crutch caught on the step leading into my house when he took me home. I fell right in front of him and started crying; I was mortified. After he helped me up, we went into the living room and sat down on the couch to talk.

He started by asking, "Why do you use crutches rather than a wheelchair? If we ever get married, I can get you a wheelchair through the government at no cost."

"You can?" I replied, astonished by his remark.

"Yes. I already talked to my commanding officer, but we must be married."

"I am too young to get married."

"I am just telling you what he told me," Tom said.

"I have fought with my parents for years about letting me use a wheelchair, but they are dead set against it."

"What is their problem? Wouldn't it be easier?" He asked.

"It would be much easier, but my parents feel using a wheelchair would be like me going backwards. Mother told me about all the hard work she and I did to get me to use crutches. I try to understand her point of view, but that does not mean I agree with her."

"Wouldn't using a wheelchair be better for your back?"

"That's what I've told them for years. I could also wear normal clothes and shoes. No matter how much we argue, they will never give in."

"I know we haven't known each other very long, but I'd be honored if you would be my wife. Will you marry me?" He asked unexpectedly.

"You're kidding, right?" I said, laughing.

"No. I'm not kidding," he said. "Marrying you would be a dream come true. I have never met anybody like you. I have given this a lot of thought."

"You're an able-bodied man. Why in the world would you want to marry a handicapped girl like me?" I asked.

"I don't think of you that way. You are a beautiful person inside and out, and I love you and your family. I never had a family like yours when I was young or even now for that matter."

"Then my answer is yes!" We hugged and kissed each other. We were so excited. We agreed not to tell my parents until Tom found a ring for me.

One evening after having dinner with my parents, Tom and I showed my engagement ring to them and told them we wanted to get married. To say they were upset is putting it mildly. They said that Tom was a nice enough person, but they thought I was too young to get married, and they would not give their permission. Tom was almost 21 and had been in the military since he was 18. On the other hand, I was not quite 16 and had been sheltered most of my life. Mother thought that because this was the first able-bodied man that paid attention to me that I was not using my head. Daddy even asked Tom why he wanted to marry a handicapped girl. That really hurt me. I did everything I could that night to convince them that this was the right decision. I even threatened them with getting pregnant if that was what it took to get them to sign the papers. My parents asked us not to say one word about our engagement until they had a chance to talk to their pastor. We had no choice but to agree. I took my ring off, kissed Tom good-bye, and went to my bedroom. After writing in my notebook, I cried myself to sleep.

My parents had multiple appointments with their pastor. On a few occasions, I went too. Their pastor wanted my view on why I wanted to get married so young. I told many lies during those sessions. I knew the real reason I wanted to marry Tom; I wanted that wheelchair! Marrying Tom was the only way I knew I would get one! After more hours of counseling, my parents finally agreed to sign the required papers so that Tom and I could get married. Mother and Daddy never gave us their blessing. At the time, I did not care.

The day finally came that I could wear my engagement ring. I wanted everybody to see it. I will never forget how proud I felt when I went to school and to the Wheelacade and showed off my ring. Nobody thought I was serious, and many made snide remarks. Some thought I was pregnant. Why else would a 15 year old get married? In time, they would find out differently! Having the knowledge that somebody loved me, besides my family, was the best feeling! Now I could have my own home, be my own boss, and finally have that wheelchair that I wanted so badly.

Tom rented a one bedroom duplex about five blocks from my parents' house. My parents and grandparents gave us some furniture and that along with two bridal showers gave us a modest, but good start. We had a small wedding at my parents' home. Karen was my maid of honor. She was excited for me. She knew all my thoughts and feelings. She agreed with some and not with others; but, in the end, she supported me. I was living in a dream world. I had no idea about how to be a wife. I knew all about washing, ironing, cooking, and cleaning; but, regarding sex, I was in the dark.

We spent our first night in a hotel in San Diego. As a virgin, I did not know what to expect. Rather than making love, Tom forced himself on me. As soon as he left the room to go swimming, I noticed I was bleeding. I called my mother immediately to find out what was wrong. She said not to be alarmed, that this sometimes happens when you are with a man sexually for the first time. I really needed my mother now more than ever. It was good to know that she was still there for me.

The next morning we caught a train to Texas for our honeymoon. This was the first time I was on a train, and I had motion sickness all the way there. I never felt so sick in my life. The only reason I agreed to go to Texas was that Tom wanted me to meet his family. I had never been that far away from my family before. I was scared to death.

When we arrived, we caught a cab to Tom's childhood home. It was 120 degrees, in the afternoon, in the shade! I normally do not sweat, but now I was sweating because the humidity was so high. When Tom introduced me to his family, they seemed nice enough, but looked shocked when they saw my crutches. I just knew by their reaction that Tom never told them I was disabled. That night while getting ready for bed, I asked Tom if he told them I was on crutches. He said that he did not see the need to. I was furious! He told me he did not tell them because he did not think of me as being handicapped. Sweet as that sounds, it was still deceitful. I let him know, as far as I was concerned, he should have told his parents about my disability.

My feet swelled for two days due to the heat and humidity. They looked like two little balloons with tiny toes hanging out the end. My feet hurt so badly, they were throbbing. I could not wear shoes and I felt awful! I told Tom I had to get back to California because of my feet. I was not telling the truth, but I did not care. I wanted to get back to my family. I wanted to go home! I missed everyone something awful. Thankfully, Tom agreed, and we left the next morning.

I arranged for my parents to pick us up. When I saw them, I was never so happy to see anyone in my life. We went to their house for dinner. Nana and Granddad were also there to welcome us back. I felt more relaxed being back close to my family. Marriage was not all I thought it would be and being away from my family for the first time was hard. I figured I would have to pay a high price to get that wheelchair that I wanted so desperately, but I never expected to feel the way I felt after getting married.

I decided to take a year off from school mainly to honor my parents' wishes. I could have been a three-year graduate, but my parents always dreamed of the day that Neil and I would graduate together. Neil could not graduate in three years because he planned to go to college, and he could not get in all the necessary classes. I only needed my regular classes and some business courses because I wanted to be a secretary. I had no intention of going to college.

"I don't mind taking a year off from school," I told my parents.

"Are you sure?"

"I am positive. Taking time off from school and homework will help me in my transition from student to homemaker and wife."

Just as Tom promised, on my 16th birthday, he surprised me with my very own wheelchair that he got through the military. Tom and I knew my parents were against my using a wheelchair, but we did not care. I was married now. My parents did not have a say in what I did. I was being very defiant. I continued to use my crutches only when I visited Mother and Daddy. At our home, I found using the wheelchair made it easier to do household chores because my hands were not holding crutches.

Along with having my wheelchair, Daddy had a unique stool made for me. I could sit on it to make my housework even easier. The stool had four legs with four caster wheels attached. When I sat on it, I could rest my feet on the crossbar and push myself around the house by holding onto the walls and furniture.

"Why didn't I have this stool years ago?" I asked Daddy.

"You didn't need it because you didn't do that much housework when you were living with us," he said, laughing.

With this new stool plus my wheelchair, I became a whiz at housework. My friends would kid me when they came over about my house being so clean. I took after Mother and Nana, or so I thought. I knew that I was trying to be perfect in this area to make up for the physical imperfections I had. I could do something really well, so I worked hard at it. All seemed to be going quite well until Tom started drinking rather heavily and causing dissension between us. I knew down deep that I had gotten married for all the wrong reasons, but I would never admit that to anyone, least of all my parents. As far as they knew, my life with Tom was perfect.

I eventually went back to high school as a senior. I still was not driving, so Mother or Neil would pick me up and drive me to school. Tom had to leave earlier than I did, and there were times he would have duty on base and spend the night. Getting back in the groove was a little hard at first, but my girlfriend, Karen, was a big help. I never told any of my classmates that my marriage was on rocky ground.

After a few weeks of struggling at school on my crutches, I decided to use my wheelchair. What a joyous day! It seemed like I waited a lifetime to be able to do this. My days seemed happier because I could do more things with ease. I could carry my own books. I could leave class at the same time my classmates did. Now they piled me high with their books. I could wear regular shoes and stylish clothes right "off the rack" from stores. I had less back pain because the stress from standing was off my spine.

I enjoyed school because I got good grades. I also realized that most of my heartache while attending school was due to my disability. If only I had this wheelchair sooner. If only Mother and Daddy would have consented to me using a wheelchair, I probably would have never gotten married. I was happier now, and I noticed my classmates started to treat me differently too. This newfound freedom changed my attitude. One day when it rained, I no longer had the fear of falling. I wheeled myself right out into the rain, leaned my head back, and sat there feeling the soft pressure of raindrops fall on my face. The rain mingled with my tears of joy.

One evening I ate dinner at my parent's home because Tom had to stay all night on base. After dinner, my parents apologized to me for forcing me to use crutches for so many years. I assured them I understood. I knew that they were only doing what they felt was best. On the other hand, I did not want them to think poorly of me because of my using a wheelchair. Mother saw with her own eyes my newfound independence. The first time we went shopping together, while using my wheelchair, I could shop with ease. I could carry my own packages as well as some of hers in my lap. On the other hand, the wheelchair posed other problems such as access to public bathrooms. That obstacle seemed small at the time. As long as I had Mother's approval, that was all I needed.

Many times, I felt like my emotions were on a roller coaster. One day I would be up; the next day I would feel down. I thought I finally found what I was looking for. What else could I possibly want? At times I felt confused about using my wheelchair and insecure about my marriage. Was my newfound happiness regarding my wheelchair just going to burst like an over inflated balloon? Was there something missing or lacking in my life? Every once in awhile I felt this strong, almost uncontrollable desire to find "it," but what was the "it" that I was so desperately searching for?

One night while in bed, I thought about Jesus and I started praying, "Lord Jesus, it's been a long time since I've talked to You. Not because You haven't been there, but because I shut You out of my life. Please forgive me. I am truly sorry. I have made some terrible choices lately, and now I have to learn to live with those choices. Many times, I have asked myself, what were you thinking? If only I had turned to You sooner for guidance, maybe I would have done things differently. Please stay with me. Wrap Your arms around me and hold me ever so tight as I continue to accept my disability, explore my independence, and make better choices. Amen."

6

HILLS AND VALLEYS

The last few months in high school were free of stress. Compared to elementary school and junior high, the students in high school were more understanding. Using my wheelchair at school helped my psyche. I continued to do well academically. I was a whiz in my business classes. I felt very proud of myself when I received two certificates for typing over 120 wpm at a nearby college. When God took away my legs, He gave me extra power in my hands. My typing skills were extraordinary. It takes a lot of arm power to walk with crutches or push a wheelchair. It will also take a lot of strength when I get my car. I will have to fold up and lift my wheelchair, all 57 pounds, and put it in the car.

The day of my senior prom and after-prom finally arrived. The sun was shining, the birds were singing, and butterflies were dancing through the air outside my bedroom window. It was springtime and everything seemed right with the world. Mother had helped me find a dress and kept it at her house. She and Daddy paid for it; they knew Tom and I could not afford it. It was the most beautiful dress I had ever seen. The dress was a pink strapless gown with ruffles all the way to the floor. When I sat in my wheelchair with its removable arms removed, the fullness of my dress made my wheelchair invisible. All signs of my disability magically disappeared!

Early in the evening Mother picked me up and took me to her house to get ready for the prom. Tom was going to come straight from work to her house. I was so nervous because I knew I could not dance.

"If I cannot dance, what is Tom going to do all night?" I asked Mother.

"Everything will be fine! Tom agreed to go and it is only one night. He goes to your dance practices, and dance shows, and he does not seem to mind. If he did, he would not go. He could dance at the prom if he wants to. He knows Karen and could dance with her," she said.

"You're probably right. I just don't want any problems," I said.

"There won't be any problems. I am so glad you decided to get ready at our house. I can help you and take a bunch of pictures of all of you."

When Tom arrived, he and my brother put on their tuxedos. Boy, did they look handsome. Neil had to leave to pick up his date and then brought her back to the house. Mother had the time of her life taking pictures. We all looked pretty darn good. I felt like a queen!

We took two separate cars and met at the prom. We had a wonderful evening. Afterwards, we went back to my parents' house to change clothes and go to the after-prom. The theme was, "The Year of Flappers and Gangsters." Our outfits, which Mother helped put together, were hysterical, but cute. We all had a ball.

The next day, reality destroyed the glamour of the night before. Tom was drinking again and complaining because he did not dance at the prom.

"I knew this would happen! I told you to dance. I even suggested you dance with Karen," I reminded him.

"That would be disrespectful for me to leave you alone and go off with someone else and dance knowing that you couldn't."

"Lots of guys were dancing with other girls besides their date. The girls sat and talked when their boyfriends were off dancing with somebody else. Nobody was glued at the hip," I said, trying to convince him. "We're all friends. It was no big deal. You could have danced with any number of girls," I added.

"I would have felt like a jerk!" He replied, getting angry.

"There was no liquor, but you had your flask! I'm surprised you didn't get caught."

"Why do you always bring up my drinking? There were other guys drinking too," he said, trying to convince me that he was not doing anything wrong.

"I don't care about the other guys. My only concern is you. When you do not drink, you are so nice to me; but, when you drink, you act like a different person. Your drinking scares me because I get the brunt of it. Remember a month ago. You came home drunk and punched me so hard that you dislocated my jaw, and I had to go to the orthodontist."

"Yeah, so what!" He replied.

"I guess it is no big deal to you. Believe me I have tried to understand. My parents drink. So does Granddad. In my opinion, you drink excessively! I tried alcohol and do not like it. If you drank once in awhile I wouldn't care, but you don't know when to stop."

He gave me this awful glaring look. He knew I was right. When he gave me that certain look, I knew I better shut up, or I would pay the price.

A few weeks after my prom, Tom came home from work drunk. He was verbally abusive to me. This was happening so often I was concerned for my own well-being.

One day, I was outside sitting on the front lawn pulling weeds out of our flower garden when Tom suddenly came over to me. He had this awful smirk on his face and started yelling at me. Then he took my wheelchair away, brought it into our house, and left me outside all by myself. At first, I thought he was playing around. As more time passed, I became frightened. Feelings of helplessness came over me. It was as if somebody had taken my legs away. I felt paralyzed with fear. What was I going to do?

I yelled at the top of my lungs, "Tom, bring me my wheelchair!" There was no response. "How am I going to get into the house?" I yelled again.

After awhile he yelled back, "If you want to come inside, I'm sure you will find a way!" He was laughing his head off while peering at me through our front screen door.

I built up enough courage and literally crawled on my hands and knees into the house. I felt angry, embarrassed, and humiliated. I could not believe he did this to me. Tears were streaming down my face. It reminded me of the time in elementary school when that one kid hid my crutches, and I felt helpless. It is amazing how one incident can trigger old memories.

When I finally got into the house, I started screaming at him, "How could you do that to me? It's like you took my legs away!"

"Easy," he said, continuing to laugh, "I just did it! You looked pretty funny crawling into the house."

"You're drunk!" I screamed.

"So what if I am. What are you going to do about it?" He sneered.

"You have no right to treat me like this!" I yelled back.

"I can do whatever I want. You're my wife!" He yelled.

"I'm sick of the way you treat me. You hit me whenever you want. Today your actions towards me are unforgivable. Men do not treat women this way and then say I love you. I am your wife! How could you do this?"

"I can and will do whatever I want to you or anybody else. You're not going to stop me," he yelled, pointing his finger at me.

"You're not going to treat me like this anymore!" I yelled. "I want out of this marriage! I want a divorce, the sooner the better! I do not know why I married you in the first place. I guess I do. I wanted my wheelchair. I paid a high price to get it. I was so stupid. It is obvious that you do not love or respect me. I am out of here. No, on second thought, you get out! You brought nothing to this marriage, furniture or otherwise, except for my wheelchair, so get out! Do you hear me? Get out and don't come back! You'll hear from my attorney!"

"Fine," he said, as he grabbed some of his things, got in his car, and drove away.

I could not believe what had just happened. How in the world was I going to tell my parents? What was I going to do? I told Tom he would hear from my attorney. "What attorney?" I thought. I did not have an attorney. I could not afford to live on my own, and I was supposed to get an attorney. To top it off, I was still in school. I will have to ask my parents if I could move back home with them. How would I ever be able to do that? I sat there for a long time. I wanted to call my parents, but I was crying so hard I was afraid I would frighten them. I knew I had to calm down. I was such a fool and made a huge mistake getting married so young just so I could have a wheelchair. I dreaded telling my parents. I knew they were going to say, "I told you so." I decided to wait a few days to see if Tom would come back and apologize.

Tom did not call or come home. In the back of my mind, I wondered if I even wanted him back. Our marriage was over. I wished I could have a long, lasting, and loving relationship like my parents and grandparents had. Tom's drinking changed all my expectations. Maybe he is an alcoholic. I said those marriage vows "in sickness and in health." Should I stand by him? I was so confused.

When I finally told Mother and Daddy, they were very angry about Tom's drinking. They were even more upset about what Tom did to me and encouraged me to come home. Finishing school had to be my priority now, so I could get a job after graduation.

In the weeks that followed, I went through a lot emotionally. I had to put all my household items in storage. We found a storage garage by my high school for ten dollars a month. I guess I could have sold everything, but Mother, Daddy, Nana, and Granddad gave me all the furniture, which for me had a lot of sentimental value.

Living at home with my parents again was going to be an adjustment after being on my own. I was confused and felt like a failure. I knew that my family would help me through this difficult time. They were always there for me, and this time was no different. Daddy always said, "Live in my house, you live by my rules." Those words kept ringing in my ears. I was not used to rules after being married. Now I would have to answer to my parents once again.

If things were not bad enough, I found out that because I was under age, one of my parents had to act as my legal guardian and file for divorce on my behalf. That did not sit well with Mother or Daddy. They were genuinely upset. I was too. I never thought I would be going through a divorce at such a young age. They tried to convince me that it takes two to make or break a marriage.

After settling in, Mother and Daddy tried to give me my space. They knew I was hurting. At school, the kids heard I was getting a divorce. After praising my husband and telling everybody how wonderful it was to be married, I felt humiliated. I never told a soul about the things that Tom did to me physically. Now I had to put up with my so-called friends, snickering and making snide remarks. I did not need that right now. I felt bad enough. During this time, I learned who my true friends really were; they did not judge me.

In June of 1960, Neil and I graduated from Helix High School with honors. We both carried a 4.0 grade point average (GPA). Mother, Daddy, Nana, and Granddad were so proud. Dreams came true for all four of them as they watched Neil and I graduate together.

Graduating from high school made me feel as if I accomplished something extraordinary in my life. Afterwards, we had a party at our house.

College was out of the question for me. I told my parents, "Neil has the brains in this family." Because of a football scholarship and the financial help of our parents, his dream came true. Neil was going to attend college in Los Angeles, but he said he would come home on weekends and during the summer.

Four days after graduation, I felt proud to have landed my first job as a secretary. My typing skills really paid off. Connie, from the Wheelacade, put in a good word for me. She also agreed to drive me to work until I found a car.

Finding a car can have some challenges. If you cannot use your legs due to a disability, the law requires that handicapped people drive with hand controls, and the car must have an automatic transmission. With one hand on the steering wheel and one hand on the hand controls, there is no way to operate a stick shift. I also had to find a two-door car so I could fold up my wheelchair and put it behind the passenger seat by myself.

When I got my learner's permit, I asked some of my friends at the Wheelacade to teach me to drive because they had hand controls in their cars. I knew I would be safe because of the knowledge they all had driving a vehicle while being disabled. I was going to purchase my hand controls from George, a friend of mine at Wheelacade. He owned a company, located in San Diego, called Manufacturing Production Services Corporation (MPS) that designed and installed hand controls.

Daddy and I spent weekends looking around town until we finally found the perfect car. It was a 1952, light green Dodge that fit me perfectly. I was so excited! This car was going to give me more freedom. I could come and go now without always having to ask somebody to take me places. Now I could pick up my friends and go out with them. Connie and I could take turns driving each other to work.

After Daddy drove my car home, I called George, at MPS Corporation, to make an appointment to have my hand controls installed. Hand controls are just that. They have two levers bolted to the steering column. One goes to the brake and one to the gas. You steer the car with one hand and operate the hand controls with the other. Pushing the controls towards the dash applies the brake and pulling the controls towards the driver's seat operates the gas. After having my hand controls installed, I immediately went down to the Department of Motor Vehicles. After taking the written test, I had to wait for an inspector to take the driving portion. I believe he made my driving test last longer than most because he was in awe of how my hand controls worked. Once I got my driver's license, I drove around town for hours. I felt very proud of myself.

One evening, I sat in my bedroom wondering why my marriage had failed. I knew going through what I did made me stronger, but I wanted answers. I realized that when members of my dance group married, each couple, except for one, married their own kind, meaning both were disabled. I only knew one other couple that had a mixed marriage as mine was. I finally agreed to date some guys from my dance group. We usually just went out to dinner or a movie. I did not want a serious relationship and made that quite clear. I used my crutches and my date used a wheelchair; or, if we went shopping, then we would both use our wheelchairs. One wheelchair went up on the back seat and one went on the floor behind the passenger seat. Our favorite hangout was a drive-in restaurant called Oscar's. We literally drove in, parked our car, ordered through a microphone box, and ate in the car. Girls on roller skates delivered our food on a tray that hooked right on the open window of the car. When we finished eating, we turned on the headlights, and the girl would come out and retrieve our tray. This was ideal for those of us who were disabled.

Once in awhile I would stay out late at night and did things that I should not have. My parents got really upset with me one time because I left the house with one guy and came home with another. Daddy said, "If you ever do that again, Young Lady, I'm going to toss you out on your rear!" I knew when Daddy said something he meant it. I never did that again. Mother let me get away with far more than Daddy did. Mother was a softy and wanted to do whatever it took to make me happy. I took advantage of her. When I got older and looked back, I was not very proud of myself.

Mother tried hard to reason with me about dating. She was very happy that I mostly dated handicapped men. She felt I would be happier being with my own kind as she put it. She just wanted me to slow down and enjoy life. Nana tried to reason with me too. Quite honestly, I wanted to work during the week, and go out on the weekends and have fun. Who, at my age, wanted to stay home watching TV or playing cards? I did not feel I was doing anything wrong. I did not come home drunk or pregnant. I had not been with a man sexually, except when I was married. I never wanted to embarrass my parents by having a child out of wedlock. I knew that would kill them. I had too much respect for them to cause them that kind of grief.

One evening, I was in bed, when all of a sudden I felt God tapping on my shoulder. "Lord Jesus, is that You?" I asked silently. "I know it has been a long time since I talked to You. Please forgive me. I need Your advice, Lord. Because of my family's deep love for me, I try to listen to them, but sometimes it is hard. Please help me to be a better daughter and granddaughter. I accomplished quite a bit lately, but getting divorced still haunts me. I feel like such a failure. Without my family, I do not know what I would have done. Thank You for their presence in my life. As I grow, I will still have many hills to climb after going through the valleys. Even when I turn away from You, there is great comfort knowing You are always there. Amen."

7

SINKING DEEPER

On weekends, my girlfriends and I would try to meet boys and go to parties. I was becoming rebellious. My actions were showing it. My weekdays were busy at work. On Wednesday nights, I still went to the Wheelacade. Those in the group married with children now could not make it to many of the shows, but we still practiced our routines. Without as many shows, we did not push ourselves as hard. The Wheelacade was becoming more of a social gathering. That was fine with me.

There were many service men in San Diego, due to all the bases in the area. It was during this rebellious time when I met another military man who was to become my husband. Jim and I only dated a short time. When he asked me to marry him, I agreed to as soon as my divorce was final. When we told my parents, they were extremely upset. Mother and Daddy felt I did not know Jim long enough. They did not like him one bit and felt I was making another huge mistake. My decision to marry again was causing a lot of dissension in our home. I did not care. I was going to get married, with or without my family's blessing. I told myself, later they would accept Jim.

Jim and I found a small apartment to rent in San Diego. Daddy would not help me move because he was against this marriage. Instead, Jim arranged for some of his friends to help unload my storage unit and bring everything over to the apartment. Before we were married, Jim had decided to move in rather than stay on base. I continued to live with my parents. Down deep, I knew I was hurting them, but I did not care. I was searching for something. What that was I did not know. My parents and grandparents had always been supportive, but this time they drew the line. They made no bones about how they felt about me getting married again. This was the second able-bodied man that asked me to get married. I was not going to pass up this opportunity, no matter what my family thought or what it would cost me.

"You always pick these military guys. Why can't you marry somebody from the Wheelacade?" Mother asked.

"I honestly do not know," I answered.

What I did not tell my mother that day was I wanted desperately to have a normal life. Marrying somebody disabled like myself made me feel like I was settling for second best. Trying to prove myself to those around me made me make some terrible choices.

Jim and I went to the Justice of the Peace to get married. My parents attended our wedding, but my grandparents did not. Mother warned me that I was "going from the frying pan back into the fire," but I would not listen. This strong desire to prove myself was becoming an obsession. Why my parents could not understand my feelings was beyond me. I wanted desperately to be married and start a family of my own.

Jim was a nice person when I met him and continued to be throughout our courtship and for the first few months of our marriage. He was so sweet and caring towards me and treated me with a lot of respect. He never belittled me. He encouraged me when I faced challenges. Then, after a few months, he started to display a terrible temper. As the days and weeks followed, Jim would yell at me more and more. I was shocked. He had never shown any anger problems before. As time passed, my parents still did not warm up to Jim. My brother despised him and my grandparents stayed downstairs in their home whenever Jim and I visited Mother and Daddy. This added to my heartache.

One weekend my parents and grandparents were planning to drive to the University of California in Los Angeles to see my brother. Besides visiting him, Mother and Daddy wanted to give Nana and Granddad the "grand tour" of the college. They wanted me to go, but I told them I could not. Jim would always get upset whenever I did anything with my family. Making excuses to my parents was becoming the norm for me. Sadness filled my heart when they left for Los Angeles and I had to stay home. I was in a terrible position of choosing between Jim and my family.

As more time passed, things were getting worse in my marriage. I was staying away from my parents and grandparents even more. I did not want them to know how Jim treated me. Down deep, I missed my family and decided to talk to Jim.

"I've always had a close relationship with my family, so it is hard for me to give all that up because we're married," I said, trying to explain my feelings.

"Then maybe you shouldn't have married me," he said.

"Maybe I shouldn't have, but we're married so why can't we compromise and try to get along when we visit them?" I pleaded.

"You're too much into family," he said. "Since I joined the military, I don't even talk to my parents and haven't for years."

"That's nothing to brag about. My parents and grandparents have always been there for me."

Suddenly and unexpectedly, Jim grabbed me by the hair, pulled me out of my wheelchair, and threw me to the floor. Pain wrenched my entire body!

"What's gotten into you?" I yelled, as tears streamed down my cheeks.

"You and your family drive me nuts!" Jim yelled.

I was petrified! I started to scream. The more I screamed, the more he kicked and hit me. Finally, I cried out, "In the name of God, please stop!"

With that plea, he stopped and walked away leaving me all battered and bruised, lying on the floor. A short time later, Jim left the house. I knew I could not contact my family now. If my family saw my bruises, they would kill Jim.

I thought to myself, "What am I going to do now?" Here I was again in an abusive marriage. Why did I not listen to my parents? They told me not to jump into another marriage. I knew I was trying to find something, but I did not know what. Was all this happening because I am disabled? Both Tom and Jim knew I could not walk. Why did they treat me so nice when we dated, then treat me so cruelly and so viciously, after we were married? Nothing made sense to me anymore. I was sinking deeper into despair. The next morning I called in sick at work, so they would not see my bruises.

Jim and I had our share of fights for quite some time, but we always managed to make up. This time, Jim stayed away for a few days. When he did come home, we did not say much to each other. When my bruises lightened, I returned to work. Connie knew something was wrong, but I would not tell anybody anything. I did not want to admit failure again. Mother called me a few times asking me to come over. I continued to make excuses. It was easier to stay away.

One day I had just arrived home from work when the doorbell rang. A man served me with divorce papers. I did not understand what was going on. When Jim got home, I asked him about the papers.

"Why did you file for a divorce? I have done nothing to deserve this. You are the one who treats me like dirt. I have been the best wife I could be!" I said, yelling at him.

"I filed because I need to move out and get away from you before I do more damage to you than I've already done," he explained.

"Let me be the judge of that. I do not want a divorce. Maybe we could try counseling. I know we can make this work."

"I want you to sign the papers anyway. If you want to try to make this marriage work then that is okay with me, but I want the divorce to go forward. I'll stay here sometimes, but stay on base most of the time."

"That's crazy! If you want to work at this marriage, then you need to be here, except when you have duty!"

For a month or so, I felt that our relationship was doing better because he was not attacking me. Maybe our marriage was going to be okay. Some nights Jim stayed away. That bothered me, but I did not want to upset him so I kept quiet. I felt if I complained that he would get mad and I would pay the price. I was living on eggshells. Going to work took my mind off some of my problems. I even signed the divorce papers, even though we were still living together as husband and wife. I was willing to do whatever it took to keep this marriage intact. I knew if I got a divorce, I would be admitting to failure again. That would have broken my spirit.

One evening, after dinner, Jim went into another one of his rages. I was scared to death. I was taking a bath, and Jim walked into the bathroom with a wet dishtowel and started hitting me with it while laughing. My skin started to welt. I started crying, fearing what he would do to me next. Before I could even get out of the tub, he left the room, and returned with a pot full of hot water and poured it over my head. As the water flowed down my naked body, I screamed with pain! I tried to get out of the tub again, but he would push me back down into the water. I could not fight him. Here I was a handicapped woman alone with her husband, an able-bodied man that had gone mad. I did not know what he would do next. I screamed aloud to God, "Please, God, help me! Make Jim stop!" With that, Jim left the room. I waited about five minutes. Hearing nothing, I got out of the tub. When I finished putting on my pajamas, I went into the living room where Jim was sitting watching TV as if nothing had happened. We needed to talk.

I started by saying, "There is no way for us to have a normal married life when you go into these rages for no reason. I don't understand how you can show so much love to me for weeks and then turn 180 degrees."

"I know," he said, hanging his head. "I'm so sorry."

"I don't think you're sorry. If you were, you would do something about it. I have asked you to see a counselor. I told you I would even go with you."

"I don't need help!" He yelled.

"It's obvious to me that you do," I said, "and if you feel you don't, then things will never change. This is happening too often. I don't know what I'm doing to provoke your outbursts."

"I don't know why I do this to you. I have not told you, but I've gotten into some fights on base too."

"Jim, this is getting out of hand. Please, can we start counseling? Let's work together to save our marriage," I pleaded.

"Absolutely not," he said, getting off the couch and starting to pace around the room.

We talked for over an hour, but nothing changed. I knew our marriage was over. I had no choice, but to leave. I could not take the abuse anymore. I feared that one day he might get more violent and even kill me.

"Before things get worse, I think we should go our separate ways," I said, hoping he would understand and not get mad and hurt me again.

Jim got up off the couch, packed up some things, and left. When he left, I could not stop crying. I honestly thought everything would work out. Having to face the truth was hard. I sat there for the longest time, thinking, "Here we go again!" Doubts about my own self worth haunted me. I felt like a failure. Am I expecting too much from these men? Is God punishing me? Then a light bulb went off in my head. Maybe God was punishing me for quitting church. I had no answers. Maybe I was the one who needed counseling. I wanted to die. I think a part of me did that day.

I continued to stay in our apartment because the rent was paid. I also went to work. Once in awhile I talked to Mother on the phone. I knew I would eventually have to face my family and tell them that Jim had moved out and filed for a divorce. I could only imagine how my parents were going to react. On the other hand, they might be glad because they never liked him.

One day after work, I drove over to my parents' house to tell them what was going on. Nana and Granddad were also there.

"I don't know how to tell you this, but Jim and I are getting a divorce. He has a violent temper. I can't take it anymore," I said, starting to cry. "I haven't told you a lot of what's been going on. I wanted to spare your feelings. Now, I must tell you that Jim has hurt me many times physically. I even had to take time off from work because of the bruises I sustained. I did not want anybody at work to know we were having problems."

"Oh my goodness!" Mother said, coming over to comfort me.

"You poor, sweet thing," Nana said.

"You obviously married a monster," Granddad said.

Questions were coming from all of them, except Daddy. He just sat there, taking it all in and shaking his head in disgust. I could tell he was fuming!

Mother asked, "Why didn't you come to us sooner? I cannot believe you went through this by yourself. Daddy and I had our suspicions, but we never thought it was this bad!"

"I couldn't tell you," I said. "I kept hoping and praying that we could work things out. A couple of months ago Jim served me with divorce papers, which I signed, but afterwards we seemed to work things out."

"Divorce papers!" Mother said. "Why did you stay?"

"It doesn't matter. I only signed the papers to make him happy. I told him I refused to leave because, no matter what, I wanted to make this marriage work. After the last beating, I came to the realization that our marriage was over. I could not stay with him any longer, so he left!" I said, trying to explain my situation.

"This sounds worse than a soap opera," Mother said.

"I even tried desperately to get Jim to start counseling," I said. "It was pretty scary to watch him change right in front of my eyes."

"Don't make excuses for him Sharon!" Mother yelled. "No man has the right to abuse a woman. To top that off you are disabled! What in the world was he thinking? He must be mad!"

Daddy finally said, "I could kill that man for what he did to you! We need to go over to your apartment right now and get your things. I do not want you there another night. God forbid if Jim comes back and wants you to forgive him or some fool thing."

"Okay," I said. "Let's go."

Then Daddy said, "Wait a minute. I'll only allow you to come back home if you agree not to see Jim."

"I promise Daddy. I'll do whatever you say."

After agreeing to the stipulations Daddy set down, we jumped in our cars and went over to my apartment to grab as many of my things as we could. Daddy said he would get my furniture later and put it back in storage.

When we arrived back at their house, we unloaded all my stuff into their garage. Then we all met back in the living room. My entire family was glad I was home with them where I was safe.

"I am so thankful to have all of you. I really didn't want this to happen," I said, with tears streaming down my face. "I really needed to come home. The next time I want to get married you have to lock me in a closet and throw away the key."

"That's going a little extreme," Mother said. "You have known our thoughts about Jim for a long time. It sounds as though you did your best and that is all you can do. We are upset you had to go through so much heartache."

After talking for a while, Nana and Granddad went downstairs to get ready for bed. Mother came in my bedroom to help me put a few things away after Daddy went to bed.

"I don't know what I would do without you," I told her.

"I told you we would always be here. We are true to our word," Mother said, giving me a hug, and then she added, "Try to get some sleep."

"Okay. Goodnight. I love you," I said, feeling safe and secure once again.

The following weekend Daddy and Granddad got the rest of my things out of the apartment and met Mother and me at the storage unit. After everyone left, I was beside myself with grief. The dissolution of a marriage is like a death. I failed again and had to go through the grieving process. Next, I had to pick myself up and put all my energy into work and family. I often wondered where my parents got the strength to go through all these trials with me. Many parents would not have been this supportive.

One day, after I came home from work, Mother and I talked while she was getting dinner ready. It was during this time she suggested that I go back to church. I told her I had been praying a lot lately, but for whatever reason, I had this feeling if I went back to church, people there would judge me even more.

"Years ago when I went to church, I was judged because I danced and played cards. Now I have been married twice. I quit drinking altogether, but I still smoke. There is no way any church will accept me."

"Daddy and I smoke and they don't look down on us."

"Mother, I feel like I have to be perfect to attend church. I came to that conclusion years ago. Jesus loves me, but the people will never accept me with all my faults."

"Sharon, if God only wanted perfect people to fill His church, then it would be pretty empty. There is not one person alive that is perfect. Christ died for our sins. If we had no sin in our life, then Christ died for nothing. I think you are using your lack of perfection as an excuse. Those are my feelings, for whatever they are worth."

"I think I know what you're saying. Go to church with all your sins and God will change your life to the way He wants it to be."

"That sums it up. God wants to heal people's souls. He loves you no matter what. He died for you, a sinner. Just think about it and let God direct your heart," Mother said.

"Thank you so much for those encouraging words. Maybe church is what is missing in my life. Ever since I quit going, my life has been a mess!" I said.

"Why don't you set the table? Your daddy will be home any minute and he likes to eat when he gets home."

"How well I know that," I said, laughing.

When this day ended, I went to my bedroom to be alone. For the longest time, I lay there looking up towards heaven, trying to figure out the direction my life had taken over the past few years. Why did both these men abuse me? I tried to be the best wife I could be, and yet I failed. All my efforts to stay married still ended in divorce. Now I felt the guilt of two broken marriages. I will have to live with that for the rest of my life.

Before I sank deeper into despair, I reached for my Bible hoping for answers. I opened it to Matthew 11:28-30, which states, "Come unto me, all ye that labor and are heavy laden, and I will give you rest. Take my yoke upon you, and learn of me; for I am meek and lowly in heart, and ye shall find rest unto your souls. For my yoke is easy, and my burden is light." Then I prayed, "Lord Jesus I am weary and so, so tired. I am tired of failing and I desperately need You in my life. Please forgive me for my transgressions. You have given me this special family and all I do is hurt them. What is wrong with me? Please help me. Please direct my path. You know my heart. Please help me find peace in my life. Thank you, Lord Jesus, for loving me and always being there for me. Amen."

8

A CHILD IS BORN

One Saturday morning I was lying in bed having a pity-party. I felt I was entitled. How quickly I forgot all the good in my life when my second marriage fell apart. Dwelling on the negative was suffocating me. I had to force myself to look at the positive. I was so thankful for my family. In addition, I did find love. I remember hearing the words, "It is better to have loved and lost, than to have never loved at all." I was hoping I would be able to forgive Tom and Jim, one day.

It was during this time when I really found out who my friends were. Karen was still a great encourager and a good friend from high school. I did not see her as much anymore, but we talked on the phone from time to time. She spent the majority of her time with her fiancé now. Connie was always there for me. We saw each other daily at work and I treasured her friendship. She was a great listener and never judged me.

I often wondered why my life consisted of so many problems. I read about Job in the Bible many times. Job went through one torment after another, yet God was faithful to him. There were times I cried out to my Lord and Savior, too, just like Job did. No matter how hard I tried, things would not change; or, if they did, it was short-lived. I felt that I was never good enough. Many times, I wondered if God could even hear my pleas for help, or if He ever loved me. I felt like God had let me down. I had to find the strength from way down deep inside my soul to keep the faith like Job had. I had to believe that God would take care of me no matter what.

As each day passed, I was a robot: Get up, go to work, come home, visit with my family, and go to bed; then repeat the same routine the next day. I had no desire to go to my dance club or go out with my friends anymore. I was not feeling like myself for quite awhile and blamed it on stress. Then I realized I had not had my monthly cycle for a few months. I decided to see my doctor. Sure enough, my suspicions were right. I was pregnant! I was thrilled and scared at the same time. I had to believe that God would take care of my unborn child and me as well. I was convinced that God sent this child to me. Maybe God was sending me this special gift to make up for the trauma I had endured. If God had not wanted this pregnancy to happen, then He would not have allowed it. I finally realized why I stayed with Jim even though he handed me those divorce papers to sign. God planned this pregnancy long before I even knew about it.

After I came home from the doctor, I said nothing to my family. I needed time to absorb the news. I wish I could have shared this happy moment with my husband. If I had my way, I would never tell him. Then it dawned on me that I must have been pregnant when Jim abused me. "Thank you, God, for taking care of me and my unborn child," I prayed silently. Now, more than ever, I needed Jim to stay out of my life and my child's life as well. The fear of Jim hurting my child the way that he had hurt me made chills run up and down my spine.

I went to bed early that night. As I lay there, I put my hand on my stomach knowing that within me was a gift from God. Through all the misery, God blessed me with a child. Those words, "You're pregnant," kept ringing in my ears. God sent this child to me, and nobody could ever take him or her away from me. Wait until I tell Mother, Daddy, Nana, and Granddad and my brother too. Soon, we will have four generations living in one house!

The prospect of being a single parent, who is handicapped besides, blew me away! I had two great examples of mothers right in front of me: Mother and Nana. I made a promise that night to God and to my unborn child. I would do whatever it took to be the best mother. I was determined to keep that promise no matter what it took. I did not care if I had a boy or a girl. I had this vision, in my mind's eye, of ten little fingers and ten little toes with tiny eyes looking up at me. This child will be mine forever.

Since moving back home, I felt more peaceful. I did not want any stress to affect my unborn child. I had to tell my family eventually that I was pregnant. I wondered how they would react. I wanted them to be excited too. This would be my parent's first grandchild and my grandparent's first great grandchild. How fortunate I was to have my family; they were there for me no matter what.

As usual, I started asking myself questions. When would be the right time to tell my family? How long could I keep my pregnancy a secret? I was not showing yet which was a godsend in itself. According to my doctor I was around two or three months pregnant. Did I dare call Jim? I had no choice. A child had to be included in the divorce papers because we were still married when I conceived. The thought of telling Jim scared me. I had no idea how he would react. I had no idea how I would react if Jim wanted to have a part in his child's life. How was I going to continue working after the baby came? I did not know how to answer any of these questions.

After dinner, one evening, was the perfect time to talk to my parents without any distractions.

"Mother and Daddy, I have something to tell you," I said.

"What now?" Daddy asked, acting skeptical. I did not blame him.

Mother chimed in too, asking, "What's wrong?"

"I haven't been feeling myself lately, so I went to the doctor. Come to find out I am fine, but much to my amazement I am pregnant! The doctor is not sure, but thinks the baby will be born sometime in July next year. I think I got pregnant around my birthday."

"I can't believe it! I am thrilled for you," Mother said. "I think you will be a great mother, but you're going to face more challenges being handicapped and single."

"I know," I replied.

"How could you let this happen?" Daddy asked.

"Because Jim and I were having so many problems, you can bet that I didn't plan this. It just happened!" I told him.

"No kidding!" Daddy said, leaving the room to grab a beer.

"I have so much going through my head right now. I do not know where to begin. You can continue to stay here as long as you want. I do not want you out on your own, above all, with a new baby. We want to be a part of your life and our grandchild's life too. I cannot believe I am going to be a grandmother! I am so excited! Please know everything is going to be okay. We will be with you every step of the way," Mother said, coming over to give me a hug.

"I am the luckiest girl in the world. To be a part of this family is truly a blessing. Thank you for being so supportive."

Daddy came back, after he grabbed a beer, and said, "I agree with your mother. I heard her from the kitchen. We want you here. We do not want you alone in some apartment somewhere. We will not even discuss any other option with you. You and your child will live here with us and that is final!"

"Thank you so much. Everything is so overwhelming. When I first found out I was pregnant, I could not believe my ears. That is why it took me so long to tell you. I think I was in shock. I do believe, however, that God has a plan for my life. I don't know what that is, but I have to have faith that God will see me through whatever happens."

"God will, Sharon. God is always there. We are the ones that push Him away. Please don't make the same mistake that I did when you got polio."

"I won't. I believe that God wants me to have this baby. If He did not, then I wouldn't have gotten pregnant."

"Have you told Jim yet?" Daddy asked.

"No, I haven't. I called my attorney and he said that the divorce papers need modification because there is a child involved now. He told me not to worry. I don't want to, but I'll have to call Jim and let him know eventually."

"I wouldn't want to tell him either, but he is the father and has every right to know," Daddy said, and Mother agreed.

"I'm hoping that Jim won't want anything to do with the baby. It is obvious he does not want anything to do with me. We have not had any contact for some time. I am hoping it will stay that way when the baby comes. I want nothing from him; neither alimony nor child support. No way will I ever leave Jim alone with our baby. He can be so sweet and then turn on a dime and become this person I don't even know," I said, with conviction.

"I've got to go downstairs and tell my parents the news," Mother said, as she left.

"Daddy, I hope you're not too disappointed with me. I know I have caused our family a lot of grief, but it was never intentional. You have to believe that!" I said.

"Sharon, you have been through the war over the past few years. You have had some bad luck and made some terrible choices too; but, of late, you have been doing nothing but going to work. See, I do observe things that happen around here, even though I'm not around as much as your mother is," he said, with a grin on his face.

"Words are cheap. To say I am sorry for all I have put you and Mother through is senseless. You both know how sorry I am. I can only hope and pray that in time things will get better," I said, trying to reassure him of my intentions.

"Things will turn around for you. Don't ever give up hope."

Soon, Mother came back upstairs. Nana and Granddad were right behind her. They were thrilled! Nana and Granddad were always happy when good things happened to me. They felt this baby was going to bring me a lot of joy.

We sat talking for quite a while. It was so nice to talk about happy things for a change. Laughter filled our home. Finally, I was bringing happiness to Mother, Daddy, Nana, and Granddad.

Shortly after Christmas 1961, my regular doctor said that because I was a post polio victim and pregnant, he wanted me to see a specialist. I was alarmed, but he assured me that he was just being extra cautious.

When I saw the specialist, Dr. Wells, he said everything was fine, but he wanted me to use my wheelchair full-time. He did not want me to fall while using my crutches. I told him about my parents' house. He knew I would have some challenges using a wheelchair in their home, but he figured we would work it out. I was more concerned that I was not showing yet and had not gained much weight. In a way, I was glad because I was not ready yet to tell anybody, especially anyone outside my family, about my pregnancy. Dr. Wells reassured me that everything was okay. He felt I was carrying the baby in the curved area of my back and that was why I was not showing. Maybe that curve was finally serving a purpose.

The day came for me to call Jim. I could feel my heart pounding, and my hand shook as I dialed the phone. When he answered, I told him I had to talk to him about our divorce. Much to my surprise, my lawyer had already contacted his lawyer, so he already knew about the baby! It was obvious that he did not care because he would have called me. This was a good sign. This is what I had prayed for. Jim agreed, first, to leave the original divorce papers as they stood and not re-file because our child would be born before the final decree. Secondly, he agreed to pay no alimony or child support, which is what I wanted. Lastly, he did not want to have anything to do with his child or me. Even he feared for our safety. This was a big load off my mind. He went on to explain that since he left me he had to see his commanding officer because he stabbed someone in the mess hall and might go to jail. At that moment, I silently thanked God for getting me out of that marriage.

In Mark 9:23 it states, "Jesus said unto him, If thou canst believe, all things are possible to him that believeth." Down deep in my soul, I did believe. I felt my faith was coming back stronger each day. I knew God was watching over me. Another Scripture I held onto was Matthew 19:26 that states, "But Jesus beheld them, and said unto them, With men this is impossible, but with God all things are possible." From that day forward, I knew I would have to hang onto those words and hang onto God for dear life.

Around springtime, Mother, Nana, and I were sitting in the kitchen talking when the phone rang. After Mother hung up the phone she said, "That was Tom! He's back in San Diego after being overseas. He wants to see me and catch up on old times."

"Why would he want to see you, his ex-wife's mom?" I inquired. "He was married to me. No way do I want to see him, and you shouldn't either," I added.

"It'll be fine. Do not worry so much. It has been quite awhile since you have seen him and maybe he has changed. Tom was a very likeable person. Things would have been better if you had never married, but that's water under the bridge," Mother said, while fussing around the kitchen.

"He doesn't even know I got married again," I told her. "He doesn't know I'm pregnant and going through another divorce. Wouldn't that be wonderful news for him to catch up on?" I added in a snide way, getting very irritated with my mother.

"Listen, he's coming to see me, not you," Mother said.

I pleaded with her, "Mother please do not tell him anything about me!"

"Okay," she said, "Stop worrying."

When Tom arrived, I stayed in my bedroom until my curiosity got the best of me and I went into the kitchen. Tom asked me to sit down with him and the rest of the family. I agreed. Thankfully, nobody let on what happened to me while he was gone. He said that after we divorced, he went to Long Beach and then overseas for nine months. He still looked handsome, and I felt all those old feelings resurface. I thought to myself, what hold does this man have on me? I know he was my first love; but, more than that, I wanted my wheelchair. Maybe that clouded my judgment. I also remembered how things had been between us before he started drinking.

Later, after Tom left, Mother said I would eventually have to tell him about my marriage and being pregnant. I told her I probably would never see him again.

A few days later while I was at work, Tom visited Mother again. When I came home, Mother said Tom came over to tell her that he still had feelings for me.

"I don't understand. Why is this happening?" I said.

"All I know is what he told me," Mother said.

"My mind is swimming!" I said, totally confused.

"Sharon, I don't know why he's back."

"He treated me so badly when he was drinking. Can somebody change that much?"

"I believe drinking was Tom's downfall," Mother said.

"Do you know if he is still drinking?" I questioned her.

"He said he hasn't had a drink in over a year! He realized how awful he treated you and got help. I give him credit for that. He is older now and more mature."

"You actually asked him about his drinking?"

"Yes. I sure did," Mother said.

"I can't believe you did that," I said, as I left the room in total amazement.

Over the next few weeks, Tom continued to come over. Our conversations were light. I did not need anything to stress me out right now.

One evening, Mother and Daddy went out to dinner with friends. I think they made plans deliberately so that Tom and I could be alone so we could talk. We hashed over many things that happened to the two of us since we went our separate ways. Luckily, I still was not showing, so Tom was not yet aware of my pregnancy, or my marriage to Jim. I knew that if he continued to come over, I would have to tell him.

A few weeks later, I decided to be upfront with Tom. I told him about my partying days, my marriage to Jim, and my divorce. Then I told him I was pregnant. He thought I was kidding.

"You're just saying that."

"No, I am not. I would never kid about something that important."

"You're pregnant?" Tom said, in a surprising tone. Then he asked, "Why are you getting a divorce?"

"We are divorcing because Jim physically abused me. He would be nice one minute and then blow up the next. It scared me to death."

"I know I treated you badly, but I only did that when I was drunk. I know that is no excuse. After we divorced, I got help and have not had a drink in over a year. I learned that alcohol and I do not mix. Can you ever forgive me? I am so sorry," he said, with conviction.

"I forgive you, Tom. Maybe I should have stayed with you. You had a disease, but I just could not."

"I understand," he replied. "I was a mess. I know that now."

"My marriage to Jim is over. The divorce will not be final until after our baby is born. Jim has agreed to leave the baby and me alone. I am thankful for that. I want nothing from him! He just got into some serious trouble again and might go to jail. I hope you understand when I say it's better if he stays out of my life and my child's life."

"I sure do, especially if he's a violent man. I would not want somebody like that around my child!" Tom said.

"You know, Tom, I've always wanted a home, husband, and a family, but things never worked out for me."

"Maybe things did not work out for us because we were too young; and, of course, my problem with alcohol," he said.

All of a sudden, Tom got off the couch, went down on one knee and put his arms around me. He whispered in my ear, "If Jim doesn't want you or his child, I do!"

"What?" I blurted out in utter shock.

"We could get married again," Tom said.

"We can't get married. My divorce is not final and won't be until after my baby is born," I said.

"So then we'll wait and get married after your divorce is final."

"Not so fast," I said. "We have a lot of talking to do before any decision is made about anything. My hormones are wacky right now. All I do is cry. This is no time for me to make major decisions."

"Okay. Calm down," Tom said, "but please give it some thought."

"I will. You can count on that. Now please go," I said.

The next morning I talked to Mother and Daddy about everything that happened the night before. Mother was more into "girl talk" than Daddy was, so Daddy made an excuse to leave us alone. Mother totally understood my frustration. Mother said one thing that really stood out in her mind was that Tom thought enough about his problem with alcohol that he sought help and quit drinking. That meant a lot to her. She pointed out that he took that problem and turned it around. I had to agree with her, but I told her I was not going to rush into another marriage.

"My priority now is my unborn child. I will see what happens after my baby is born," I told her.

"I agree with you 100 percent. This is a major decision and one that should not be taken lightly."

Over the next months, there was a lot of joy in our home. I was feeling much better and felt more positive. All of us were anxiously waiting for my baby to be born. I was lucky; my health was good. Even in my eighth month, I did not wear maternity clothes, just big blouses. I only gained 17 pounds. I kept asking my doctor if something was wrong, but he assured me that I was okay and the baby was fine.

In June of 1962, I decided to terminate my employment. It was hard leaving everyone, but I knew this day would come. They were like my second family. It was a good thing because a few weeks later I started labor with a bang! Literally, it was on July 4. After five days of mild labor, my doctor told me to go to the hospital. My doctor wanted to check the positioning of the baby, so he ordered some x-rays. My doctor's suspicions were correct. My baby was in a double breech position. There was no way I could have natural childbirth. He told me he would schedule me for a C-Section the following day.

My emotions were running wild. The other women had their husbands with them. I was there with nobody, except my family. Thank God, I had them. They were helping me through a very emotional time. Mother was feeling sad because I did not have a husband by my side as the other women did. To top that off, Tom could not be there because he was aboard ship on maneuvers. Mother could sense my sadness. She knew how important it was to her when Daddy was with her when my brother and I were born. Mother wanted the same for me too. After many tears, a lot of hugs and kisses from my family, the nurse came into my room and wheeled me out so Dr. Wells could perform surgery.

Thankfully, the surgery went fine. When I woke, the first thing I inquired about was whether I gave birth to a boy or a girl.

"You have a beautiful baby boy. He weighed in at 7 pounds, 10 ounces and he is doing fine," my doctor said, congratulating me.

"Oh thank God! I want to see him now!"

"Not right now my dear," he said, "you must rest. You just had major surgery. You can see your son tomorrow."

My family and I were floating on cloud nine. They would go see my son and then come back to see me. After my surgery, I felt good considering all I had gone through; but, by the end of the day, I was beat!

The following morning the nurse brought my son to me. He was the most beautiful baby in the world. His head was a mass of black hair. He was so big. I could not get over how perfect he was. Sure enough, he had ten little fingers and ten little toes. He was looking up at me just the way I had pictured it would be. I wanted to shout to the world, "My son is born! He is here, born this tenth day of July 1962!" Thankfulness filled my heart. God sent me this beautiful, healthy baby boy, and everything I had been through was worth it!

In the Bible, the book of Psalms is full of songs written by King David. Every time I read Psalms, it gives me comfort. I felt it only fitting to name my son David, after King David in the Old Testament. A long time ago, I promised God to be the best mother I could be and that was a promise I planned to keep.

After everyone left, I prayed a prayer of thanksgiving to God. "Lord Jesus, thank you for this beautiful gift. David is so perfect in every way. It is hard for me to believe that for the first time in my life, I have something that nobody can ever take away from me. Please keep my son safe in Your protective arms. Amen."

9

FROM DESPAIR TO JOY

When David was two days old, Tom returned from maneuvers and immediately came to the hospital. He was so excited. You would have thought David was his own son. Proudly, he said, "I can't wait until we get married and the three of us are a family."

"We will talk more about marriage when I get out of here. Right now, I want to concentrate on my son. He is truly a gift from God. I can't believe the amount of love I feel towards him," I said.

After we visited for a while he said, "You need your rest. I'll see you tomorrow."

I had to stay in the hospital for ten days. I was glad because as the days went by I could tell my stomach was more sensitive than I thought. Due to my disability, I used my stomach muscles more than the average person did, especially when "transferring" my body from one location to another. I also experienced some trauma in the hospital. One day my nurse grabbed my arms trying to assist me to the toilet. I fell to the floor because I had no strength in my legs to support me. On the way down, I hit my head on the toilet rim and knocked myself out. When I told Dr. Wells what happened, he arranged for Mother to stay with me. I still had severe abdominal pain; and, every time I transferred, the staples pulled.

The day finally came for me to take my son home. What a glorious day! Everyone was excited. With two sets of grandparents, I would have plenty of help caring for my son. At first, I was all thumbs, but I learned fast. It struck me odd that people could go to school to learn all sorts of things, but there was no class for how to be a good parent. Fortunately, I had my mother and Nana to teach me. David was such a good baby. My breast milk soured while I was under anesthesia, so David used a bottle. Even then, God knew it would be easier because Mother and Nana could feed David while I gained back my strength.

It was summer, so Neil came home from college. When he held David, I felt tears in my eyes. David looked so tiny compared to my 6'2" brother who was such a big brute. While I was changing David's diaper, Neil leaned down to give him a kiss. Suddenly, David peed on his chest. I roared with laughter. Neil did not think it was the least bit funny. "Yuk," he commented as he walked away to wash up.

One day I woke with a high fever and a swollen left leg. The fear of polio gripped the heart of my mother. She thought it might be polio resurfacing because some scientists felt you could get polio more than once. Mother called my doctor, and we went right in. He said that I had phlebitis, an inflammation of the veins. This was causing my fever and the pain in my leg. He said that I could stay at home as long as I took warm baths and prescribed medication.

When Mother and I returned home, Neil had to help Mother get me in and out of the tub because the pain was so bad. My leg weighed a ton. There he was again, my brother, my big protector. I could always count on him. Thank God, I was not alone; my family was there to help me.

One afternoon my girlfriend, Karen, came for a visit.

"My goodness Sharon, Your leg is huge! When are things ever going to be normal in your life?" Karen asked.

"I don't know," I replied. "You can bet I'm ready. I thank God everyday for Mother and Nana. They have helped me so much with David. If I were alone right now, I don't know what I would do."

Karen then asked, "Are you and Tom getting married again?"

"He wants to, but I'm still leery. We can't get married now anyway until my divorce is final."

"Please let me know what you decide. I have to run. Take care of yourself. I hope you find the happiness you deserve."

Tom and I talked for months about remarrying. We hashed and rehashed our past, and talked at length with my mother and Daddy. Finally, we decided to get married again. Mother and Daddy gave us their blessing. I called Karen and Connie. They knew Tom and thought because he stopped drinking that things would work out this time. They were both happy for me.

My parents said we could live with them until we found a place to rent. We were so thankful for their support. A few days later, we were married in a small ceremony at my parent's home. We decided not to go on a honeymoon. Our number one concern was having David's last name legally changed to match ours. David's father was in jail now and did not protest. This was another answer to my prayers. God was watching over my son and me.

Eventually we found an apartment in El Cajon, about 20 minutes from my parents' house. It took forever to find just the right place. Using a wheelchair meant there could be no steps. The doorways had to be wide enough for my wheelchair. There had to be added space throughout the house to get around. I needed a place where I felt comfortable and could manage without the help of my parents and grandparents. Now, I had two people depending on me. This apartment fit every need. I was overjoyed!

After a couple of months, Tom came home and said his ship was going into dry dock and we had to move to Long Beach. I could not believe my ears. We were finally into a routine and now we had to move again. Moving two hours away from my family scared me to death. We always lived within a few miles from one another. Mother came over to help me with David if I needed her. If we moved to Long Beach and I needed help, I would have nobody. I explained my feelings to Tom. He tried to understand my point of view, but he wanted his family with him. I understood his feelings, but the fear of moving terrified me! We finally decided that Tom would stay in Long Beach aboard ship during the week and come home on weekends until David was a little older. God was really watching over us during this time. A few weeks later, I found out I was pregnant again.

Days later, Mother invited the three of us for dinner. We felt this was the perfect time to tell Mother and Daddy. After we ate, we told them our news. They were thrilled, but concerned about me physically.

"Because Tom is in Long Beach all week, why don't the three of you move back in here?" Mother suggested. "I do not like the idea of you and David being alone all week, especially now that you are pregnant. When Tom comes home on weekends, he can come here just as easily."

"I think you have come up with a great idea. Sharon cannot be moving right now. She needs to be close to her family and her doctor," Tom said.

"We can work out all the details later," Daddy interjected.

"Tom, I hope you do not think we are interfering. We know you have obligations in the military, but I think we've come up with a good alternative," Mother said.

"Listen, Tom, while you're gone this week, the gals can pack up your stuff. We will have everything ready to take to storage when you come home next weekend. How does that sound?" Daddy asked.

"Fine, I guess. If everybody is in agreement then let's do it," Tom said, looking at me for some input. "What do you think, Sharon?"

"Do I actually get a say?" I asked jokingly, and then added, "Mother and Daddy, we are so lucky to have both of you in our lives. This arrangement will take a big load off our shoulders."

Afterwards, Mother went downstairs to get Nana and Granddad to ask them to come upstairs. We told them the news about the baby and about moving in with Mother and Daddy. They were thrilled!

Within the next month, we settled in at my parent's house. Tom was commuting, and things were working out better than we ever thought possible. This was a good decision because this pregnancy was not an easy one. I gained a lot of weight right away and began wearing maternity clothes at two months. My doctor was not pleased about my getting pregnant so soon because I would have to have another C-Section. I, on the other hand, was delighted. David would have a brother or sister to share his life with, and they would be close in age.

As time went by, I could feel a strain developing between Tom and me. He was not coming home every weekend. I started to feel threatened. I wanted to get my stuff out of storage, pack my belongings, grab my son, and move to Long Beach; physically, I could not. When I shared these feelings with Tom, much to my surprise, he discouraged me from moving. Feelings of doubt overwhelmed me. My woman's intuition told me that something was wrong. I wondered why Tom did not want me with him. I had to trust God that everything would work out.

When I shared my fears with Mother, she said that I always thought the worst. Maybe she was right. The sad part is that all my suspicions came true. Tom came home one weekend and told me he had fallen in love with another woman and filed for divorce. I started screaming at him and crying at the same time. I went completely numb. I wanted to die! It was like an instant replay of my past. I was pregnant again, and I would have another divorce to add to my list of failures.

"What in heaven's name did I do to deserve this?" I screamed at him. He just sat there and said nothing! That infuriated me more.

"We talked for months about getting remarried and I thought you wanted a home and a family like I did," I said, pleading with him.

"I thought I did too," he said, "but things have changed."

"Now you want out of this marriage after convincing my parents and me how much you loved and cared about me and wanted to be a father to David. My God, we even had David's last name changed. You said you loved David as if he were your own. Now you want to leave David and your unborn child and me. What's gotten into you?" I asked with so much anger pouring out of me.

"It's not like that. I've thought about this a long time."

"Are you doing this because I didn't move to Long Beach?" I asked.

"No, it is not that," he said.

"Then why are you doing this?" I asked.

"I just can't deal with all this. Our marriage didn't work before, and I was a fool to think it would work this time."

"You can't deal with what?" I asked.

"You are disabled and confined to a wheelchair!"

"The whole time we've known each other I have been disabled; first on crutches and then in a wheelchair," I yelled, with tears still streaming down my face. I was crying so hard I thought I was going to vomit.

"Listen to me! I need to be free to be able to live a normal life with a normal woman. I am sorry. My girlfriend and I have more in common than you and I do!"

Listening to Tom as I sat there, all I could hear was the word normal. Tears kept flowing as I said to him, "You are going to be a father! You were so quick to judge Jim when he left me when I was pregnant, and now you're doing the same thing!" I said, screaming even louder.

"Yes, I did judge Jim. I will be there for David and my child. I will pay child support, but that is it. You will be receiving papers from my attorney. I know you're hurt, but I know you wouldn't want to stay married to a man that doesn't love you."

With those words, he got up, walked out, got into his car, and drove away. I literally wanted to die! Tears would not stop flowing. I felt like my world had fallen apart.

When I told my family, they were in shock. Nobody could believe this was happening to me again. They had no words to comfort me. My life was falling apart, and I did not know what to do. How could I ever face anyone again? People are going to think there is something terribly wrong with me. I had no strength left to prove them wrong. I cried for days. My body wrenched with pain.

The main thing that haunted me was Tom's preference for an able-bodied woman. He did not want to be married to me, a handicapped woman. If only he had decided to leave me for another reason. I kept falling into a deep dark hole. I could not fight my despair, and I did not really care. I know with every inch of my being, if it were not for my children, I would not be here today. They kept me from taking my life. The devil was pulling me in one direction and God, in another. I was lost. I did not know if I would ever regain my faith again. Many times, I cried out to God, "Why have you forsaken me?" I could not pray. I was in a terrible state of mind, and I did not know if I would ever come back to God.

Over the next few months, I asked myself what is normal. I felt normal as far as being a wife, a mother, and a homemaker. I could do all the things required of me; and, I was darn good at it too. It was going to take me a long time to get over the stigma that Tom left me for an able-bodied woman.

Because of David and my unborn child, I had to find the will to go on and keep the promise I made to God that I would be the best mother I could be. God knew I needed to make that promise to Him a long time ago. I tried to be thankful for both Tom and Jim because without them I would not have my children. I swore I would never date another able-bodied man again as long as I lived! I do not know what I would have done without my family. They stood by me, never dreaming that my life would have so much turmoil in it. I felt like I had been through the war and they had gone through everything with me.

Months later, after the initial shock wore off, and the anger subsided, I remember trying to pray again. I wrote down a prayer in my journal: "Lord Jesus, I don't know why all this has happened, and there are times that I feel very angry with You for allowing it to. Please forgive me. Thank you for David, Lord, and my unborn child. Bless their souls; my children are saving my life. Amen."

David was the light of my life. At times, I would sit by his crib and just watch him sleep. He brought me so much joy. Being disabled was a challenge in caring for David, but I always found a way to do whatever was necessary so that he would be a happy and contented child.

It was easier for me to be in a wheelchair full-time to care for David. The biggest challenge was when David and I went out together, just the two of us. Back in the 1960's, I carried him in an infant seat. When I left the house, I would place David in his infant seat. When we got in the car, I would put David on the floorboard first, in front of the passenger seat. Next, I would transfer to the passenger seat, fold up my wheelchair, and put it behind the passenger seat. Then I would slide over behind the steering wheel, and raise David up onto the passenger seat. Once our seat belts were secure, we took off.

When we arrived at our destination, I reversed the process to get out of the car. When we went shopping, people stared at us; they were in awe. I had David across the arms of my wheelchair in his infant seat while I pushed my wheelchair. People would stop me just to look at him. He was so cute. I was the proudest mother in the world. I was also grateful to God for the extra strength in my hands and shoulders that He had given me.

A month or so later, I decided to venture out to our local drugstore. Getting the wheelchair in and out of the car was becoming a challenge now because of my protruding stomach. When I arrived, I took the wheelchair out of the car; but, as I tried to transfer, I was too heavy. My hip hit the side of the wheelchair and I landed on the pavement. My wheelchair went flying out of my reach. There I sat startled. This had never happened to me before. I yelled for Mr. Sexton, the owner of the drug store, to come out and help me.

Other customers were gathering around now to see what all the commotion was. Mr. Sexton saw my wheelchair up against the side of the building and brought it to me. The more I tried to get off the ground and into my wheelchair, the harder I laughed. After about five minutes, Mr. Sexton and one of his employees managed to literally pick me up and put me back into my wheelchair. I went in the store, got my prescription, and went home. I now knew I could not go out alone again until I had my baby.

When I got home, I told Mother and Nana what had happened.

"No more shopping by yourself in your condition," Mother told me.

Nana sat there shaking her head in disbelief. She could not believe what I had to endure on a daily basis.

When David was about nine months old, he was starting to get into more things. He was pulling himself up onto the furniture. Standing there, I could tell he wanted to let go and walk, but he was still skeptical.

"Come here!" I called to him.

Mother stood at one end of the living room and said, "Go to Mommy." All of a sudden, he walked over to me. Mother and I were crying. What a wonderful day it was for my mother and I to watch David take his first steps. A few minutes later Nana came in. She realized what had happened. She had tears in her eyes too.

I continued to see my gynecologist. He was concerned that I was overweight. I was well over 200 pounds. He kept asking me about my diet. I told him I was careful because the weight was hurting my mobility. Whenever my independence was threatened, I would freak out. After some lab work, Dr. Wells said that I had toxemia. He told me he would monitor me and assured me that everything should be okay.

The day came for me to go to the hospital and have my second C-Section. Dr. Wells decided to take my baby a few weeks early because of the toxemia. Mother stayed with me in the hospital so that I would not have an instant replay of what happened to me when I gave birth to David.

The birth went fine. I lost 60 pounds during the surgery because I had so much fluid. After surgery, Dr. Wells gave me a shot so that I would go through afterbirth labor to help me lose weight and keep me from getting phlebitis again. For two days, I was heavily medicated. Once I woke up and became more aware, Dr. Wells told me I gave birth to a son. I was thrilled! I prayed for so long to have another boy. David would have a brother to play with and they were only 53 weeks apart.

"Did you tie my tubes?" I asked.

"No, I couldn't. Under the law, you and your husband both have to sign the papers. I am sorry, Sharon. I cannot emphasize how important it is that you never get pregnant again. You are at high risk for excessive bleeding, toxemia, and phlebitis, so be careful."

"I don't think I'll be getting married again. Can you please tell the nurse to bring me my son?" I asked.

"I can't do that right now," Dr. Wells said.

"Why, what's wrong?" I asked, feeling my heart start to pound.

"Things aren't going well for your son right now," Dr. Wells explained, with concern written all over his face.

"What's wrong?" I asked, pleading with him for some answers.

"As you know we took him a few weeks early. He was born blue due to the lack of oxygen to his lungs. He is having difficulty breathing. We have your son in ICU."

"I can't believe it!" I cried out.

"We will know more in a couple of days. I must tell you, there is a chance that he might not make it."

With tears streaming down my face, I cried out, "No! This can't be!"

"I'm sorry, Sharon. I have to be honest with you."

"Please let me see my son!" I pleaded.

"You have to rest. The nurses are caring for your son in ICU. Right now, I want you to take care of yourself."

"My son can't die!" I yelled.

My stomach was beginning to hurt because of the incision, so Dr. Wells ordered a sedative for me and said, "Listen, we are doing everything humanly possible to give your son the best chance to survive. They will not take him out of the incubator until we are sure he is physically ready. Try to stay calm. The only thing you can do right now is pray. It is out of our hands. Here comes the nurse with your medication."

"I still want to see him. Even if I can't hold him," I said.

"Not today, but tomorrow we will have a nurse wheel you down to ICU. After you get some rest, our staff pediatrician will be by to see you. I will go find your mother. I think she went to the cafeteria." With those words, he left.

I lay there for the longest time, crying my heart out. My stomach wrenched with pain from the surgery, but I could not stop crying. God answered my prayers and gave me a son, and now there was a chance I might lose him. Doubts of God's love came streaming back. Why does God always make me question Him? As I drifted off from the medication, I asked God, "Why me?"

When I woke up, Mother was sitting by my bed. She took one look at me and knew that Dr. Wells told me about my son. She did not say a word. She came over and held me. She knew words were senseless. I was thankful I did not have to be alone.

The following day, with Mother by my side, I finally was able to go to the ICU and see my son. There in front of me was another gift from God! He was so tiny, but he was mine. Nobody could take him away from me. God spared my child and I was so grateful. I could only stay for five minutes. I felt more optimistic when I left.

"Have you decided on a name, Sharon?" Mother asked me.

"Yes. I have decided to name him Neil with the middle name of Hartley. He will have the names of my brother, my grandfather, and your maiden name. I hope that pleases everybody."

"Everyone will be elated," Mother said.

I can just imagine family gatherings when somebody calls out Neil," I told her. "My son Neil, my brother Neil, and my granddad Neil will all respond."

Finally, the day came when the nurse brought my son to me. I waited so long to hold my beautiful baby boy. As I looked down at his sweet face, my heart filled with love. I could tell he was more fragile than David was. Later, the pediatrician said Neil was doing much better and physically his future looked good. I had two healthy boys. What more could I ask for? I could not take my eyes off him. He was so tiny, but still had those ten little fingers and ten little toes. I just wanted to eat him up.

As I lay there holding Neil, I said a silent prayer to my Lord and Savior. "Sweet Jesus, thank you for this gift that You have given me. You blessed me with two fine boys. Please forgive me for doubting You. Please forgive me for all the times I felt You had forsaken me. Thank you, for taking me out of total despair and bringing joy back into my life again. Amen."

10

PEACE AT LAST

I was anxious to leave the hospital after ten days and head home. I was sitting in my hospital room waiting for Mother and the nurse to bring Neil to me. As I looked out the window, my mind wandered. It was a beautiful summer's day in July of 1963. The sky was clear, and there was a slight breeze coming through my open window. I enjoyed living in southern California. Raising two children was going to have its challenges. I realized I would have to use my wheelchair full-time now.

As my mind continued to wander, my thoughts turned to Tom and Jim. God healed my soul from all the hateful feelings that I had towards these two men. I needed to be as positive around my boys as I could be. I wanted them to be happy and content no matter what my situation was. I knew some day I would have to tell them about their fathers, but that would have to wait until they were old enough to understand.

Shortly after Mother arrived, the nurse brought my son to me along with my discharge papers. I was so happy to be leaving the hospital with a healthy baby. As Mother and I drove home, I could tell I was getting apprehensive. I did not know if I were excited or scared to death. I had been caring for David with very few problems. Caring for two children, especially diaper changes and bottle-feeding, was going to be a challenge. I knew that God was in control. I had Him and my family to lean on.

When we pulled up outside our home, I felt more relaxed. David was standing out front with Nana and Granddad waiting for us. He referred to my parents as Ammy and Pappy now that he was talking.

David yelled, "Hi Mommy. Hi Ammy. Where is my brother?"

"He is right here," I said, cradling Neil in my arms. "As soon as we get out of the car and into the house, you can hold him. Come here first and give me a hug. Then go inside with Nana and Granddad. We will be in as quickly as we can," I said, hugging him.

When we got inside, David was so happy to see us. He spent the longest time examining his new baby brother. He wanted to kiss him every few minutes and be right by his side. He kept rubbing the top of Neil's head saying, "Ah." To watch David interact with his brother was precious. There we were, sitting in the living room of my parents' home with four generations present. We felt blessed.

As the days went by, I began getting my strength back and was amazed at my accomplishments. Mother was right again! I had some doubts in the hospital regarding my capabilities of caring for two children, but everything worked out. Being disabled did not hinder my taking care of my boys. I had to do things differently than able-bodied people, but I got the job done. At first, some things seemed difficult. After a few tries, however, I did okay. Being in a wheelchair made it easier for me to dress, bathe, change diapers, and feed my boys. As each day passed, I learned my own way of doing things.

About a week after I got home, friends started coming over to see my newborn son. I was so proud of him! Everybody was happy for me.

David was so easy to care for. He could entertain himself for hours watching cartoons if I let him. Having two sets of grandparents, David was never lacking in the toy department. David knew his mommy was in a wheelchair. He instinctively pushed his toys close to the walls to make a pathway for me to get through. Everybody that saw this thought it was cute. David showed empathy towards me and for my disability at a very young age.

Neil was doing really well until he developed colic. Poor thing would cry for hours because of gas pains in his stomach. He cried from four o'clock in the afternoon until midnight for weeks. We could tell what time of day it was when he started crying. Even the medication that the doctor prescribed did little to help. Mother, Nana, and I tried everything we could to comfort him. Nothing we did seemed to work. Eventually the colic subsided. It was none too soon. Our family found silence in our home to be an added pleasure after this experience.

At times, I felt so helpless when my sons had a problem that I could not fix. My mother warned me that I would have many times like that. "Wait until they are teenagers!" Mother said.

"Personally, I don't want to think that far ahead," I told her, chuckling. "Look at my teenage years. I do not even want to remember those years."

Later that evening, after the boys were in bed, Mother and I talked.

"I always feel like I have to fix my boys' problems. If they cry, I want to do whatever it takes to make them stop. When they get sick, my heart bleeds. Even when Neil had colic, it seemed like no matter what I did, nothing worked. I felt so helpless. I made a promise to God to be a good mother. I want desperately to keep that promise," I said.

"Listen, Sharon, you're a great mother. Years ago, I went through those same feeling when you got polio. I felt it was my fault. I felt that God had forsaken our family. I tried everything humanly possible to help you walk. Those were hard times for your daddy and me. It took me years to realize that I could not fix everything. You're going to have to learn that as well."

"I cannot imagine what you and Daddy went through," I said. "I think I understand more now that I'm a mom. You must have been beside yourself with worry."

"Six years old is very young to have your child's life completely changed right before your eyes," she shared.

"I know how I felt when I almost lost Neil when he was born. I felt a part of me was dying. I was never so scared in my life."

"I believe that children don't totally understand what their parents go through raising them until they have children of their own," Mother said.

"That's true. I did not understand. I only thought about myself. Not to mention getting married at 15!" I said.

"Let's not go there," she said, rolling her eyes back in her head. "When there is nothing you can do to help your child, it's the worst feeling in the world. All you can do is your best. The rest is up to them. Even before they are teenagers, they will make some bad choices. They, alone, will have to take responsibility for those choices. Do not feel guilty over every little thing that happens in their lives."

"You know me, I feel guilty about everything. I always take the blame. Look at my marriages and divorces," I pointed out to her.

"You went through a lot, but that's in the past. You have to let all that go and concentrate on the here and now," Mother said, giving me a hug.

I thanked her for listening to me. She was the best listener and always tried to reassure me that everything would be okay. I appreciated her wisdom. She knew a lot about mothering having raised twins. My boys were not twins, but they were very close in age. Having Mother and Nana to help me was a blessing.

That night I grabbed my Bible alongside my bed and started reading through it. Whenever I read the Bible, it gave me peace. I turned to the book of Psalms. Psalms always comforted me. King David always seemed to cry out to his Lord because of the trials that he went through. In Psalms 40:13-14 it states, "Be pleased, O Lord, to deliver me; O Lord, make haste to help me. Let them be ashamed and confounded together who seek after my soul to destroy it; let them be driven backward and be put to shame who wish me evil." Then, I prayed, "Lord Jesus, please deliver me, be with me and help me not to ponder on what other people think or say about me. Make me strong to overcome the hardships of my past and help me to accept whatever comes my way in the future. Help me be a good mother. Help me to have a positive outlook on life so that my children will not suffer from my transgressions. Amen."

Because my boys were close in age, I had my hands full. Many days seemed to whiz by. I could hardly catch my breath. I knew in a short time, they would be able to play and enjoy each other's company. That would give me more time to relax. When I told Mother this, she laughed and said, "You're dreaming. When they are small, their problems are small and when they get bigger, their problems will get bigger."

"You could have gone forever without telling me that," I said, laughing.

When my brother, Neil, went off to college, Mother kept his bedroom the same because he came home during vacation breaks. This summer was different because he was working part-time, taking extra classes, and wanting to spend any extra time he had with his fiancée. Mother called Neil one day and asked him if David could use his room while he was gone. He agreed. Most of his things were at college anyway. I missed my brother coming home this summer, but was glad David could use his room. This made it easier on all of us. David could take naps in there during the day and sleep in there at night. He would not be disturbed when I had to tend to Neil. Another advantage would be more space for me to maneuver my wheelchair in my own room.

I loved being a mother. It was not easy, but being a mom was so rewarding. I was thankful that Mother and Nana were there to help me. We did a lot of laundry because both boys were in diapers. Nana and Mother took care of the laundry because there were two steps to go down into the garage where the washer and dryer were. They did the laundry in the garage while I sat and folded the clothes at the kitchen table. We made a great team.

Not only was it easier caring for my boys in the wheelchair, but I also noticed my back was doing better. The curve in my spine was not hurting as much. I knew quite a few people from my dance group who married and had children. All of them were in wheelchairs full-time, except Connie and her husband. They both used crutches and wore long leg braces. Karen, my other girlfriend, marveled at how I cared for my boys. She was pregnant now and waiting for her first child to be born.

When one of the boys had to go to the doctor, Mother would always go with me to help while Nana stayed home with the other one. Getting one child and me into the car was enough for one day's work. I knew that eventually I would have to go out by myself with my boys. If for no other reason, I would need to practice doing things without my mother always there to help me. Being independent was extremely important to me. The saying "Where there's a will, there's always a way" is very true.

As a post polio victim and a young mother, I made sure my children had all their vaccinations, especially those for polio. My doctor said less than 18 cases of polio occurred among the over 50 million persons that took the full course of vaccine for polio. How could I not be thankful to have this opportunity to immunize my boys?

When Neil was around three months old, I decided to venture out to a local store with the boys by myself. First, I would have David sit in the back seat of the car while I placed Neil in his infant seat on the floorboard in front of the passenger seat. Next, I would transfer into the car from my wheelchair to the passenger seat, fold up my wheelchair, and put it behind the passenger seat. Then I would slide over to the driver's seat. With Neil still in his infant seat on the floorboard, I would instruct David to jump over the front seat so I could put a seat belt around him. I would secure Neil the best I could on the floorboard. Then when we got to where we were going I would have to get all three of us out of the car and then back in again to head home. Once home, I would have to get all of us out again! Mother used to say, "Now I know why God made young mothers," when she watched me. How right she was. By the time I got home, I was exhausted! I told Mother I had better take her along with me until Neil got a little older.

Our next shopping trip consisted of going to the mall. This time Mother went with us. The only thing that bothered me was people staring at us. Maybe they were just in awe seeing me in a wheelchair carrying two children. Maybe they were curious, but nobody said anything; they just stared. I often wished they would ask me questions because then I would know what they were thinking. There were times I really wondered why I bothered to go shopping. I felt so conspicuous because most of the time I was the only one in a wheelchair. When Mother went with us, she would have her hands full of packages, so David would stand on my foot pedals facing me and hold onto both arms of my wheelchair as I pushed my chair. Neil would be in his infant seat that fit perfectly across the arms of my wheelchair. Sometimes, David, holding onto the wheelchair, would walk along side of me. He knew never to let go, and he never did. Instinctively, he knew his mommy had special needs and needed his cooperation. Around the house, David loved to stand on my foot pedals and take rides around the house while I did housework. We had so much fun together. Soon Neil will be walking and enjoying these same experiences too.

On October 18, 1963 my girlfriend, Karen, and her husband became proud parents of a baby girl, on my birthday no less. I honestly think God took this occasion to heal me even more. You see, I was jealous of Karen because she was married and her husband was by her side during her pregnancy and the birth of their child. Jealousy reared its ugly head and damaged my soul. God knew I needed healing. Only because of Him could I finally share in her joy.

Around Thanksgiving, I decided I had to try to get my old job back. Tom was behind on his child support, and I needed to pay off my doctor and hospital bills. I could not continue to take advantage of my parents. I had no choice, but to approach Mother. She appreciated the fact that I did not want to take advantage of her and Daddy, but wondered if I could manage working full-time. I told her I could if she could watch the boys for me. I assured her that I would care for them when I got home and on the weekends. She agreed.

A few days later, I called my ex-boss. "Hi Dave, this is Sharon. Remember when you said I could have my old job back whenever I wanted it?" I reminded him.

"Yes, I remember. Why?" He asked.

"I'd like to take you up on your offer."

"Let me get back to you in a few days," he said.

Later that week Dave called and said I could start work on Monday. Connie still worked there. I was ecstatic!

"Thank you," I said, "you will not regret hiring me back."

"I'll see you on Monday!" He said.

I immediately told Mother and Nana. They were happy for me. Nana told me not to fret about the boys. She would help Mother. They both knew I needed to go back to work to help my self-esteem and not feel like a freeloader!

After Christmas, I felt more peaceful. I wanted to honor my children by placing them before God. Whether their circumstances were good or bad, they needed God's presence in their lives. I told Mother and Daddy I wanted to have David and Neil christened. I felt it was important. They agreed. I had really wanted David christened the year before. When I found out I was pregnant, I figured I could wait and have both children christened at the same time. I contacted St. Andrews Episcopal Church, where Mother and Daddy attended, to set a date. I also contacted my brother and he agreed to come with his fiancée.

What a wonderful day it was to watch my boys christened on February 2, 1964. I remember the pastor saying, "Lord bless these two young sons of Sharon's. Be ever so close to them. They have gone through a lot and so has she. All of them will need Your love in abundance. These two darling boys are truly a gift from You to Sharon. Your love will be with them forever. Be with this entire family, Lord. I ask you to bless these two boys in the name of the Father, the Son, and the Holy Spirit." While the pastor sprinkled their heads with "holy" water, he said, "Now the God of peace be with you all. Amen." I felt a deep peace knowing that God would always take care of my boys. To have my whole family present, witnessing this joyous day, brought tears to my eyes.

Later that evening I took out my Bible and looked through it. I felt God was trying to speak to me. It had been awhile since I picked up my Bible. How easy it is to put God on the back burner when life gets so busy. There in John 14:27 it states, in part, "…Let not your heart be troubled, neither let it be afraid." God gave me a real sense of peace during the christening of my two sons. I prayed, "God, my life is in Your hands. I cannot change a single thing that has happened to me in the past; it is over and done. I really want things to be better for my two children and me. Please make that happen. Amen."

Over the next few months, our lives were going to change. The doctor diagnosed Nana with severe arthritis in her spine. She had a hard time climbing up or down the long flight of stairs that led from her and Granddad's house to ours. Everybody thought it might be time to consider moving to a one-story house. Nana also pointed out that it would be easier on me if we could find a house with no steps. We all agreed. The only stipulation was we wanted to stay together.

Before my parents hired a real estate agent, I asked if we could wait long enough to have a small combined birthday party for David and Neil. They would be turning one and two years of age. I wanted their birthdays to be extra special. Everyone agreed. We loaded everyone into two cars and headed for Mission Beach. Belmont Park Amusement Center is right by the beach so the boys sitting on my parents' lap had the opportunity to go on a bunch of different kiddy rides. The boys had a blast! The management prohibited me from going on any of the rides because of the park's liability policy. I had to focus on the positive. Watching my boys laugh and scream while they rode various rides with my parents made my heart soar.

As the boys were getting older, it was becoming easier for me to do things. When we went out, it was easier to get them in and out of the car. When we shopped, Neil would sit with his little butt sitting right in the wheelchair seat between my knees, and David stood on the foot pedals holding onto the arms of my wheelchair. The people around us looked at us in awe!

In a short time, my parents' realtor found the perfect place. It was two houses on one lot with a one-car garage and patio area separating the two houses. Mother, Daddy, my boys, and I would be living in the big house up front; Nana and Granddad would live in the little house in back. If not under one roof, all four generations would still be close living together on one piece of property. This would make it easier for Nana because she had a smaller house to take care of. Granddad agreed to take care of the yard while Daddy worked. I was excited because one of the bedrooms was huge. Mother and Daddy said that I could have it for my boys and me. There was enough room in there for my twin bed, two cribs, and two dressers; and, I could still maneuver my wheelchair.

When I first saw the house, I was concerned about the steps. There was only one out front, but four in the back. Daddy put in a ramp in the back to accommodate my wheelchair. With this ramp, my friends in wheelchairs could now come over and visit.

Our new houses were older and needed work before we could move in. Everybody pitched in at different times during the week. On the weekends, we all went together and had the best time. David even tried his hand at painting. I do not know who had more paint on, David or the walls. The object was to have fun and we did. This was a new adventure for our family. We were anticipating the day we could move in.

On August 8, 1964, Mother and Daddy took off for Los Angeles to see Neil marry Margaret. Nana, Granddad, my boys, and I stayed home. It was too hard for Nana to make that long drive. For me, taking two children would be too hard too. Mother and Daddy promised all of us that they would take pictures of Neil and Margaret's special day. I phoned my brother telling him I was sorry I could not come. He knew I would be there if I could. He assured me that he and Margaret would come for another visit once we had moved into our new home.

That evening I went back to that Scripture that meant a lot to me in John 14:27 that states, "Peace I leave with you, my peace I give unto you; not as the world giveth, give I unto you. Let not your heart be troubled, neither let it be afraid." I felt so blessed. Things were going really well for my children and me. My boys were healthy and happy. I had a great job and all of us were excited about moving. We were looking forward to starting another adventure together. As each day passed, I felt closer to finding peace at last.

11

THINGS ARE LOOKING UP

Moving day arrived in September of 1964. Moving four generations out of one large house into two smaller ones was a monumental job. Having two little ones under foot was a challenge too. I was happy we moved. Now I could do more with the boys and help Mother do the laundry because the laundry room was inside the house. This helped my self-esteem. I felt more independent. I knew there would always be certain things that I could not do, but accepting that was hard. Whenever I had to ask for help, it made me feel inadequate.

Our two houses on one level made it ideal for me using a wheelchair. Having the ramp in the back of the house also allowed me access to the entire back yard and my grandparents' house. Friends of mine confined to wheelchairs could finally come and visit me. The bathroom was the only barrier. The bathroom had two doors, but neither door was wide enough for me to enter. Daddy could not widen either door because of where the wiring was in the wall. This meant I had to "hop" onto my four-legged stool or "crawl" on the floor whenever I had to use the bathroom. When I bathed the boys, I would crawl over to the tub to bathe them. The boys still loved to crawl around the house with me. They did not think of me as different. They thought we were just having fun.

I remember one day when both boys were in their bedroom and getting quite mischievous. I told them to knock it off, a reprimand which they totally ignored. I went wheeling into the room at a very high rate of speed. That got their attention! Instantly, and I mean instantly, they both flew under one of the cribs. I stopped my wheelchair, got down on the floor, and crawled towards them. Their eyes kept getting bigger, the closer I got. In a stern voice, I said to the two of them, "Don't you ever do that again! You cannot escape from me so do not even try. Mommy cannot walk, but I can still get to you." David, put his arm around Neil's shoulder and said, "Okay, Mommy. We'll be good." They were the sweetest boys. It was hard for me to keep a straight face while disciplining them.

The boys loved our new home. They could go outside more and play because the entire property was fenced. Four gates had locks on them for their safety. They loved to visit Nana and Granddad too.

One day, Neil was standing by the couch. All of a sudden, he released his hold and took his first steps.

I yelled, "Mother, come quickly. Neil is walking!"

Mother came running into the room. We both had tears streaming down our faces again, just like when David took his first steps. To see my children walk, especially that first time, was memorable. When you are disabled, it is a vision that stays with you forever. I was thankful I was there to witness it.

David was easy to care for. He was still content watching TV, looking through a book, or playing with his toys. Neil, on the other hand, could not sit still for long periods. He was far more active and seemed to get into everything. One day I came home from work and Mother told me Neil disappeared. She explained that she looked for Neil for over an hour with no luck. She was beginning to panic. Finally, Neil, completely covered with black ash, poked his head out of the living room fireplace. He obviously was having the time of his life because he never made a sound. Mother told me that when she found him she wanted to laugh, cry, and spank him all at the same time. I could only imagine how frightening that was for her. I would have given anything to have a picture of what he looked like at that moment. Mother, bless her heart, sure had her moments taking care of my boys. She never complained. She told me that caring for the boys kept her young.

Another time Mother panicked when she could not find Neil, so she called Nana and Granddad to come over to help her. When Nana came in the back door, she heard a noise coming from the dryer. There Neil was, inside the dryer! How he managed to get in and close the door was anybody's guess. Neil kept everyone hopping. To see my parents and grandparents interact with my boys was a joy.

Mother and Daddy loved their new house. It was easier for Mother to care for. She now had more time to enjoy her grandchildren. Daddy used to pinch my mother on her butt all the time and she would say, "Not in front of the children, Bill!" Mother and Daddy were always hugging and smooching. What a great witness they were to all of us.

Nana and Granddad enjoyed their "little" house. It reminded me of a dollhouse. Nana was a meticulous housekeeper, as was my mother; you could eat off their floors. Granddad would tease Nana about cleaning, but she would tell him, "I haven't got anything better to do, so leave me alone!" Nana and Granddad were so cute. Granddad was more active; he loved to take the boys for walks. He also went to the Senior Center to play cards or shuffle board. He cared for all the landscaping on our property. Our places looked like pictures in a home and garden magazine. Because of Nana's arthritis, she preferred to stay home. She was content spending time with my boys, her daughter, and me. She also loved to crochet. Their presence in my life and in the lives of my boys was a gift from God. The little things they did showed me what true love meant.

As Daddy left for work, he would come into my room to wake me. I did not want to use an alarm clock because it would awaken the boys. After I was ready, I would get the boys up, take care of them, and then leave for work. I tried to do as much as I could to help Mother. She had enough to do during the day while I was gone. Every night when Daddy and I came home, dinner was on the table. We always made a point of having our evening meal together as a family. While eating we discussed what each of us did during the day. Later I would help Mother clean up the kitchen and bathe the boys. This allowed her more time to spend with Daddy.

Mother and Daddy bought a camper shell for their truck, so that we could enjoy family times, especially at Waddell's Trailer Park, located 45 minutes away. Trees and mountains surrounded the park and off to the side was a huge swimming pool. In the middle of the park was a recreation center with a full kitchen, tables, chairs, a fireplace, dartboard, shuffleboard, and a billiard table. Sometimes, Mother and Daddy went alone and other times we all went. David and Neil loved it there. They loved the water. I liked being able to get into the pool and swim with them. Now our family could go to the beach, to the mountains, or to Waddell's Trailer Park.

Later I talked to my parents about getting a second job to enable me to pay off my doctor bills sooner. They agreed to take care of the boys no more than three nights a week and only for a few hours. I called George, who owned MPS Corporation. George hired me part-time. He agreed to my request of two hours, three nights a week. I did office work and made appointments for persons that needed hand controls. George agreed to hire me because he wanted to stay open a few hours in the evening for those that had to work. This job was so rewarding. Every time a product sold, I knew another disabled person was able to be more independent because he or she could now drive.

I had the best of both worlds working at two places. There was a mixture of handicapped and able-bodied people. We shared our highs, our lows, our hopes, and our dreams. The handicapped people shared ways to accomplish various tasks. This gave able-bodied employees an education on what it was like being handicapped and the daily challenges that disabled people faced. To have that kind of closeness was special.

MPS Corporation decided to have a drawing to give away a new set of hand controls to a veteran at the Long Beach Veteran's Hospital. Warner, one of the partners, asked me to be their model in a magazine layout in the PARAPLEGIA NEWS. He also asked if I would go up to Long Beach and draw the winning ticket. I could not believe it! I told him that I felt honored, but I would have to ask my parents if they could watch the boys. He asked me to let him know as soon as possible.

While eating dinner, I told Mother and Daddy about my conversation with Warner and that my picture was going to be in a magazine. They were thrilled. After a short discussion, they encouraged me to go and said they would take David and Neil to Waddell's Trailer Park over night so that I would have the entire day to myself.

"Thank you so much," I said, "I'll call Warner after we're done eating."

I socialized occasionally, but only with handicapped men. I was still leery about dating able-bodied men. I did not want an instant replay of what I went through in the past. I know I should not judge all men by two, but I did. Sometimes I wondered if I would ever get married again. I had my doubts, but I still longed to have a loving relationship with the opposite sex as my parents and grandparents had. Seeing the love they shared was special. I was finally starting to feel good about myself and that frightened me. I felt if things were too good, then that was a sure sign that something awful was going to happen. I put a protective wall around myself. I did not want to be hurt again.

The only place I felt secure was with my family and my boys. I never had to worry about my boys because they were always around family and getting the best care possible. Mother and Daddy were my boys' heroes and they loved them dearly. Daddy and Granddad were the only father figures my boys had. I was hoping I could quit my second job soon so that I could be home with them more. I felt I was missing so much. In the meantime, Nana and Granddad were there to help Mother. Granddad enjoyed playing with the boys and taking them for rides around the back yard in his wheelbarrow. Despite everything that had transpired in my life, I felt David and Neil were well-adjusted children. As I sat there looking out my bedroom window after a light rain, I noticed a rainbow off in the distance. "Thank you Jesus," I said aloud, "You are watching over us! Maybe, only good things will happen from here on out. I hope so."

The day came for me to go to the Veteran's Hospital in Long Beach, California. Mother and Daddy took the boys to Waddell's Trailer Park as they promised. Red, Marene, and Warner came by my house in separate cars to accommodate all four of our wheelchairs. We followed each other to Long Beach.

I always enjoyed being with Warner. We knew each other since I was 11 years old when I joined the Wheelacade. While driving, Warner seemed more interested in how I was doing. This surprised me because he usually did not say much.

"Why are you so interested in me all of a sudden?" I questioned him.

"I am just amazed at how you have survived so much over the years. Most people might have gone off the deep end," he said.

"With two small children I couldn't give up. Believe me there were times I wanted to. If it weren't for my boys and my family, I might not have made it," I replied.

"You deserve the best. I think your family is wonderful and I know they have helped you a lot. I don't know any woman that has gone through as much as you have."

"Believe me, Warner, I spent years trying to find someone that would just love me for me and accept my disability, but I guess that's not going to happen."

"When the time is right, it will happen," Warner assured me.

Upon our arriving, the hospital administrator greeted us. He was glad we arrived safely and reminded us the banquet started at two o'clock. The four of us went to freshen up.

As I entered the banquet hall, it was packed. Veterans came from miles around to attend this highly publicized event. I had never seen so many handicapped men and women with so many varied disabilities all in one room at the same time. It was an amazing sight. Some veterans stayed in the hospital full-time. Others left the hospital after completing physical therapy and lived on their own. Following a fantastic meal, various speakers gave talks encouraging the veterans and thanking them for their service to our country. These men and women sacrificed a lot and came back with many emotional and physical scars.

Finally, the time came for me to draw the winning ticket out of a huge glass bowl. The winner came up front with a big smile on his face. He was recently injured and very young. Having hand controls would give him his independence once he left the hospital. I know what that did for my self-esteem. I felt like a million bucks!

Being out in public brings many challenges that all disabled persons face. I knew there were those represented here today who would eventually leave the hospital. Many would face barriers like finding a parking space that would accommodate their wheelchair; access to public buildings and bathrooms; and obstacles in socializing. I faced barriers every day. If I wanted to visit a neighbor, I could not if there were steps leading into their home. I would get so frustrated. Many times, I felt like I did not have the right to pee because my wheelchair could not fit in a private home or public bathroom. Handicap people put on a happy face and act as if everything is okay, when it is not! Some of these veterans had no idea of what they were going to face once they left the hospital.

After giving out the rest of the door prizes and listening to the final speaker, we were able to mingle with the patients. Some were paraplegic and confined to wheelchairs. They had no feeling from the waist down. That meant they had no bladder or bowel control. Many had to use urinal bags attached to one leg or wear a catheter 24/7. They also had to learn a special technique in order to have a bowel movement. Others were quadriplegic. That meant they could not use their arms or their legs. The level of their injury determined what they could or could not feel. Most quads had no feeling from the neck or shoulders down. Some were fortunate to be able to use one arm, but most quads could not use either arm. I also talked to a couple of amputees. One amputee told me he could still feel his legs even though they were both gone. I was amazed!

Later we visited people on the wards that could not come to the banquet hall. Some of these poor people lay in Stryker beds all day. A Stryker bed is a circular bed that makes it easy for a nurse to rotate so that the patient will not get bedsores. Some of these patients had absolutely no will to live. All the quadriplegic patients were dependent on their nurses.

They had to be hand fed, dressed, and bathed. Some had to wear diapers. Some were on ventilators. Some were depressed and lay in their beds weeping uncontrollably. I learned from one of the doctors that some patients could possibly get back some movement in their arms or legs once the swelling went down around their spinal cord. Some doctors even believed that some mobility could come back up to five years later.

Can you imagine being 18 to 20 years old and have your entire life, as you knew it, taken away? I could not. They remembered what it was like to be able-bodied before they were injured. Their lives changed forever. After that day, I felt fortunate to be a post polio victim and not remember what it was like to be normal. My disability seemed ever so slight in comparison. After being with these brave souls, I knew I had to make a conscious effort not to whine or complain.

The day was slowly ending, and I knew we would be heading home soon. That evening many of the veterans that lived outside the hospital had parties planned. Warner wanted to head back, but I did not. I did not have to worry about the boys, so I wanted to make the most of this day.

"Sharon," Red said, "Marene and I are going to go to one of the parties. Come join us. We can take you home later."

"I would like to, but I have to call Granddad. I'll need him to help me when we get home to get my wheelchair out of the trunk."

"Hurry up, so we can let Warner know if he should leave or not."

I called Granddad. He said he would be more than happy to help me when I got home. He encouraged me to stay and have a good time. I told him I would call him when we left the party so that he would know about what time I would be home.

I told Warner I was going to stay and thanked him for taking me. Red and Marene assured him they would make sure I got home safely. He said good-bye and left. One of the able-bodied veterans helped us with our wheelchairs and off we went to have a little bit of fun after experiencing such an emotional day.

It was at a party at a Veteran's home where I met Chuck. He owned a home in Garden Grove, not too far from the hospital. Chuck was a quadriplegic, but he had the use of one arm and both shoulders. He lost the use of his right hand, but was quite mobile considering his disability. Later that evening, I learned Chuck's disability was due to an automobile accident that he had while he was in the military. Because his injury occurred in the military, he received a monthly disability check and the government paid for his medical needs as well. I felt a little envious. Then again, I did not lay down my life for my country.

There was an attraction between Chuck and me immediately. He had a positive attitude and he was extremely good looking. He had a noticeable tan and curly black hair. His tight shirt revealed his muscular physique. He told me he used to be a boxer in the military before his accident. Because of his boxing career, he had great upper body strength. This helped

Chuck push his wheelchair or transfer. As the evening progressed, Chuck was spending most of his time with me. He was very complimentary and made me feel special.

After spending a few hours at the party, Red, Marene, and I said our good-byes and thanked Chuck for a wonderful evening. Marene told Chuck if he were ever down our way, he could stay with them. Chuck thanked them and said that he would definitely take them up on their offer. Then I called Granddad to tell him I was on my way home. Chuck's brother helped load our wheelchairs into the car and we headed home.

Red and Marene were such compassionate people. I knew Marene was a post polio victim as was I. She lost the use of her right hand, forcing her to learn to write with her left. Red was a pilot in the military and became a paraplegic when his plane went down during the war.

"We that are paraplegic are all put in one basket. People assume things about us that are not true," he said.

"Like what?" I questioned him.

"There are some paraplegics that cannot have children, but some can. It all depends on where the spinal cord was damaged."

"That sounds like me. People think because I had polio that I have no feeling in my legs. They also think I can't have children," I said. "Awhile back somebody asked me if my boys were adopted."

"See, Sharon, that's what I mean. If people would just ask questions, they wouldn't sit and wonder."

"People probably think we don't want them asking us personal questions," I said.

"They will never know unless they ask. We know that every person that is handicapped is different to some degree," he replied.

Then Marene said, "I can only imagine how you must have felt when people thought your boys were adopted, especially after all you went through to have them."

"And here I am working two jobs, plus caring for my boys."

"You should get married again," Marene said.

"Sure," I said, laughing. "No, thank you. I have had my share of being married. I do not need any more problems. Right now things are going very well for me. As soon as I can quit my second job, things will be even better."

"You cannot quit working at MPS. We need you! Red and I are stockholders," she said, teasing me.

"I know, but I really want to be at home with my boys."

"That day will come. Maybe sooner than you think," she said.

"I hope so," I replied.

"It is only my opinion, Sharon, but I feel that most of the hurt you went through was because you were married to able-bodied men. You need to be married to someone of your own kind that can understand you better," Marene said.

"I've thought the same thing. Able-bodied men still scare me."

"Who knows, maybe Chuck's the one," she said, grinning from ear to ear. "He sure is cute and seemed to take a liking to you. Maybe our trip today was a turning point in your life and things will look up for you."

"That would be nice, but I live too far away to have a relationship with Chuck."

"Where there's a will there's a way, and don't you ever forget that!" Marene said.

"Thanks, Marene, but right now I'm content and happier than I've been in a long time. My boys are doing well and my family has been a godsend. I am glad I went today, but I am anxious to get home. It has been a long, emotional day. Seeing those veterans with so many physical problems was hard. My heart went out to them."

"We feel the same, Sharon," Red said. "We go up there quite a bit to try to encourage them not to give up. Some are so young."

"That's a wonderful thing the two of you do," I said. "Well, here we are, home already. Thanks for the ride."

"It was our pleasure," Marene said.

"If you want to go back, just let us know," Red added.

Red honked the horn when we arrived at my grandparents' house. Granddad came out, got my wheelchair out of the trunk, and we said good-bye.

As they drove away, I talked to Granddad, as he walked with me to my house.

"Thank you for waiting up for me," I said, giving him a hug.

"It was my pleasure," Granddad said.

He unlocked the door for me and made sure I was safely inside before he went home. The house seemed so empty with everyone gone. I felt exhausted when I finally got into bed. Before I went to sleep, I said a prayer for all of the veterans at the hospital. Today I realized how lucky I was. My disability seemed ever so slight in comparison. Maybe Marene was right. Maybe things were finally looking up for me.

12

SMOOTH SAILING FOR A WHILE

The next day, late in the afternoon, my parents brought the boys home from Waddell's Trailer Park. David and Neil were anxious to see me, as much as I was to see them. They were so excited about their short vacation. They went on and on about how much fun they had. It took very little to make them happy at this age. I wanted to savor every precious moment. God really blessed me with these boys.

As soon as the boys were asleep, I spent time with Mother and Daddy. I wanted to tell them all about my day at the hospital. "After yesterday, I thank God I'm a post polio victim. I cannot imagine being a paraplegia or quadriplegia. Can you imagine not having feeling in your legs or arms and no bladder or bowel control? I would not want to change places with any of them."

"We can always find somebody worse off than we are," Mother said.

Then I told them that Red, Marene, and I went to a party at Chuck's house.

"Chuck is considered a quadriplegic. He has no feeling from his chest down. He does have the use of his shoulders and one arm. He had to learn to write left-handed. In order for him to push his wheelchair, he had a special hand-rim fitted with rubber tips about two inches apart. Using that hand-rim allows him to push his wheelchair with the palm of his bad hand. It is something to see!" I said.

"Why doesn't he use an electric wheelchair?" Mother asked.

"I asked Chuck that same question. He told me if he went into an electric wheelchair, he might gain weight due to the lack of exercise."

"That makes a lot of sense," Mother said.

"Where does he live?" Daddy asked.

"He owns his own home in Garden Grove, not too far from the hospital. His brother, sister-in-law, and their two children live with him. He said they help him. I didn't ask what that meant, but he seems to be very close to his family."

"Kind of like you," Daddy said, and Mother agreed.

"That's for sure. He said he would call me, but I doubt it. We live too far from each other. Marene said I should get married again, but to a handicapped man. I think she is playing matchmaker. I told her I was perfectly content, but he was mighty cute."

"Maybe he will call you," Daddy said.

"I gave him my phone number, so I'll wait and see."

Much to my surprise, a few weeks later, Chuck started calling me regularly. I know his phone bill must have been outrageous. Then one weekend he came down to see me and meet my family. He stayed at Red and Marene's house.

As time went by Chuck came down more often. I learned more about him and his family. Chuck's brother and his family lived with him and one sister lived close by. His parents and two other sisters lived in Arizona. All his siblings were married, but Chuck was not, and never had been. He was very close to his family. They meant a lot to him. They all came together when he was injured. He told me he did not know what he would have done without them. Not everybody had close families like Chuck and me.

Many people in my dance group did not have close families. One man's mother put him in an orphanage when he was only six months old because he got polio. For whatever reason, his mother could not handle what happened to her son. I guess it was better for him not to be around somebody that did not love him. It is hard to say how people react until you walk in their shoes. Chuck knew many at the hospital that had no family support. Some had sweethearts and received "Dear John" letters after they were injured. Some were married and, after their injury, their wives left them. Some were at the hospital while their families lived hundreds of miles away. There was a lot of heartache there.

Chuck did not have to work which allowed us more time to spend together. At times, he visited his family in California and Arizona. When Chuck went to Arizona, his brother went with him. Chuck could not travel overnight by himself due to the severity of his disability. Hotels or motels could not accommodate his needs. Day trips he could manage by himself.

When Chuck and I were together, we talked about everything you could imagine. I told him about my belief in God and about my baptism as a young child. I told him about leaving the church afterwards because the church condemned dancing. I told him about the valleys and the mountaintops that I had gone through. I explained to him why I had to work two jobs. I eventually told him about my marriages and that my boys had two different fathers. I told him about the time I wanted to die when my husband left me for an able-bodied woman. He could relate to the despair that I once felt. He, too, had no desire to live when he was first injured. We spent months talking. I felt that was a good sign. We were becoming very close.

After dating for a little over a year, Chuck asked me to be his wife. He loved my children and me very much. Not only did he want me to be his wife, but he also wanted to adopt my boys. He said to me, "I will never be able to father a child due to my disability. I feel these boys have been through enough. I want to be the father that they never had. I only want that if it's okay with you," Chuck said.

"I knew we were getting close, but I didn't think you wanted to marry me. We haven't been dating that long," I said.

"We've been dating for over a year. I would like you to consider being my wife and to quit working."

"Regarding MPS, I was going to quit long before this, but raising two boys is expensive. I wished I did not have to work my second job. Hopefully, that will stop soon," I said.

"Sharon, I'm serious. I have more than enough money. I will be glad to pay off any doctor bills you have. I want you to be able to stay home more with your boys. If you quit your second job, then we'd be able to spend more time together too," he said, trying to convince me.

"This sounds too good to be true," I said, smiling.

"Well it's true and you still haven't answered the biggest question. Will you marry me?" Chuck said, reaching out to hold my hand.

"Yes, I'll marry you," I said, trying to get closer to him. With both of us in wheelchairs, we had to line up our wheelchairs just right in order to hug and kiss each other. I added, "I'm not only willing to be your wife, but I would be honored to have you adopt my boys. I have not heard one word from Jim in years. Tom only sends me child support once in awhile. I'll give notice at MPS, but I'm keeping my other job."

"Whatever you think is best. Right now, you have made me a very happy man! Next time I come down, we will go pick out a ring for you. I can't wait to tell our families and Red and Marene," he said. "Let's go tell your parents and grandparents and the boys right away."

"I'd like us to talk to my parents and grandparents first. I do not want the boys in on this just yet."

"Whatever you think is best," he replied.

Chuck needed to get back to Red and Marene's house to get his things. Before we said good-bye he asked, "Are you sure you want to tell the boys about our engagement without me?"

"Yes, please let me do this. I know they really like you, but your being my husband and their stepfather is going to be an adjustment. Let me feel them out first. I will make sure Mother is with me, so I can get her input. Now get going. Be safe and call me when you get home," I said, waving good-bye.

After David and Neil were sound asleep, I told my family that Chuck had asked me to be his wife. That is when I found out that Chuck called Daddy the day before to ask for my hand in marriage. Daddy gave Chuck his blessing and told Chuck that because of our disabilities we would make the perfect pair. I respected Chuck for talking to Daddy first. It was old-fashioned, but sweet, nonetheless. My family was glad that we had found each other. They felt we had a good chance at happiness because we were both disabled.

It was a long, emotional day. I still had to tell the boys at some point what was going on. I needed to talk to Mother alone. Maybe tomorrow, I had to get to bed.

The following day after dinner, I asked Mother to meet me in the living room.

"What's up?" Mother asked.

"I need to discuss some things with you," I said.

"Fine, but first I have a question. Has Chuck been married before?" Mother asked.

"No. He said that he saw too much heartache when he was in the hospital. Guys that were married later divorced after they were injured."

"How sad," Mother said. "That sounds similar to what happened to you."

"That's for sure. Some people can deal with people being disabled, but some can't," I said. "I think marrying Chuck gives me the best of everything. He owns his own home, and it is wheelchair accessible. He also has financial security. I will not have to worry about having any more children due to his disability."

"I'm concerned about that," Mother said. "Sex is a big part of any marriage. You must give that some serious thought."

"Mother, I'm pleased as punch! I have not had sex since Tom left and I am fine. I do not think you need to make love in order to love somebody. You can show love in many ways other than sexually," I said, trying to convince her.

"I should keep my mouth shut. That is between you and Chuck," she said, pulling back. "The two of you will have to work that out."

"Chuck wants to adopt David and Neil. That was quite a surprise, but I am glad. Neither Chuck nor I want to have to deal with the boys' biological fathers. David and Neil do not even know them. Chuck's adopting them will be wonderful. Chuck said adopting David and Neil would be a huge gift from me to him."

"It sounds absolutely wonderful for all of you," Mother responded.

"Mother, I have to talk to David and Neil and see how they react when I tell them that Chuck and I want to get married. Do you think they will be okay with it?" I asked her.

"Most of the time children adjust better than adults do. I think they will be okay. My main concern is where all of you are going to live. That might be the hardest thing for them and you," she said, acting genuinely concerned.

"We've talked for hours about so many things, but that's one thing we haven't talked about. We had better make that decision soon. I am not sure if I want to move to Garden

Grove. I know it's not that far away, but I really like it better down here close to my family," I said.

"You and Chuck should discuss moving before you even tell the boys that you're engaged to be married," Mother suggested.

"You're absolutely right! I am not going to make the same mistake I made years ago with Neil's father. I did not move to Long Beach, and look what happened. If I have to move to Garden Grove, then that is what I will do. I'll do whatever I have to, to make a good life for me and my boys."

"Well, my dear, it's getting late. We better call it a day." We hugged each other and said goodnight.

I went into my bedroom where the boys were sleeping. I got down on my knees on the floor next to my bed and took out my Bible. Using a flashlight, I opened my Bible and slowly moved my finger down the page. There it was, "Delight thyself also in the Lord, and he shall give thee the desires of thine heart." Psalms 37:4. Then I prayed, "Lord Jesus if this marriage is Your will for me and my boys, then I pray I am making the right decision. I trust You to work out all the details. I want to be happy and be a full-time mother to my boys. I pray this marriage will last and that Chuck, David, Neil, and I will have a happy future together. Amen." I crawled into bed and lay there with thoughts running through my mind. I hoped that I had given myself enough time to heal emotionally from the past. God knew I needed someone to share my life with me. God brought Chuck into my life for a reason. Only God knew what that reason was. I had to trust God that I was making the right decision. I refused to start worrying about problems that Chuck and I might face. Instead, I chose to hold onto God and let Him take care of our future.

The following week when I went to work at MPS, I sat down with George, Red, Marene, and Warner. Rather sheepishly, I handed them my two-week letter of resignation. Much to my delight, they totally understood. Red and Marene were thrilled that Chuck and I were getting married. They said that I could quit now if I wanted to. I told them that after everything they did for me, I felt I should give them time to find someone to replace me.

When I got home, I called Chuck to share the good news with him. "In two weeks or less I'll be able to spend evenings with my boys again. This is the best gift you could have ever given me," I told him.

"I'm excited too. Now I can come down on Friday nights and you will not be at work. You will be able to spend more time with me." Then he asked, "Did you tell David and Neil about us getting married?"

"No. Mother suggested that all of us should sit down with the boys and tell them. That way we will be telling them as a family unit. If the boys see we're all happy, then they will be happy too."

"I am so glad. I really wanted to be there," he said. "I am so excited! I want to shout from the rooftop that we're getting married and I'm going to be a dad!"

"That will come sooner than you think. We still have to discuss our living arrangements. Mother asked me if you were moving down here close to La Mesa, or if I was moving up to Garden Grove. I can't believe we have not discussed this."

"We'll discuss that when I come down this weekend. In the meantime, I have to go. Somebody's at the front door and I am here by myself. Take care of yourself and my boys! I love you," he said, as he hung up the phone.

The following weekend Chuck and I discussed our living arrangements. Chuck wanted us to move to Garden Grove because his home was wheelchair accessible. He promised me that if things did not work out, we could move back closer to my family.

"It's going to take time for me and the boys to adjust," I explained. "I am deeply concerned about the boys. They are very attached to my parents, plus Nana and Granddad."

"I know that, but don't you think they need to be around children more?" Chuck asked.

"Definitely," I responded.

"There are lots of kids in my neighborhood. I think that would do them the world of good."

"You're probably right. Don't forget, David and Neil have mostly been around adults."

"I think it's a wise decision. We are only about two hours away from your family," Chuck said, trying to convince me.

"I'm going to go out on a limb, trust God, and agree to move."

"Oh, Sharon, I am so happy!" He said.

Chuck and I found something I had never shared with another man. We had mutual respect for one another. We were very aware of each other's innermost thoughts and feelings. We both have had our share of challenges, so we felt we could handle this one too. All Chuck and I could do was our best. We knew we would never be normal as far as society was concerned. We knew we would face challenges every day. Some challenges we would overcome; others we would not. We both had a strong desire to live the best life we could.

Two weeks later, Chuck and I, along with my parents and grandparents, sat down with David and Neil. We told them that Chuck and I were getting married and that Chuck was going to be their daddy. On a child's level, they seemed to understand. We tried to keep it light. David and Neil were young, so just seeing me happy was all they needed. That same day we broke the news to everyone that I had agreed to move to Garden Grove. They all told us they would miss the boys and me, but understood why I had to go. After we finished talking, Chuck surprised me by placing an engagement ring on my finger. Even though we had talked about picking out a ring together, this ring meant even more to me because Chuck picked it out by himself.

A little over a month later, I quit my full-time job. This job was harder to give up because I was there for a long time. They helped me get through my lows and celebrated my highs. I was going to make a point of spending time with them, as well as those from my dance group, before I headed north. I wanted to spend time with my girlfriend, Karen, too. My brother, Neil and his wife were excited when I called to tell them the news. Neil said they would try to come down for our wedding.

I had so much on my mind. I could only hope that I would find the time to do everything. Not working would allow me more time to see my friends, plan my wedding, and get everything ready to move. I knew my life was going to change drastically. Trusting in God was going to have to be my priority.

While Mother and Nana watched the boys, I started to commute to Garden Grove. Granddad went with me, so I would not have to drive alone. I never dreamed that I would be moving here one day. Chuck's house was ideal for wheelchairs. The boys and I would be living in a lovely home on a cul-de-sac. That meant David and Neil could play safely. Looking around the house, I knew I would have my hands full taking care of my husband, my children, and a new home. "Oh Lord give me the strength that I need to do all this," I prayed silently as I looked around Chuck's house. I had some skepticism because I had pretty much been under the protection of my parents most of my life. At 23 years of age, it was time for me to spread my wings.

On this first visit, I also had a chance to meet Chuck's dog, Duke, a white German shepherd. My only concern was that he would be too big for the boys. Chuck assured me that Duke would be fine. He was always gentle around his brother's two children. Two weeks before the wedding, Chuck brought Duke down to meet the boys. The boys fell in love with him immediately.

A few days later, Chuck arranged with some of his friends to drive down with him to La Mesa, rent a U-Haul, unload my storage unit, and take everything to his house in Garden Grove. Chuck and I followed them so I could tell them where to place the furniture. As my furniture arrived, Chuck's brother was moving out his furniture to move into his new house. He would continue to stay with Chuck until we got married. Everyone was running around like chickens. By the end of the day, we were beat and Chuck still had to drive me home. He planned to spend the night at Red and Marene's house. We were so thankful for their generosity.

During our planning stage, Mother and Daddy agreed to keep the boys for a couple of weeks after Chuck and I got married. This would give us time to settle in. Later they would rent a U-Haul and bring the boys' furniture and toys when they brought the boys to Garden Grove.

Over the next few days, my parents, grandparents, and I were busy getting everything ready for our wedding. Daddy and Granddad were cleaning up the outside of the house, while Mother, Nana, and I were busy doing the inside. We ordered a cake and flowers. My dress was pale peach lace with a matching heart-shaped headpiece with a short veil attached. It was gorgeous! Chuck rented a tuxedo and stayed at Red and Marene's house until we met at the church.

On March 26, 1966, Chuck and I were married in my parents' church. As we came out of the church, Chuck surprised me with a brand new black Cadillac as a wedding gift. I was shocked! Afterwards we drove to my parents' house for our reception. The only sad part was that my brother could not be there. We had some close friends in attendance along with Chuck's entire family. The boys were so excited. Chuck's siblings were all married and had children, so David and Neil had cousins to play with now and I became an aunt.

When the time came for us to leave, I tried to keep my emotions in check, but I could not. It was hard saying good-bye to everyone, especially to David and Neil. I could not put it off any longer; we needed to leave. We loaded our wheelchairs, gave some final hugs and kisses to everyone, and left. As we pulled away, my eyes filled with tears. I tried to convince myself that they were tears of joy. I knew I had made the right decision to move, but it was still hard leaving everybody behind.

Chuck and I talked all the way to Garden Grove. He reassured me that everything would be fine. When we finally pulled into the driveway, at Chuck's house, we saw a huge sign. Much to our surprise, the sign read: "Quarantine! Honeymoon Sickness!"

"Oh, Chuck, how sweet is this?" I said.

"That's how my friends are. We are always looking out for one another. They know how happy you've made me."

"We'd better get inside your house, I said. "It is getting chilly out here and frankly, I am exhausted. It's been a long day."

"Why not go inside our house!" He said, with a big smile.

"By golly, you're right. It is our house now. I've got a whole lot to get used to, don't I?" I said, realizing that was an understatement.

"Yes, you sure do," he said. "We both do."

For obvious reasons Chuck could not carry me over the threshold. Instead, after getting inside, we prayed a short simple prayer that God would watch over our families, the boys, and us. With God's help, we prayed that we would have smooth sailing ahead. We asked God to help us through the many challenges that we were undoubtedly going to face as we started our new life together.

13

ADJUSTMENTS GALORE

I awoke the following morning with my husband by my side. I should have been the happiest woman in the world, but I had mixed feelings. I was trying very hard to be positive. I had a man that loved me. I had this beautiful home to live in with my husband and my boys. I did not have to work anymore. I could be home now with David and Neil. I already missed David, Neil, my parents, and grandparents. This was crazy! I just saw them less than 24 hours ago!

I quietly snuck out of bed, so I would not disturb Chuck. In the stillness of the early morning hour, I wheeled through the entire house, trying to picture what I wanted it to look like after I put my feminine touch in each room. My parents and grandparents gave me all this furniture years ago. There was sentimental value attached to each piece. Having these things meant that a part of my family would always be here with me.

I went outside first to feed Duke and give him some water. He was so big, about 150 pounds, but the sweetest dog. As I sat there petting him, I still felt anxious about the boys moving up here. I was hoping that Duke would help them adjust.

My thoughts continued as I entered the kitchen, "How are the boys going to react when my parents bring them up here? How are the boys going to feel when they leave to go home?" No matter what, I would have to put on a happy face when the boys arrived. I wanted them to be thrilled about being here with Chuck and me. Having Chuck as their daddy was going to be another adjustment; not just for them, but for Chuck as well.

My daydreaming was interrupted when Chuck yelled, "Honey, where are you?"

"I'll be right there," I hollered. "I'm in the kitchen making a pot of coffee."

After I had finished, I went into the bedroom to see Chuck.

"How are you?" He asked. "Come over here and give me a kiss."

"I'm doing okay," I said, as I leaned over to kiss him. "I sure do miss my family."

"Why don't you call them?" He suggested.

"I will. Our phone bill will be astronomical with me calling everybody."

"That's okay. Don't worry about that. I knew leaving the boys was going to be hard. They will be here soon," he said, to comfort me.

"I wheeled through the house this morning. There is a lot of work to do. I am glad the boys are not here yet. I want to make our place homey before they come up."

"Go ahead and get your shower. Then you can help me with mine. When we are done, we can go shopping. How does that sound?" He asked. "Later in the week you should call my sister and sister-in-law and see if they could go with you."

"I will," I told him. "Now let me get started or we'll never get out of here."

This time alone allowed Chuck and me to adjust to living together. Now I was not the only one with a disability. For years, I knew every handicapped person had different challenges. There was no way Chuck could live by himself. I did not have a clue what it was like to live 24/7 with a quadriplegic. I knew that Chuck had no bladder control and had to wear a urinal bag. I also knew he had no bowel control, but I figured he had that under control. I assumed he could take showers and dress himself. I knew that he could get in and out of bed by himself because he stayed at Red and Marene's house. I saw how he got himself and his wheelchair in and out of his car with no help. I was correct in some of my assumptions, but wrong in others.

I started working on getting our home organized. I took my time unpacking and arranging closets and cupboards. Chuck and I shopped almost daily that first week. We had to learn how to get two wheelchairs in and out of the car by ourselves. When we went shopping, I pushed the cart and filled the basket. Lastly, we would put items we purchased in the trunk, get in the car, and drive home. When we got home, we had our wheelchairs and packages to unload. It took a lot of energy just to go shopping. When Chuck's sister or sister-in-law helped, life was a lot easier for us.

Every day I could see an improvement in our home. My biggest job was setting up the kitchen. Because I had a lot of strength in my hands and shoulders, I literally would lift myself up onto the arm of my wheelchair and sit there. Next, I would pick up my legs and put them in the seat of my wheelchair. Then I would lift myself up onto the countertop. This process helped me reach items in the upper cupboards. When using the stove, I would sit on the arm of my wheelchair so that I could see inside the pot. I could literally lift a full pot of spaghetti in boiling water off the stove with one hand. I would then push my wheelchair with the other hand to take it over to the sink. I could do all the same things that able-bodied people could do, but I had to find my own way of doing things. Mother always said, "If you want to do something bad enough, you would find a way." She was right. Mother and Nana were very proud of their homes. I wanted to be just like them. I knew I was making up for my being disabled. I could not walk, but I was going to be perfect in other ways if it killed me.

I talked to the boys and Mother a few times a day. I talked to Daddy from time to time. I also called Nana and Granddad. Once when I talked to Nana, she told me Mother was getting anxious about the boys moving to Garden Grove. She made me swear not to tell Mother about our conversation.

The day finally arrived when Mother and Daddy brought the boys up with the rest of their furniture and belongings. Chuck arranged for his friends to help Daddy unload the U-Haul when they arrived. They arrived early. It was great to see everyone.

"We are so glad you are here," I told David and Neil, as Chuck and I gave them each a long hug and tons of kisses.

"We sure have missed you guys," I said.

"Me too," Chuck said.

"Thank you for taking care of David and Neil," I told my parents.

"It was our pleasure. We loved every minute," Mother said.

"Is this going to be our new house?" David asked.

"Yes, it is. I want to show you and Neil your new bedroom," I said, motioning them to come into the house.

Right away Neil jumped onto my foot pedals and took a ride to the bedroom while everyone followed.

As we entered their bedroom, I said, "This is where you guys will be sleeping."

"Oh boy," David said. "This room is huge!"

"It won't look quite so big once we get your beds and dressers in here."

"If you like this room, wait until you and Neil see your playroom," Chuck said.

When they entered their playroom, they were amazed. We had purchased a couple of children's desks, tables, and many toys for them. Maybe it was bribery, but we did not care. We would do anything to make their transition easier.

After showing the boys and my parents our home, Mother and I visited while Chuck's friends and Daddy unloaded the U-Haul.

"You're going to have your hands full taking care of this big place," Mother said, looking around.

"Not just taking care of the house, but taking care of Chuck and the boys. I'm glad Chuck doesn't have to work because he can help me watch the boys while I do household chores or cook dinner," I said. "I have no idea how much help Chuck needs. I am glad he can dress and undress himself, but I have to help him shower and do other things. Please say an extra prayer for me once in awhile."

"You can count on that. Please pray for me too. It's going to be rough leaving the boys today," Mother said.

"I know that. You have been with the boys almost every day since they were born. In a few months, the boys will be having their birthdays. I want you, Daddy, Nana, and Granddad to come up. I will call Neil and Margaret to see if they can come too. Chuck is also going to call his brother and sister and invite them and their families."

"It sounds wonderful, but we will be back before then. We would not miss the boys' birthdays for anything. I cannot speak for Nana and Granddad. You can call them later."

"I will," I assured her.

"Oh, Sharon, I'm going to miss you so much. These past two weeks have been hard, but at least I had the boys to keep me busy. We must stay in touch. I know you will be busy, so you call me when it is convenient. Tomorrow Daddy and I are going to go to Waddell's for a few days. He knows I am on edge about the boys moving. I am happy for you and Chuck, but it still makes me sad to let those two darling boys go. I'm trying to be brave," she said, choking up.

"I understand. I really do. Do not get me crying. I wonder how the boys are going to react when you and Daddy leave. Both of us have to put on a brave face when that time comes," I said, trying to comfort her.

"I will. I won't break down. I promise," Mother said.

"Come on let's see what the guys are up to," I said, as we went inside.

To surprise the boys, Chuck and his brother had built them each a go-kart. When Chuck showed the go-karts to the boys, they were excited. Immediately they took them out front and became best friends with the neighborhood children. As we watched the boys interact with the other children, we realized how much they needed other children in their lives.

After unloading the U-Haul, Chuck's friends stayed to help Daddy set up the boys' beds, visit, and have a beer before they returned the truck. Once they left, Chuck and Daddy kept the boys occupied in the backyard. This gave Mother and I time to set up the boys' bedroom and playroom. When we were done, we asked the boys to come in and see their new rooms.

They both came to a screeching halt when they looked in their bedroom.

"Wow, Mommy, where did you get these?" David asked, stroking his bedspread.

"Mommy, our beds look like real cars," Neil added.

"Daddy Chuck and I saw them and thought they would be perfect for your new room."

"Can we see our playroom again?" Neil asked.

"Sure, follow me. We just rearranged some things and put away the toys you brought up with you," I explained.

"This room is really cool," David said.

"Sure is," Neil said.

"I'm glad you like it. Now go play. Ammy and I are going to finish up a few things and then call for pizza."

"Yeah! Mommy is going to order pizza," David said, as the boys ran outside.

David and Neil seemed genuinely happy that day. After we ate pizza, I knew the time was nearing for my parents to leave. I felt a knot in my stomach. Reality was about to set in for David and Neil. The boys thought they were leaving with their grandparents, but when we told them they were staying with us they did not like it one bit. Putting on that brave face as Mother and I talked about earlier went right out the window. With their arms outstretched reaching for my mother, both boys started to cry.

"Don't leave us," they pleaded, as Chuck and I were hanging onto both of them. I thought I would die inside. David and Neil did not want any part of Chuck or me.

Mother got down on her knees, holding the boys, one in each arm and said, "You must be brave. You need to stay here with your mommy and Chuck. Pappy and I will come back and see you. You can also call us whenever you want."

The boys finally calmed down, but that evening was absolutely awful for all of us.

As each day passed, I had to make many adjustments. At times, my head was spinning when I assessed everything that I needed to do. Daily David asked for Ammy and Neil asked for Granddad. Chuck and I encouraged the boys to play with their new friends. That helped, but they still had some rough days.

My new role as a full-time mother, wife, and homemaker now was hard for me. I realized how easy I had it living with my parents. When I came home from work, Mother had everything done. It was different now because it was my responsibility to do everything. Every day Chuck or one of the boys called me to help them with something. Some days I yearned for some peace and quiet. Other days seemed easier. David and Neil were still considerate of us being in wheelchairs. They still kept their toys around the outside walls, so we could get into their playroom to play with them. They were good at putting their clothes in the hamper. The little things they did were very sweet.

One afternoon I was feeling exhausted, and Chuck called me on it saying, "You're going to kill yourself taking care of this house. You look so tired. Who cares if our house is clean? Our house looks better than most. You have enough work just caring for me and the boys."

"Okay. Okay. Enough said. I am going to try to do better."

"I am genuinely concerned that you are going to put yourself into an early grave. What would the boys and I do without you?"

"I'm sorry. This has not been one of my better days." I explained.

"Please, take care of yourself. I'm serious!"

"I will," I said.

I know I was unreasonable about the house, but I felt if my house was not clean that it would reflect poorly on me. I could not handle that.

David and Neil were like oil and vinegar. They got along extremely well, but their likes and dislikes were opposite. David hated to get his hands dirty; and, if he did, he would run to the nearest sink to wash up. On the other hand, even if Neil had to go to the bathroom, he would not take the time to do so. After weeks of trying to get my little sweetheart to come in more often, I finally resorted to threats.

One day Neil and I were in the bathroom, trying to get him cleaned up because he was too busy playing to use the potty. His little bottom looked like he had a mud pie glued to it. After undressing him, I said, "You see that?" I asked him, as I showed him what was in his pants.

"Yes," Neil replied, as I flushed the toilet.

"You see anything now?" I asked.

"No," he said, starting to choke up.

"Listen to me Young Man and don't start crying. The next time you do 'that' in your pants you're going to go down there," I said, pointing to the toilet water as we both watched me flush the toilet again.

I probably ruined my son for life, but it was either he or I. Even though I was not very diplomatic, it worked. After that, whenever David used the bathroom, Neil was right behind him.

I called Mother and told her what happened. She could not stop laughing.

"You would have to be here to see the look on Neil's face. It was hard for me to keep a straight face, but I did."

"Sounds like things are going better."

"I am adjusting. To make things easier, I help Chuck with his shower in the morning. Then I take care of myself while Chuck and the boys eat breakfast. In the evening, I help David and Neil with their baths and get them ready for bed. I seem to have more free time for myself during the day."

"That is great! I'm glad you're taking time for yourself."

"I am learning. I had better get off the phone. The house is too quiet. I had better check and see what the boys are doing. See you all soon for the boys' birthday."

"I can't wait," Mother said. "Daddy and I enjoy our day trips to see all of you, but this time will be special because of the boys' birthday. I love you."

"I love you too. See you soon."

We had been living here four months now, but I still yearned to be closer to my family. I was always thrilled when Mother and Daddy would come up for the day, but it was still hard to say good-bye. The boys still did not want them to leave either. In time, I was hoping that would change. Chuck's one sister still lived close by, but she and her husband were busy at work and raising four children. Chuck's brother and his family moved back to Arizona. My brother and his wife were busy with studies and work. At times, Chuck and I felt lonely for adult interaction. A neighbor would come over from time to time, but most of the time it was just the boys and us.

Just before the boys' birthday party, we decided to get them an above-ground swimming pool for the backyard. We felt that would be a great gift for the two of them because they loved the water so much. Mother, Daddy, Nana, and Granddad and my brother and his wife came to celebrate their birthdays. David turned four and Neil turned three. The party was a huge success. Besides the pool, Chuck made each of the boys a small four-sided trailer that they pulled behind their tricycles. Everyone was amazed at the talent Chuck had, especially with the use of only one hand.

After spending the day together, everybody had to head home. This time things were better. Everybody was cheerful and said they had a nice day. I was so relieved that the boys did not start crying. Instead, they ran up to their grandparents, and their aunt and uncle, gave them hugs and kisses and went running off to their playroom. As I watched everyone leave, I had to admit that my children and I were doing a little better.

A week after the boys' birthday, Chuck said he wanted to talk to me after I got the boys settled down. When I had finished, I went into the living room to talk to him. Chuck said, "Sharon, it's no secret you're not totally happy living here. You have adjusted, but you are still homesick."

"You know me so well," I said. "Go on."

"After seeing how happy you were when all of your family was here made me realize that we really need to be closer to them. I know that would make you and the boys happy."

"No doubt about that!"

"You and the boys are important to me. I think we should check out the possibility of moving. We probably should have never moved here."

"Isn't hindsight great?" I chuckled.

"Being close to your family is where your heart is. You also have friends down there from work and the Wheelacade. Most of them are married now with kids. We would have adult friendships. The boys could play with their children. Most of my friends that live here are single. We have nothing in common with them," Chuck explained.

"I have stayed in touch with my friends, but it isn't the same as living close by," I admitted. "Now that the boys are getting older it is easier for us to tote them around. We could visit my friends that have disabilities because their homes are wheelchair accessible."

"There has got to be a house down by your folks that will work."

"Wait, just a minute. I need to go get my Bible." I came back into the living room and told Chuck, "Here it is, in Psalms 55:22, 'Cast thy burden upon the Lord, and He shall sustain thee; He shall never suffer the righteous to be moved.' If we are supposed to move, then God will make it happen. I believe that."

"I do too," Chuck said, with conviction.

"We need to lay this decision at the feet of Jesus," I said.

"I say let's call a realtor," Chuck said. "When I went to church as a young boy my mom always said, 'God helps those that help themselves.' We should get the ball rolling. In the meantime, call your folks and see if they can check out some areas close to them. We might be able to find a builder to help accommodate a home for our wheelchairs."

"I will call Mother tomorrow. My head is swimming! I am so excited! I doubt if I will be able to sleep a wink tonight. Mother is going to flip when she hears we are thinking about moving back. I will swear her to secrecy. I do not want the boys to know what's going on until we know for sure."

We finally climbed into bed. We had come a long way in our first few months of marriage. We had one adjustment after another, but we managed to conquer every challenge. In the process, we learned a lot about each other.

14

GOD KNOWS THE DESIRES
OF OUR HEART

The following morning, after very little sleep, I could hardly contain myself. I was so happy. I felt God answered my prayers. I did make a conscious decision to move here, but I was not content. God knew the desires of my heart. Over these past few months, I had learned a lot about myself and I was becoming a stronger person. Now, my daily prayer was that God would work out all the details and make our dreams come true.

After I got the housework done, I called Mother to tell her the news. "Mother, I have a surprise to tell you. Hang onto your britches! Chuck and I had a long talk last night, and we are going to see about moving back."

"Oh my goodness! Sharon, you can't imagine how long I've prayed about this. I have spent many nights on my knees asking God to bring you all back here. I miss all of you so much. When are you planning to do this?" She inquired.

"First of all, you can't tell the boys anything about this. You have to promise me. You can tell Daddy, Nana, Granddad, and even Neil. You must swear everybody to secrecy."

"I will. Believe me. I'll do whatever it takes."

"Mother, I'm so excited. Chuck just left to talk to a realtor. Chuck feels because there are so many veterans up here needing a house when they leave the hospital, our house should sell fast. I hope he is right."

"Where are the boys? Can they hear you?" She asked.

"No. They are in their playroom with their friends."

"Okay. Tell me what we can do. We're at your beckon call."

"Our biggest challenge is finding a new house that is wheelchair accessible or a used house that can be redone to accommodate our needs. Can you see if there is any new construction going on around your area? That would be our first choice. If we find a new house that isn't quite done, then maybe the builder would be willing to make some changes."

"I'll have Daddy make some calls to his "mucky-mucks," as he calls them. They might know if there are any new developments."

"Anything you could do would be great. Listen, I better go and check on the boys. They are too quiet," I said, laughing.

"I know the feeling. Are you going to call your brother and grandparents?"

"Yes, I will. Please call me, if you find out anything."

"You will be the first one I call. I love you."

"I love you too. Bye for now."

After making lunch for the boys and their friends, I waited for Chuck to come home. Chuck returned with a huge smile on his face. He gave me a "thumbs up" so I knew things went well with the realtor. "I wanted you to know," I said, "I called Mother. She and Daddy are going to check out some things for us. I called Nana and Neil too. Nana was thrilled, as was Granddad. Neil was at work, so I left word with Margaret. I do not think our decision came as much of a shock to anybody. You need to call your family too."

"I'll do that later. Right now I have to get some papers and go back to the realtor's office so she can check comps in the area."

Within a few days, Mother called and told us Daddy found a new development in the town of Fletcher Hills, about 20 minutes from their house. My parents talked to the builder and he said he would be willing to make changes for our wheelchairs, as long as our requests are reasonable. The builder suggested we come down, as soon as possible, before he puts the final touches on the one house that he thought would work for us.

The next day we were on the road again. We dropped the boys off at Nana and Granddad's, while Chuck, Mother, Daddy, and I went to meet with the builder. As we drove down the street, we were delighted to see the house was on a cul-de-sac just like ours in Garden Grove. Some houses were already finished and there were children playing out front.

We went through the entire house while the builder made notes on the floor plan of things that we needed done. Everything was fine, except for four things: First, was cement work. We had to have a ramp poured leading to the front door and from the garage to the house. We also needed to have cement poured around the entire outside of the house, except for the covered patio area. Next, the builder had to widen one bathroom door. Then, we had to have the master bathroom shower redone with a smaller lip, so Chuck could wheel his wheelchair closer, making it easier for him to transfer to a shower chair. This would be a major plus for him and for me too. Finally, we asked for Parquet wood flooring throughout, except in the kitchen, bathrooms, and laundry room. Those rooms could have linoleum as originally planned. We did not want carpet because it was too hard for us to push our wheelchairs on.

The builder said he would go over the list, come up with a price, and get back to us in a few days. God led us to this one particular house with this builder. I had to believe this was going to be our new home. It happened so fast. Chuck gave the builder some earnest money. We signed the papers contingent on him agreeing to do what we noted on our list.

After the builder left, Chuck, Mother, Daddy, and I stayed for a while looking around.

"Look, Mother, this kitchen is huge! Look at all the cabinets and the laundry room is in the middle of the house," I told her.

"This house is a lot bigger than your house in Garden Grove. Are you sure you'll be able to take care of it?" She questioned me.

"I'll have to. We even have more rooms here. Gee, I will have to buy some more furniture," I said, laughing.

"I am sure you won't have a problem doing that," Chuck chimed in.

Daddy went and checked the outside of the house for us because Chuck and I could not get to the un-landscaped dirt areas on the property. When Daddy came in, Chuck asked, "Does everything look okay?"

"Does to me," he said.

"If the builder can make our changes, we are going to have to put our house on the market right away," I said.

When we got back to Nana and Granddad's, Daddy took the boys outside so Mother and I could tell Nana and Granddad about the house. They were happy for us. Before we left, we ordered in pizza, ate, visited for a while, and headed home to Garden Grove.

Within a few days, the builder called. We each got on a separate phone. The three of us reviewed the items we needed done. After talking for quite awhile, the three of us came to an agreement.

When we got off the phone, I said, "Chuck, if all goes well let's plan on going to the new house next week."

"We should leave early. That will give us time to meet with the builder and have time to visit your family before we have to head back," Chuck said.

"The boys will be beside themselves when they find out we're moving closer to their grandparents."

"Let's be patient. I know that's hard right now, but we don't want to let on to the boys that anything is going on," Chuck said.

"I agree. I'd better get some more done before it's time to cook dinner."

Within a few days, we were on the road again. The boys thought these frequent trips to see their grandparents were neat. After dropping the boys off at Nana and Granddad's, we, along with my parents, met the builder at the house in Fletcher Hills. Then, we proceeded to the escrow company and my parents went on home. When we were done, I called Mother and Daddy and asked them to bring the boys back over to our new home. They were ecstatic!

As I watched my parents' car drive up the street, I could see David and Neil pointing their fingers at us. Mother and Daddy had huge smiles on their faces. As soon as they pulled into the driveway, David and Neil jumped out of my parents' car and raced over to us.

"What are you doing here?" David asked, with Neil right behind him, asking, "Why are you here?"

"Whose house is this?" David asked, somewhat bewildered.

"Be still you two. This is "our" new house! We wanted to surprise you," I said, enthusiastically.

"We can't move here. It's not done," David replied, in a skeptical voice.

"It will be done soon, and then we can move in."

"Yippee! Granddad can give me wheelbarrow rides again," Neil shouted, jumping up and down.

"I can only imagine how you both feel," Mother said, with tears in her eyes.

"We are so happy," I said. "Where did Daddy go?"

"I think he's roaming around inside your new house."

After showing the boys the house and making sure our "to do" list was complete for the builder, we left and headed over to my parents' home. David and Neil went on ahead with Ammy and Pappy. Chuck and I sat there in awe. We thanked God for answering our prayers. We knew we had a lot to do before we could actually move in. With God's help that too would work itself out.

As Chuck and I were driving over to my parents' house, he asked me if he could start adoption proceedings. He wanted David and Neil to be his boys and make our family complete. At that moment, I think I loved him more than ever before. Could all this happiness really be happening to me? It was all too good to be true, but I loved every minute of it. After further discussion about the adoption, we decided to wait until we moved into our new house.

It was late when we got back over to my parents' house. As we exited the car, I hollered to everyone, "What a day! We are so excited! I can't believe all this is happening so fast."

"Don't worry about a thing. We will drive over to the house every couple of days and make sure they are doing everything that you have on your list. Make sure we get a copy," Daddy said.

"Here it is. I had them make a copy at the escrow office."

"Where is Mother?" I asked Daddy.

"She went in the house to get drinks for everybody."

"I'll be back in a minute," I told everyone, as I wheeled myself up the ramp to see if I could help her.

"Mother, what is wrong?" I asked, as I noticed she was crying.

"Nothing is wrong. I am probably the happiest woman in the world right now."

"God really does look after us, doesn't He?"

"Yes, Sharon, He sure does," she said.

When Mother and I came out of the house, Chuck reminded me that Duke had been alone all day. Chuck suggested we leave.

As soon as we arrived home, I tended to Duke. Once the boys were asleep, I told Chuck I needed to talk to him.

"I do not think we should bring Duke with us. There would be no place for him to run in our yard because of all the dirt," I explained.

"I agree, and it will take months before the landscaping is in. I will call my sister and see if she could take him."

"I hope and pray the boys will be so excited about moving that they will not be too upset about Duke."

"I am sure everything will work out. I think the boys adjust to change better than we do."

After I helped Chuck get ready for bed, I went into the living room to reflect on my life. Many of my dreams had come true. My life had been a long hard road, but finally things were looking up. I had God to thank for everything and my heart was overjoyed. Then I prayed, "Lord Jesus, please give me the strength to be everything that I can be to everyone. I need You Lord! I need Your strength! Taking care of Chuck, David, Neil, and a big house is not going to be easy. I need You to help me every step of the way. My family is depending on me. I do not want to let them down. Help me not to fail them. Amen." I wiped away my tears and quietly climbed into bed.

The next day Chuck called the realtor and asked her to come over. We had a nice visit, telling her about our new home and wanting to sell this one. She thought she had just the right buyer. There was a woman whose son was in the Long Beach Veteran's Hospital. He would be getting out soon and needed a home that was wheelchair accessible. We told her clearly that we could not do a double move due to our disabilities. She said that she would do her best to make sure all worked out for both parties and that she would get back to us as soon as possible.

A few weeks later, the escrow officer called to let us know that escrow closed on our new home. In order to save us having to make another trip, she told us that she would mail the necessary papers to us for our final signatures. We notified the builder. Everything was falling into place.

One evening, after dinner, Chuck told the boys that he had something to discuss with them. He sat them down and explained we could not take Duke with us. He told them not to worry because their aunt was going to take him. The boys seemed sad at that moment, but later got up and ran outside to play. We were amazed at how well they accepted our decision.

Within a week, the realtor called and said the woman she told us about wanted to see our house. When they arrived, she fell in love with the house and said that it would be perfect for her son. She said she would get back to the realtor the next day. After she left,

I was hoping and praying that everything would work out. I had visions of people coming and going throughout the house while I was trying to pack.

The next day the realtor came back with an offer. "Here is the offer the buyer made," she said, as she pointed to the figure on the paper so the boys could not hear. "It is a little less than what you wanted, but she is going to allow your family to stay here until your new house is finished."

"Chuck, we will not have to make a double move," I said.

"That is what we prayed for. I'll sign on the dotted line," Chuck said.

After the realtor left, our heads were spinning. We were both so excited! If we could have gotten out of our wheelchairs and danced the two-step, we would have. The only thing left to do was contact a moving company. I immediately went to call my mother. When Mother picked up the phone I said, "Guess what? We sold the house! The best part is that we can stay here until we move into our new house."

"Bill, Sharon is on the phone. They sold their house!" She yelled to Daddy.

I could hear him over the phone holler, "Wonderful."

"Have you and Daddy been by our house?" I asked her.

"We just got back. Nana and Granddad went too. They love the house," she said.

"I wanted you to hear the good news," I said. "Keep us posted!"

"We will. I'll be glad to help you, if you need me."

"I'm okay. Chuck's sister and her husband are going to help," I said.

"Take care," Mother said. "Good-bye."

Over the next few weeks, I was doing my best to take care of myself and not overdo. We had plenty of help. Being busy helped pass the time. We were waiting patiently for the builder to tell us our new house was ready. Finally, he called and asked us to meet him at the house for the final walk-through. We told him we would be there the following day.

We left bright and early, dropped the boys off at my parents' house and headed to our new house. When we arrived, we could not believe our eyes. All the cement work was finished. We now had total access into the house at the front and the garage. Now with all the cement, we had complete access to the back and side yards too. The floors inside were beautiful and would be easier for me to care for. We could tell that the builder took great pride in his work. The outside still needed grass, rock, trees, and shrubs. Thank goodness, the front yard was not too big. After spending a little over an hour there, Chuck gave the builder a check, got our keys, and we left. The house was finally ours!

On the way to share the good news with my family, I said to Chuck, "God knew the desires of our hearts even before we did. I am so happy. God worked everything out, even down to the smallest detail."

"That is what happens when we put God in control," Chuck said.

"No doubt about it!" I replied.

15

A DREAM COME TRUE

As we pulled up at my parents' house, Chuck honked the horn as I hollered out the window, "We have the keys to our new home!"

Everybody rushed over to the car to talk to us.

"Oh boy, does that mean we're moving today?" David asked, jumping up and down with Neil.

"Not today, but soon," I said, motioning to the boys to step away, so Chuck and I could get out of the car.

Mother said, "All of us were just talking about how excited we are that things are finally looking up for all of you."

Unknown to the boys, Mother had called the day before and suggested that she and Daddy keep the boys with them during these final days of moving. She felt it would help us not having them underfoot, and they would not be there when Chuck's sister came to get Duke. After we visited for a short time, we told the boys we had to leave.

"Do we have to leave right now?" Neil asked me.

"Not you two. You are going to stay here while Daddy Chuck and I finalize things at our other house. How does that sound?"

"We're staying here?" David asked.

Pappy is going to get the suitcases that I had packed for the two of you from the trunk of our car.

"Be good for Ammy and Pappy," I said, giving each of them a kiss.

"Come over here you guys," Chuck said. "I want some kisses too. Remember to listen to your grandparents."

"Thank you for everything. I'll call you tomorrow and let you know what is going on," I told Mother and Daddy.

"Drive safely. We love you," Mother said, as everybody waved good-bye.

When we arrived home, there was a note from the realtor. It said that the buyer of our house in Garden Grove was ready to close escrow. She also wanted to know where we stood with our new house in Fletcher Hills. She asked us to call her.

"Talk about perfect timing again!" I said to Chuck.

"I will call her first thing tomorrow. If escrow closes right away, that would be perfect. Once we know, I will call the movers."

"God is so awesome," I commented. "To have both houses done within a few days of one another is a miracle! This is truly an answer to our prayers."

"That's what I said to you months ago. If God wanted us to move then doors would open. By the sheer grace of God," Chuck said, "everything came together perfectly."

After getting Duke and Chuck settled, I got ready for bed. That night, I slept more soundly than I had in months.

Over the next few days, I packed with the help of my neighbors and Chuck's sister. Mother called to surprise me that she contacted a cleaning company to clean our new house. Having everyone's help relieved our stress.

A few days later, the movers arrived. We were fortunate to find a company willing to pick up and deliver everything to our new house on the same day. We would not have to stay over night in a motel. Within a few minutes, the realtor and buyer showed up. We handed the buyer the keys and wished her good luck. Once the moving truck was packed, Chuck's sister helped us load up our car and put Duke in hers. We said good-bye and were on our way. A new life was waiting for us in Fletcher Hills.

As we pulled out of the driveway, I said to Chuck, "I can't believe we only lived here seven months. I am really excited about starting our new life in our brand new home, closer to my family."

"I know living here in Garden Grove has been hard for you. You have gone above and beyond the call of duty," Chuck said.

"I may be handicapped, but I am capable nonetheless," I replied.

"My family marvels at how you do things. I love you very much, but I need you to promise me one thing," Chuck said, in a serious tone.

"What's that?" I asked.

"There is going to be a lot of work putting our new house together. Promise me that you will take your time. I do not want anything to happen to you. I do not know how I would ever survive without you!"

"I promise I'll take care of myself," I said.

We arrived at my parents' house around two o'clock, embraced the children, and grabbed a bite to eat. Mother said that she would keep the boys with her until Daddy came home from work. They would all meet us at the new house later.

When Chuck and I arrived at our new house, we wheeled through every room. The house was spotless. Mother surprised me by lining the cupboards and drawers with a rattan pattern that matched my furniture. "What a dear sweet soul she is," I thought.

Soon we heard the sound of a truck. The movers were here. My heart started to pound! I was so excited! Within a short time, the truck was unloaded. The movers were great. They even helped put our beds together. Everybody arrived just when the movers were ready to leave. Chuck paid the movers while I greeted my family. I could not believe my parents brought over pizza, drinks, and even a cooler filled with groceries. The boys went running through the house looking at everything! We thought our house in Garden Grove was big; this house was even bigger. With all our furniture inside and boxes placed throughout, the house still echoed.

Over the next few weeks, we were extremely busy. Mother, Nana, and Granddad came over every day to help. Daddy came after work. Chuck hired a landscaper. We wanted the front yard done first. Chuck designed the back yard to include a large sandy area with a slide, swings, and yard toys for the boys. The last section directly behind the covered patio would be a grass area planted with trees and shrubs.

By Christmas, our home, inside and out, was finished. Now it was time to relax and celebrate the birth of Jesus Christ. To be with my family was a dream come true. One evening we had a tree trimming party. Everybody came over and helped. When we finished decorating the tree, Daddy lifted David up so he could put the angel on top. Another evening we all drove to Balboa Park in San Diego to see the nativity, depicting the true meaning of Christmas. This was also a special time because my parents celebrated their 25th wedding anniversary five days before Christmas.

On Christmas morning Mother, Daddy, Nana, and Granddad arrived early. They wanted to watch the boys open their presents. I was so happy! Here I was in our new home with my wonderful family, two fantastic children, and a husband that adored me. Most of all, I had a God that loved every member of my family and me. We shared a wonderful day together.

"I cannot believe all we got done since March," I said to Chuck, while cleaning the kitchen after everybody left. "We are so lucky to have my family's help."

"God has truly blessed us with all of them," Chuck said.

"Now that the holidays are over, I'm going to try to get together with my friends from work and the Wheelacade. We really need to have Red and Marene over as soon as possible."

"That sounds like a great idea! I think it will do us good to have adult interaction," Chuck said. "Our children can play together while we talk or play cards."

"I'll get on the phone and set some dates to get together," I said.

Some days trying to take care of our home, two children, and a handicapped husband wore me out. I still felt everything had to be perfect. I was lucky because I never had messy children. David and Neil still enjoyed doing special things to help Chuck and me. For being so young, they showed a lot of empathy towards us. I believe children raised by disabled parents gain insight into what living with hardship is all about.

Over time, what bothered me the most was Chuck's problem of having no bladder or bowel control. He struggled with this daily and my heart went out to him. I wanted to do something to make his life easier, but I could not. His biggest challenge was dealing with no bowel control. Some days this caused him a lot of heartache. When he had an accident, it caused me extra work. When that happened, he was embarrassed and felt guilty. I told him it was not his fault. Chuck had to cope the best way he could.

One day, I started calling my friends. Red and Marene were top on our list. I also reconnected with Connie and her husband. They still did not have children. Karen and I stayed in touch when I lived in Garden Grove. She was busy working and caring for two children now. My friends from the Wheelacade still lived close by. As each couple had more children, it was harder to go out. Before they just had their wheelchairs to lug around, but now they had children too. We had to make a special effort to get together even though we knew it took work. In every family, the children were able-bodied. When we made an effort to get together, we had a great time. During some of those visits, we discussed some challenges we faced as handicapped adults and parents as well.

As a group, we decided every time we went out, we would check public bathrooms, parking availability, and accessibility to enter various places. We agreed to write down the pros and cons and share them with each other. All of us felt safe when we were in our own homes or visiting other handicapped people. It was when we left our homes we felt vulnerable. Yet, we could not just sit home and vegetate. Those of us with children needed to show them that we were determined adults and wanted to find ways to live as normal a life as possible.

Included in our list of concerns were parking problems. When we shopped, there were no "handicapped" parking spaces in the 1960's. Many times, we would drive around, waiting for an end parking space, so we would have enough room to open the car door wide enough to get our wheelchairs out and back in. Most public bathrooms were a problem too. They did not accommodate a wheelchair. The stall door was usually too narrow. For example, if I knew I was going out, I would not drink for fear of not being able to use a public bathroom. My friends did the same. Chuck, on the other hand, did not have to worry because he wore a urinal bag. I believe living in a world that was not handicap friendly was hard. Some cope; others cannot, depending on their disability. All we could do was hope our society would become more aware of our needs and make the necessary changes by bringing into law some guidelines that would help all of us. I had the feeling that we would be waiting a long time for that to happen.

In March of 1967, we celebrated our first wedding anniversary with family and friends. Chuck's parents drove over from Arizona. That was an added treat because we had not seen them since we got married. They were getting older and did not like driving long distances. For them to make this trip made us feel special.

One evening, a few days after our anniversary, I told Chuck I needed to get something off my chest.

"What's up?" Chuck asked.

"It seems to me that ever since we moved here, we have not been reading our Bibles or praying like we did when we lived in Garden Grove. I truly believe we have neglected God's presence in our lives."

"You're right," Chuck said. "I hadn't really thought about that."

"It's like we have everything now because of God, and then we put Him on the back burner. I feel sick inside that I have treated God like that," I said.

"You have a point. I'm as guilty as you are."

"I hope and pray that we can put God back in our lives the way He used to be," I said.

"I pray for the same thing. Now I think it's time to call it a day and go to bed," Chuck suggested.

"I'm ready. I'll race you," I said, chuckling.

"I don't stand a chance!" Chuck responded.

That evening when we went to bed, we prayed asking God to forgive us. We knew that God did not forsake us. We were the ones that shut God out. That night, we gave God all the credit for everything He did for us. Without God, we would still be in Garden Grove. Without God, we would not have our new home. Without God, we would not be close to my family and friends. With God, our dreams had come true.

16

ONE MILESTONE AFTER ANOTHER

We had been married a little over a year now. Things were going good, maybe too good. When that happened, I would wait for the other shoe to drop. Instead of counting my blessings, I wondered when God would take the good away and replace it with more challenges. My thinking was wrong. I guess after having failed before, I tended to fall back into those negative thought patterns.

As I watched my husband, I could see the challenges he had to endure. Mine seemed minor in comparison. I really do not know if I could have handled what Chuck had to go through with such grace. Chuck let things roll off his back. I, on the other hand, took everything too seriously. Nevertheless, no matter what Chuck and I faced, I knew God was in control. I tried to hang onto my faith. When the two of us felt emotionally drained, we knew we had God and each other to lean on. I was going to try, "try" being the operative word, to enjoy life, be more relaxed, and keep my mood swings under control.

After all these years, I still felt fortunate to have a close family. We did have issues from time to time, but never allowed anything to tear down the closeness we shared. Things were not always perfect. What saved our family was being able to talk through our differences.

One day Chuck brought up the idea about installing an in-ground swimming pool in our back yard. After discussing it further, we agreed to put that idea on hold. Instead, we purchased an above-ground pool similar to, except larger, than the one we had in Garden Grove. We finally found the perfect pool with five-foot sides and ten feet across. Chuck asked Daddy and Granddad to help him set it up.

The boys were beside themselves with joy when they saw their two grandfathers arrive early one Saturday morning to put the pool together. Because the pool was plastic, Daddy had to put sand underneath the pool to keep it from ripping. The boys' play area had yards of sand that they could use. The boys looked so cute helping their grandfathers carry pails of sand. A few hours later, Daddy filled the pool with water, and the boys jumped in.

On a beautiful summer's day, in the middle of July, we surprised the boys by telling them we had invited nine of their friends over for a combined birthday and pool party. They could not believe their ears! Around noon, Mother came to set up and help me with the party. All the children looked cute in their swimsuits as they carried gifts for David and Neil. I cannot ever remember hearing so much laughter as David, Neil, and their friends romped and played in the pool. Nobody wanted to get out. After a couple of hours, David and Neil opened their gifts; everybody ate cake and went back into the pool. When the last child left, Mother and I were exhausted, but we had the time of our life sharing this wonderful day with the boys.

The next day we had another party for the boys with just our immediate family. We purchased two-wheel bikes for each of them. Because Neil was a year younger than David was, Chuck put training wheels on his bike. Mother and Daddy went swimming with David and Neil while the rest of us relaxed and watched them. Mother, Daddy, Nana, and Granddad always spoiled the boys with gifts. This birthday was no exception. Chuck's family sent cards with money inside so that we could take them shopping.

In August, I received a phone call from my brother telling me I was an aunt. Margaret gave birth to their first child, a son. They named him after our dad. My brother promised they would come down around Christmas. He wanted to celebrate Bill's first Christmas with all of us. I missed my brother so much. I was hoping and praying that after Neil got his doctorate and Margaret finished school, they would move closer, so we could see each other more.

In September, the day I dreaded arrived. David started kindergarten. I wanted David to go to school, but I felt he was growing up too fast. I did not want to let him out of the "nest." I did a good job keeping my emotions in check that morning as I helped him get ready. As I drove him to school, I was apprehensive. I heard sometimes children have a terrible time leaving their mommy on that first day, but David did not shed a tear. I was so proud of him. I took him to his classroom and introduced him and myself to his teacher. "I'll see you later Mommy," David said, as he kissed me on the cheek.

With David in school half days, it gave me more time to be with Neil. Neil was still very active. He needed my attention more than David did. David was more introverted; Neil was more extroverted. The boys also responded to affection differently. Neil needed lots of hugs and kisses, more so than David did.

Nana and Granddad spent a lot of time at our house. Even though Nana still had a lot of back pain, she looked forward to spending time with her great grandchildren. Granddad loved to play with the boys, as did Mother and Daddy. Mother always made herself available to me whenever I needed help. Granddad and Daddy helped Chuck with any manual labor that he could not do. If they saw we needed help, they were right there.

Around this time, Mother and Daddy purchased a new cab-over camper so they could take the boys to other places besides Waddell's Trailer Park. They loved taking the boys to the beach, the mountains, and out to the desert. Sometimes the four of them were gone all weekend. Other times, they went away for a week to give Chuck and me a break.

Chuck continued to have accidents because of his lack of bowel control. This usually only happened once and awhile, but lately it was happening more often. This upset him because it caused me extra work. It was hard to hide these personal mishaps from the boys, but we did the best we could. I could tell this was wearing me down. I thought I should be stronger, but all the extra work was hard on me. I never complained because Chuck felt bad enough as it was. I kept my mouth shut because I had no idea how to discuss this sensitive subject with him.

My brother, Neil, Margaret and Bill came down to celebrate Christmas in 1967 with all of us. This was Bill's first Christmas, which made it extra special. He was four months old, so he was smiling and interacting with everybody. Because there were four generations present, the LA MESA SCOUT, the local newspaper, did a story on our family gathering. The article was in the December 28, 1967 paper with the headline that read, "Christmas This Year Celebrated by Four Generations." To see all our names in print was thrilling.

After the holidays, a new year began; Chuck came to me and said, "I think we should go to church."

"I cannot go," I said, with conviction. "If people at church found out I had been married to Tom, Jim, and you, they would crucify me."

"We need Christian fellowship. We had put God on the back burner, and we said we were going to change that. What do you suggest we do?" Chuck asked.

"I don't know. It would be good for the boys. I need time to think. Okay?"

"Fine, but keep in mind, people don't have to know about your past," Chuck said, "I'm going to get on the phone and see if there is a Baptist church in the area that will work."

"Don't call La Mesa First Baptist Church. I went there already and there are steps."

"I'll let you know what I find," Chuck said, as he wheeled into our office to start making some calls.

As I thought about going back to church, I knew Chuck was right. We did need to worship our Lord and Savior, Jesus Christ, and have Christian friends.

Another night while I was fixing dinner, my mind wandered again. I started questioning if God really wanted handicapped people to go to church. None of my handicapped friends went. There were too many barriers. Steps and the accessibility to bathrooms caused problems, so it was easier to stay home and watch church on TV. Chuck did not have to worry about bathrooms, but they were a big concern for me.

Chuck finally found a church in El Cajon that he thought would work. After much soul searching, I told him I would go the following Sunday. Going to church pleased Chuck, but at first, I could take it or leave it. I had a deep fear that somebody at church would find out about my past and look down on me. Chuck thought I was crazy, but I could not help how I felt. The boys were excited about going to Sunday school while we were in church. To see them happy made me happy. As time went by, I felt less fearful.

God led us to this church for a reason. We fell in love with David and Neil's Sunday school teachers, Rick and Char. They had two beautiful daughters almost the same age as our boys. We got along splendidly. Our new friends were both able-bodied, so they had no problem toting their children around. The eight of us spent a lot of time together at our homes.

The children played for hours in the playroom and loved swimming in the pool. They were so adorable together. Their oldest daughter was the same age as Neil. Their other daughter was one year younger. David was like the big brother to all of them. We had our hands full when our children were together. The four of us used to kid around thinking, what if the children paired up later when they were young adults and got married? That would be a hoot! Rick was like a brother to Chuck and Chuck felt the same way about Rick. Char was the sister I never had. We spent hours shopping together with our children. We shared the most intimate details about our lives and helped each other all the time.

There were times we did not go to church, but we never felt guilty. We believed that God knew the desire of our hearts. If we missed a Sunday here and there, God knew why. If Chuck and I could not go, Rick and Char took David and Neil with them.

For some reason, I started having problems with severe diarrhea. Unlike Chuck, I had total feeling. I could tell when the urge hit. Because this problem persisted more often than I would have liked, I went to my doctor. After I told my doctor what had been going on, he examined me and felt my problem was strictly stress. He said I was trying to do too much as well as caring for a husband with a disability. I told him I did not have a choice. I had three people depending on me daily. My doctor suggested I lighten my load somehow. I promised my doctor I would try.

Easter Sunday was right around the corner. I called Mother to see if she and Daddy would like to go to church with us. They agreed, but wanted to meet us at our house first so that they could give David and Neil their Easter baskets. Easter Sunday 1968 was a glorious day. I could not remember the last time I went to church with my parents. Mother looked beautiful. She wore a hot pink dress with a matching hat. Daddy, Chuck, and the boys wore suits. I wore a brand new pale blue dress and matching hat for the occasion. The six of us looked smashing!

When our pastor finished preaching, the choir started singing that old hymn, JUST AS I AM. That is when it hit me! God knew everything about me and still loved me just as I am. The only thing He wanted from me was to believe in Him and I did. As the choir sang, I looked at Chuck with tears in my eyes. Chuck looked back at me with tears in his. We nodded to one another and wheeled ourselves down to the altar. I rededicated my life to Jesus Christ that day and so did Chuck. I was baptized years ago, but Chuck never was. Now, because of his disability, he could not get into the baptistery. That really bothered him, so he talked to the pastor. The pastor agreed to come to our house and baptize Chuck in our swimming pool as soon as he could. I could not believe our above-ground pool was going to serve as a baptistery, right in our own back yard. We felt blessed!

After church, we all met Nana and Granddad at a local restaurant to celebrate Easter. We told them that Chuck and I rededicated our lives to Jesus Christ and about Chuck's pending baptism in our back yard.

"Personally, I think it's a bunch of hogwash," Nana said.

Granddad looked right at Nana and said, "If this makes them happy, then so be it! Do not interfere with how they believe. Everybody knows that you do not believe. You have told everybody that you are still waiting for that silly letter. That does not mean they should not believe in God. I believe in a 'higher power.' What that is I don't know for sure, but maybe one day I'll find out."

"Here look at this," I said, as I handed Granddad a pamphlet about how to become a Christian that I picked up at church. He looked at it briefly and put it in his shirt pocket. I knew I should not say another word. Small talk was the best way to continue this wonderful day. I am definitely a people pleaser. I was not going to make waves, especially on Easter Sunday.

After we got home, I called my brother to wish him a Happy Easter. Then Chuck called his parents in Arizona. He told them that he and I had rededicated our lives to Jesus Christ and that the pastor agreed to baptize him in our pool. They were elated! Chuck also called his brother and then his sisters. Chuck was beside himself with joy and wanted to share his good news with everybody in his family.

The day of Chuck's baptism was truly meaningful. The pastor arranged to have some of the ushers from church come over with him to help Chuck get into the pool. All of us were there, except for my daddy who had to work. Once the pastor baptized Chuck, he and the ushers said a prayer asking God to be with Chuck as he faced challenges in his life. Now that both of us were baptized and going to church, I thought that everything would be perfect from that day forward.

Shortly after, we decided to make a big step and take David and Neil to Disneyland for their birthday. We discussed this at great length with Mother and Daddy because we wanted them to join us. We felt if they came, we could try staying in a motel. If we had problems, Mother and Daddy would be there to help us. We finally found a motel that we thought would work. We took two cars just in case it did not. That way Chuck and I could return home, and my parents could stay on with the boys, so they would not be disappointed.

When we arrived, Daddy checked us in. Then we parked our cars and Daddy unloaded our stuff. There were no steps entering the room, like the manager promised, and the bathroom was big enough for us to use. Mother and Daddy had an adjourning room with a kitchenette. The boys' eyes lit up when they saw a huge swimming pool right outside our room. The six of us spent four days and three nights there having the best time. We did have challenges, but we managed with the help of my parents. If this was going to be the one and only trip we could take as a family, then that was fine. Better one than none.

Neil started kindergarten in September of 1968 and David entered first grade. David was six years old and Neil was five. Neil was a very active child at home as well as at school. His teacher called me numerous times asking me to tell Neil to settle down in class. He was having a hard time sitting still. Chuck and I had many long talks with him trying to encourage him to do better.

After David and Neil attended school for a while, I asked each of them, "How do you guys feel about me being the only mommy at your school in a wheelchair?"

"That's okay, Mommy," David said.

"I don't care," Neil chimed in.

"Boys, please listen to me," I said. "I want to make sure you are never embarrassed because I'm different from the other mothers."

"You're not different," David said. "You can do everything."

"Yeah," Neil said, agreeing with David.

"I can do a lot, but I will never be able to walk like the other moms," I said, trying to make a point. "I need the two of you to promise me something. If there ever comes a time when one of your friends says something bad or teases you about Daddy Chuck or me, you have to tell us right away. Okay?"

"I will Mommy," David said,

"Me too, Mommy," Neil said, agreeing with David.

They each gave me a hug and kiss and went off to play.

When I got home from taking the boys to school, I took care of Chuck. Whenever he needed help, I was there. With both boys in school, it was easier to care for Chuck when he had accidents. As the boys got older, it was harder to hide Chuck's problem from them. Not knowing when these accidents would happen started messing with my psyche because they were happening more often.

Some people, along with my doctor, criticized me for doing too much. My doctor said my physical condition came from stress. I could not understand his thinking. I knew I was doing a lot, but taking care of my family was very rewarding. It made me feel needed and appreciated. I did not want to give that up. I felt because I was home all day, that David and Neil should enjoy being kids for as long as possible. Mother enjoyed taking care of her family and so did Nana. I came from that mindset. I felt fortunate to be able to stay home with my boys and had Chuck to thank for that.

For us these were times of joy and times of challenges. We tried to handle each experience the best way we could. We tried to be thankful through the good and the bad. I was very thankful for the many blessings in my life. How could I not smile? Going back to church and rededicating my life to Jesus Christ was the best decision I made. God was my confidant. He knew all my deepest and darkest secrets, but He still loved me unconditionally. Chuck's baptism and rededicating his life were joyful experiences for him and me too. We had witnessed many milestones in our short married life and were looking forward to seeing many more in the years to come.

17

A LOT TO DEAL WITH

After taking the boys to school, I came home and Chuck had another accident. This one was the worst. It happened when he was getting out of bed. As I entered our bedroom, Chuck was in tears and felt awful. I did not know where to begin. I knew I would have to find the courage to talk to him. Chuck had to know these accidents were weighing heavily on me. We had to stop denying there was a problem.

After helping Chuck get into the shower, I stripped the bed and started the laundry. Once I got Chuck and his wheelchair cleaned, he went into the kitchen. Tears streamed down my face while I mopped the floor in the bedroom. I did not know how much longer I could put up with this. Thank goodness, the boys were not here. When I finished, I went into the kitchen.

I very calmly said, "Chuck, I knew you had no bladder or bowel control when we got married, but you seemed to have everything under control. During our first year of marriage, you only had an occasional accident. Lately, it has gotten much worse, and I don't understand why."

"I'm to blame. I have not been doing my daily bowel routine. I guess I got lazy."

When I heard him say that, I felt my heart starting to pound. I was fuming. Anger filled my entire body. I let him have it with both barrels as I yelled, "You got lazy! You say you love me. You say you care about me, yet you do nothing to change this situation. You know this causes me extra work, and it is not the least bit pleasant! I do not know another living soul that uses so much air spray! How could you do this to me?"

"I'm so sorry. I have no answers. It has been bothering me too."

Still fuming, I said, "If it bothered you, you would have done something about it! I guess you are too darn lazy! Why should you worry? I am here to clean up your mess. Your accidents cause me a lot of work and an abundance of stress! I cannot believe you have allowed this to go on for so long. I am a fool for not saying something before this. It is one thing to have a problem; it is quite another when you do nothing about it. That burns me!"

"I've never seen you so mad," he said, looking bewildered.

"Can you blame me? It is bad enough when you forget to empty your urinal bag and there is urine all over the floor. Bowel problems are far worse. I have tried to give you the benefit of the doubt, but no more. Knowing that you were not doing what you are supposed to do is very upsetting. I am deeply hurt."

"I can tell!" He said, coming over to try to comfort me.

"Don't come near me!" I yelled.

Chuck just sat there. He knew he could say nothing to appease me. Up to this point, we were lucky that Chuck only had one accident outside our home when the two of us went out to dinner. To say that was an awful experience is putting it mildly. Chuck was embarrassed. I was mortified. People at the restaurant probably wondered why we went out to eat. I knew all of this was causing me undo stress.

"There goes the buzzer. I am going to get the clean sheets out of the dryer and make our bed. When I get back, you'd better have some answers for me!" I said.

When I finished making the bed, I returned to the kitchen less agitated. We discussed a number of issues. First, we needed to get twin beds. I felt that would help me psychologically. If he had an accident, I would not be in the same bed. After numerous accidents, I slept as close to the edge of the bed as possible. Next, Chuck suggested he have a colostomy. I did not want that if he did not need it. He said it was no big deal. He would have surgery with no anesthetic. That freaked me out, but it made sense. Chuck had no feeling from his chest down. Finally, I suggested getting somebody in to help. Chuck did not want anyone knowing our personal business. After talking for a couple of hours, I could tell Chuck was leaning towards surgery. I told him I would support whatever decision he made.

My parents and grandparents had no clue about Chuck's accidents. Chuck wanted it to remain that way. I knew Chuck's feelings. Telling my family would serve no purpose. All this stress was causing me to have my own problems. I was starting to have attacks more frequently, usually after my evening meals. My doctor was the only person that knew what I was dealing with regarding Chuck's accidents. He eventually referred me to an internist who ran some tests and told me I had ulcerative colitis. Ulcerative colitis causes inflammation and sores, called ulcers, in the top layers of the lining of the large intestine. The inflammation makes the colon empty frequently causing diarrhea. The internist prescribed medication and a bland diet. He also referred me to a psychiatrist. I was reluctant, but realized I needed to talk to someone. I have always been a people pleaser. I was guilty of taking care of everybody else's needs before my own. I felt it was my job to keep peace in my family, not make waves.

I tried to lead as normal a life as possible, but fear of the unknown was taking over. Wondering when I would have an attack, I was getting to the point where I was afraid to eat. At least I was not having problems during the day. I could still run errands, go to my doctor appointments, go to church, and have company over. My evenings were the worst. The more Chuck continued having accidents, the more attacks I had. Every night, I thanked God I did not have an accident. If both Chuck and I were to have accidents at the same time, I did not know what I would do.

I finally made an appointment to see a psychiatrist. It helped talking to her about my problems. I did not want to burden Chuck. I could not let on to my family members that anything was wrong. I felt so torn. I prayed that the medication, a bland diet, and somebody to talk to would help me. I had to try to stay positive.

Mother, Daddy, Nana, and Granddad had an open invitation to come to our home. They usually came over after lunch. That gave me time to get the boys off to school and get the house done. If Chuck had an accident, I would have him and everything cleaned up before company arrived. I loved my family so much. They were a bright spot for me during these stressful days. David and Neil were lucky to have been born into a family that loved them and would do anything to make them happy. It was my deepest prayer that when my boys married and had children that they would have the same family closeness that I did.

I desperately needed some distraction to lift my spirits. With the holidays approaching, it seemed to be just what the doctor ordered. Right after celebrating Thanksgiving, we had our family tree trimming party and decorated the house. Mother and I started Christmas shopping while the boys were in school. We were like a couple of kids. We had so much fun together. I seemed to be doing better physically because my mind was on fun things rather than all the bad stuff. This Christmas, God provided our family with another gift. My brother called and told us Margaret was pregnant again. They were expecting their second child in May of next year.

We were still attending church. David and Neil were learning a lot about Jesus in their Sunday school class. Our friendship with Rick and Char was growing. We enjoyed our special times together away from church as well. Our children had so much fun together. Nothing uplifted my soul more than to hear my boys laughing and enjoying life.

Shortly after the first of the year, Chuck informed me that he had made a decision to have the colostomy surgery. He said he thought long and hard about his decision. He also discussed all the pros and cons with his doctors. He felt strongly that having a colostomy bag would make it easier for him to care for himself. Next, he told me that he wanted a pool installed in our back yard. I could not believe what I was hearing.

"Why try to do so much all at once?" I asked him.

"I wanted to do this when we first moved here," he said.

"Have you contacted a pool company?" I inquired.

"Yes, I did. I figured, why not get the ball rolling?"

"I do not have the strength to fight you on this. I am concerned how I am going to deal with so much going on."

"You should not worry one bit. The pool company will do all the work. It should not cause you any extra work," Chuck said, trying to reassure me.

"Can you go in the pool after you have the colostomy done?"

"Yes, the doctor said it would do me good," Chuck answered.

"I guess you've made up your mind."

"Yes, I have," Chuck, said. "The boys will be overjoyed having a big pool, and we will be able to swim with them. The sales representative is coming tomorrow to show us some ideas of what the pool will look like. I also want a ramp installed so that I can get into the pool without using a lift."

"Chuck, I can feel my stomach tighten," I said.

"You will be fine," Chuck said. "Here comes another surprise."

"What pray tell, are you going to think up next?" I asked, shocked.

"I went to see an attorney and started adoption proceedings. I have waited long enough. I want to be David and Neil's father," Chuck said. "The attorney will call to set up a second appointment so the two of us can go in and talk to him."

"I know you have wanted to adopt the boys for quite awhile, but you have not said much about it lately."

"My upcoming surgery made me stop and think. God forbid if something would happen to me. I want David and Neil to have my full benefits from the military."

"Nothing is going to happen to you," I said.

"You never know," Chuck responded.

"Oh, Chuck, don't go there!"

"Okay. Settle down!" Chuck pleaded.

"This means we'll have three things going at once: your surgery, the pool, and the adoption. I don't know if that's a good idea," I said.

"I can't think of a better time," he said, acting as if it were no big deal.

Later that night, I thought about my doctors. They all were adamant about keeping my stress down. The only question was how was I going to do that? I needed to turn to God. I prayed, "Lord Jesus, You know there are times when I do not feel like myself. You are the only reason I have been able to get through so much already. Now I need You more than ever. I place Chuck's surgery, the pool, and the boys' adoption in Your hands. Please be with all of us Lord. Grant me peace through what lies ahead. Amen." I had to trust God and to believe that He would take care of me. The adoption, however, concerned me the most because I had not been in touch with the boys' fathers in a long time.

The following day, we told both sides of our family that Chuck started adoption proceedings. Everybody was thrilled.

Just before our third wedding anniversary, Chuck had surgery. After he came home, he faced another challenge because he had to irrigate every day. That was hard for him to do with one hand. He needed my help even more now. He did his best, but he would still have accidents. Because Chuck had no feeling, he could not tell when the adhesive that held his colostomy bag in place was loose or starting to let go.

There I was taking care of Chuck, with the pool company in the back yard, and the attorney calling to keep us up-to-date on the adoption. I was still having problems of my own with colitis attacks. I continued to see two doctors monthly and my psychiatrist weekly. I would get up in the morning and not know where to start. At times, I wanted to hide so nobody could find me.

Rick and Char told us numerous times that they would help us. When we could not attend church, they made sure to take the boys with them. My family continued to come over regularly. They were glad Chuck's surgery was successful, but wondered how I was managing. They could tell I was not feeling good. Granddad came over after the boys got home from school to keep the boys out of the workers' way. The boys were patiently waiting for the pool to be finished.

We were also anxiously waiting to hear from our attorney. The adoption proceeding was causing me a lot of stress. I wondered what would happen if the boys' fathers decided not to sign the papers? Legally, Chuck had no claim to my boys. I never thought about this until the attorney brought it to our attention during one of our meetings.

Finally, a few weeks later, the attorney told us he contacted Tom, but he was having a problem locating Jim. This frightened me even more. Even though God healed my feelings toward Tom and Jim, I had the fear of what might happen. At times, I turned my problems over to God; other times I would take my problems back. Why I could not let go and let God handle everything was beyond me.

Once again, my insides went crazy. Only this time it was much harsher. A few times, I was on the toilet for over an hour. The cramps were so violent that I thought I was going to die. Sweat poured off me like water. Chuck would hand me cold washcloths to put on my face to keep me from passing out. Once, I literally did pass out. My wheelchair was right there or I would have fallen to the floor.

I stayed in constant contact with my doctors. I kept taking 26 pills a day and was still on the bland diet. Both doctors told me that there was not much more they could do for me. My psychiatrist tried to help me cope, but she could not understand why I chose to stay in my marriage. How could I not. Chuck meant the world to me.

God was truly on my side. The attorney finally called. He told us he had everything ready and needed us to meet him in the judge's chambers along with the boys. Just before we signed the papers in May of 1969, the judge talked to both David and Neil. They told the judge they wanted Chuck to be their daddy. As young as they were, they knew Chuck loved them and that he loved their mommy. From the first day Chuck met my boys, he knew they would be his one day. That day finally came. I felt so relieved knowing Tom and Jim were out of our lives forever. I did not have to worry anymore. Chuck was a very proud papa that day. We stopped by my parents and grandparents' houses after we left the courthouse. They surprised us with a special party for Chuck. All four of us had the same last name now. We were a complete family unit. Later, we called the rest of our family to give them the news. Everyone was thrilled.

That evening, after my three guys were asleep, I went out into the back yard. I needed time alone. I needed time to reflect over the last few months. I needed to thank God for bringing me through this very stressful time. I was hopeful. Maybe now that things have settled down my insides would as well.

A few days later, my brother called to tell me that he and Margaret were the proud parents of another son. Bill now had a baby brother named Stephen. I missed my brother and his family. I hardly knew my two nephews. My brother was extremely busy with school. He was due to get his Ph.D. soon. I still hoped they would move closer, but I had my doubts.

Finally, our pool was finished, and the landscaping surrounding it looked beautiful. I always looked forward to my boys' birthdays, but this year was different. Chuck and I wanted to have an adoption party, a pool party, and two birthday parties, all in one big weekend. We set a date and made phone calls inviting our immediate family to come and share our joy. Mother called a local motel to reserve rooms for those coming in from out of town.

On the day of our family celebration, everyone had a great time. Those that chose not to swim still enjoyed the happiness that was ever so present that weekend. David and Neil swam nonstop. It was their birthdays; they were getting away with murder. The boys were thrilled with the new pool, including a spa and a slide. Added to their happiness was the fact that Chuck and I could go swimming with them. This was something new and different for all of us. On a day that was so joyous, I still had the fear of the unknown. I wondered how everyone would react if Chuck had an accident in the pool. I knew now that Chuck's accidents were always on my mind, but this weekend turned out to be one that we thoroughly enjoyed.

Once the weekend was over, I needed a couple of days to regroup. The boys were out of school for the summer. Not having to get up early and take the boys to school gave me a vacation too. My boys were wonderful. They were best friends. They shared time together in the pool, watching TV, and playing in their playroom. I am so glad I had them so close together. When they were babies it was a lot of work, but now they brought me so much joy.

A few days later, after Chuck went to bed and the boys were watching TV, I decided to go outside to spend some quiet time with God. As I sat there looking up towards the evening clouds, I prayed, "Lord Jesus, You are my world. I know I could never have gotten through these past months without Your help. I have had so much to deal with. Please forgive me for worrying when I should not have. Please forgive me for doubting that You would get us through everything that needed to be done. I am so thankful that I do not have to worry about Tom and Jim anymore. They came into my life for a reason: I have two wonderful boys. Because Chuck has adopted David and Neil, Tom and Jim can never hurt us anymore. Words cannot express how grateful I feel. I pray that Chuck's physical problems get better. Please teach me to accept the things I cannot change and the wisdom to know what I can. Amen."

18

DOWNWARD SPIRAL

Chuck seemed to be adjusting to his colostomy, but he was still having accidents. This weighed heavily on both of us. Chuck had to do a daily routine to keep from having accidents. When he did what he was supposed to do and still had accidents, he felt frustrated. I tried to be as understanding as I could, but it was hard. I wanted to scream right along with him. There were times I wondered if he made the right decision. I did not want to hurt Chuck by complaining.

Trying to deal with all this stress was hard on me. I noticed my physical problems were getting worse too. I started having one attack a week. Then it was six to eight times a month. I was starting to lose weight and fear consumed me. The sicker I became, the more incapacitated I became. I was terrified to leave the house because most public bathrooms were not wheelchair accessible. The fear of having an accident after what I had been through with Chuck the past few years, scared me to death. Many days, I screamed out to God, "Take anything from me, but please don't take my independence!" Sitting on a toilet, I could not take care of Chuck, the boys, or the house. I became despondent. I took great pride in everything I did. Now due to my health, I had to let things go. Chuck and the boys did what they could, but it was not the same as having a woman's touch. The less I could do, the more depressed I became. What really bothered me was the boys could see their mommy was not well.

One night, I cried out to God for strength. My energy level was going down hill fast. I was starting to fear what my future held. I remember in the Scripture it states, "Casting all your care upon him; for he careth for you." I Peter 5:7. I knew God cared about me, so

I laid my burdens before Him daily. For whatever reason, God did not want to change my situation. How could I ever accept what was happening to me?

Mother stopped by one day. Thank goodness, Chuck and the boys were gone. Mother sat herself down at the dining room table and told me to join her. Then she said, "Sharon, I have been deeply concerned about you. I have eyes. I can tell that you have lost weight and you seem so tired. Back when we had the pool party, you were not yourself. Even Daddy, Nana, and Granddad noticed this too."

With tears in my eyes, I blurted out everything that had been going on. I told her about Chuck's accidents, the reason for his colostomy, and about my diagnosis with ulcerative colitis. I also told her I was seeing three different doctors. I explained in detail Chuck's accidents and my attacks. She could not believe her ears. I asked her to forgive me for not telling her sooner. I explained that I did not want her to worry.

"I cannot even begin to imagine what you have gone through cleaning up all those messes. That is bad enough, but your being sick on top of it, is overwhelming. My heart goes out to all of you. If only you would have told me, I could have helped you," Mother responded, sympathetically.

"How could I ask you to help? Chuck would have died if anybody knew."

"I suppose you're right. What does your psychiatrist say?" Mother inquired.

"She thinks we should separate. The thought of that causes me even more stress. I cannot imagine going through another divorce."

"This has got to be hard on you!" Mother said, coming over to put her arm around my shoulder to comfort me. "If I knew, I would have spoken to Chuck."

"I do not want Chuck to know that we talked. He would die! I am surprised that he has not had an accident when the family is with us," I said.

"I won't say a word, but if you get worse, I will," Mother said, and then she asked, "Do the boys know what's going on?"

"Sometimes I cannot hide this from them. They know to stay out of the bedroom. They know their mommy is not well. That bothers me, but there is nothing I can do about that either," I explained.

"I don't know if I could handle this as well as you have. You have more determination than anybody I know."

"Who do you think I learned that from?" I asked, starting to laugh. "You are the best shrink in the world. I should have come to you months ago. There is nobody that understands me the way you do."

"I love you so much," Mother said, putting her arm around my shoulder again. "I hear the guys coming back. We will talk more later. I will pray that things get better."

Once again, my mother was my confidant. I knew she would be there for me anytime I needed her. Just talking to her made me feel somewhat better.

I did not understand what the Lord was teaching me through this illness. The sad part was I eventually had to stop going to church on a regular basis. If I felt okay, we would go; if not, we would stay home. At least the boys were able to go with Rick and Char. Going to church meant a lot to me. Not being able to go was upsetting. Church was not the only thing I had to curtail. At times, it was the weekly things as well. If I had a bad night, I was exhausted the next day. Life, as I knew it, was changing.

Rick and Char got wind that Chuck and I were having physical problems. I think the boys let the cat out of the bag. One Sunday afternoon when the children were playing, Rick and Char asked us if we were having problems. We finally broke down and told them what was going on. They told us they would do anything to help us, and we knew they would. Taking the boys to Sunday school and coming over to our home really helped. It was obvious that they were the only ones that cared, besides my family.

It was during another visit, I had an opportunity to talk to Char while Rick and Chuck were out in the back yard watching the children swim.

"You will never know how much you both mean to us," I said. "I'm so sick, and you guys are the only ones from church that give a darn."

"Has anybody been here to see you?" Char asked.

"Nobody has come by or called," I said, starting to cry. "What's wrong with people? Every time we go to church, the pastor talks about love, yet there is so little love shown towards people nowadays. To me you cannot just say I love you. Mother always told me that actions speak louder than words."

"I agree. I don't know why people, at church act the way they do," Char said.

"We've been absent from church for weeks, and not one person has shown any concern or wondered where we were. The pastor himself has not called or come over. The pastor came here to baptize Chuck. He knows we are both in wheelchairs. You would think he would show something towards us. Not to change the subject, but the last time we went shopping, you said that you and Rick are having problems. Please forgive me for burdening you and Rick with our problems. I am so sorry."

"Don't worry! Yes, Rick and I are having problems, but it is nothing like what you and Chuck are going through. I hope that we will be able to work things out because of the girls. Since Rick came back from Vietnam, we are not as close as we were." Just then, Rick and Chuck came in.

"Listen, Sharon," Rick said. "Chuck just told me some of what has been going on. Please know we will always be there for the two of you. We're each going through some trials right now, but we have to trust God that everything will work out."

"I appreciate your concern," I said, responding to Rick's comments. "Know that we are here for the two of you too. At least we have each other to lean on. Hopefully that will help all of us through this rough patch."

After Rick and Char left, I needed some time alone. I asked Chuck to watch the boys while I went to our bedroom. The bitterness I felt was at an all time high. I felt like people at church, other than Rick and Char, were letting Chuck and me down. No words seemed to comfort me. As each day passed, I felt more emotionally drained. I wanted to eat, but could not on many occasions. I was sick of taking medicine. I felt so doped-up. I had feelings inside that I could not even explain to my psychiatrist. My psychiatrist tried to reassure me that things would get better. I was tired of hearing her say, "Give it time."

Even though I was seeing my psychiatrist weekly, my physical condition was only getting worse. One day I had three attacks. I was down to eating only 29 things now. When I cooked dinner, I would first cook a regular meal for my family. Then I would prepare my own meal. After I had an attack, however, I could only eat rice, soup, Jell-O, and a baked potato. I told my psychiatrist I was afraid to eat for fear of what would happen. She said that was normal. She assured me when I got better that I would be able to overcome those fears.

After a few more months, I was physically getting too weak to do much of anything. Mother started coming over almost daily to help me. It broke her heart to see me physically and emotionally drained. The more I talked to my three doctors, the more upset I became. With all their expertise, I felt they should have been able to help me. My regular doctor felt that I had been under stress for far too long; stress had finally taken its toll on me. My internist had done all he felt he could do other than give me more medication. I continued to talk to my psychiatrist, but it was mostly over the phone now because I was afraid to leave the house. My fear was getting the better of me.

One day I finally made it into my psychiatrist's office. She wanted to have a serious talk with me face to face. She started by saying, "You can't go on like this, Sharon."

I would argue back at her saying, "I can't stop being a wife and a mother. What would my family do?"

"You have to come to terms with what is going on."

"You are scaring me!" I said, raising my voice.

"I hope I am. You have to make some major decisions. You have lost too much weight. You are less than 100 pounds now. That is unacceptable! Something has to give or you are going to wind up in the hospital or worse. I think I need to talk to Chuck."

"I don't want you to talk to Chuck!" I said, raising my voice again. "Let's just wait and see what happens."

"Okay, but if I don't see any improvement soon, I'm calling your other two doctors to get their input. I need you to sign a medical release. Just so you know, I'll also be calling Chuck and talking to him if you don't start to improve."

"I'll sign the medical releases, but wait before you talk to Chuck," I pleaded. "Mother is helping me so I will probably get better. Bless her, she never complains. She likes to feel needed; and, right now I need her more than ever."

"You are very lucky to have such a close family. Take care of yourself and I'll talk to you in a few days," she said.

On my drive home, I had so many thoughts running through my mind. I felt backed up against a wall with no place to go. I could not understand why I was not improving. I was at my wits end and felt weepy all the time.

One evening my parents came over for dinner. About an hour or so later, I got deathly sick while they were still there. They saw me at my weakest point. Mother got me a cold dishcloth to try to cool me down because I was sweating profusely from violent cramps and diarrhea. Mother later helped the boys get ready for bed, cleaned up the kitchen, and came into my bedroom to say good night to me.

"It absolutely kills me to see you like this, Sharon."

"I'm sorry Mother. You don't need all this extra work," I said, apologizing.

"I'm glad I was here. I just wish I was helping you do something fun. I would not wish this on my worst enemy. You go to sleep now. I want to talk to Chuck if that's all right with you?"

"Right now, I could care less," I told her.

Mother talked to Chuck that evening by laying all her cards out on the table. She did not pull any punches. She was deeply concerned about me. Chuck said he was concerned too, and he was feeling very guilty. Mother told Chuck that she would prepare the evening meals from now on, and Daddy could come over after he got home from work. She felt this might help relieve my stress. Chuck agreed.

One morning while I was in the shower I started thinking about my life. Chuck and the boys relied on me. Maybe they relied on me too much. The guilt I felt when I was not able to help them was overwhelming. I spent years feeling bad about myself. When Chuck and I married, my attitude changed. My self-esteem rose to an all time high. I was doing so well. Now the tables had turned. Colitis took my independence away. I could not accept it. The harder I tried, the sicker I became.

After more sessions with my psychiatrist over the phone, she finally asked that I come into her office as soon as I felt well enough to do so. When that day came, she told me that she and my other two doctors had a consultation. They all felt strongly that I should leave Chuck.

"What? You've got to be kidding! You doctors are no doctors at all to say such a thing," I yelled, storming out of her office.

She followed me out into the lobby and asked me to come back, saying, "Come on let's talk this through."

"Okay," I said. "You really shocked me by saying that."

After we got back into her office she said, "Listen carefully. You are a fantastic person. You have come a long way with everything that has happened in your life, but doing what you are doing now is too hard on you physically. I do not think you can take care of your two boys and Chuck any longer. It is too hard on you. Your health is in peril, and you can't deny that."

"I know. I've lost a lot of weight and I look awful."

"You don't look awful. You look sickly. Something has got to give."

"But I love Chuck and I love my boys. How in the world can I ever leave him? He has given me so much. I have a beautiful home. He adopted my boys. He has given me financial security beyond anything I could have imagined. I have been able to be home with my boys. You might as well bury me, if I have to give all this up."

"I can tell you are scared, but what is worse? Living with Chuck and being sick, or leaving Chuck and being well? You have to ask yourself those questions. If it were the normal every day problems I am sure you would do okay. Chuck having so many accidents and you having to clean up feces is not easy for anybody, let alone, somebody confined to a wheelchair. The many times you told me that you woke up with feces on your nightgown, I asked myself, 'Why in the world would any woman live like that?' I have heard all your excuses. We have spent hours talking, but nothing is changing. You have to decide what is best for you and your boys."

"I am so scared!" I said, starting to shake all over.

"Sharon, you tell me you constantly worry when you and Chuck go out in public, or use the pool that he might have an accident."

"I know, but he only had one accident when we went out to eat. He has not had an accident in the pool. If that happened, I would try not to make a big deal out of it."

"But it is a big deal! Subconsciously, you are thinking about it. You are probably thinking about it more than you realize. If nothing else, your body is taking the brunt of all this because of the stress you are under. The mind and body can only take so much," she explained.

I responded by saying, "My internist told me, 'Sometimes it's not what you eat, but the frame of mind you're in when you're eating. If you eat while you're upset, sometimes the food will go right through you.'"

"I agree totally. As more time goes on, the worse it is going to get. You need to get a handle on the situation. You are doing everything humanly possible. This does not mean that you do not love Chuck, it means that you have to love yourself more."

"That makes no sense. That's doctor double-talk."

"Then I ask you this last question, Sharon. Who is going to take care of David, Neil, and Chuck if something happens to you? You must think seriously about what I have said and separate from Chuck or get a divorce. If he truly loves you, he will let you go. I want you to know the time has come for me to call Chuck."

"Okay. I have a lot of thinking to do." I said, as I left.

As I drove home, I was thinking about everything she said. "Why did God bring Chuck into my life, just to have this happen? How could I ever leave Chuck? He has been so good to my boys and me. What in the world will happen to us? How will the boys react? Are we going to have to move back to my parents' house? I had no other choice right now. How was I ever going to tell Chuck about what my psychiatrist told me?" I was going to have to reach down deep inside my soul with the help of my God to come up with some answers.

When I got home, Chuck and the boys greeted me with open arms. At that very moment, I started bawling. They looked at me as if I were crazy!

"Mommy, what's wrong?" David asked.

"Why are you crying?" Neil asked.

Chuck said, "Mommy just got home. Let's give her time alone."

Without any explanation, I went to my bedroom.

I sat in my wheelchair with my feet up on the bed. I took my Bible out of my nightstand. I desperately needed some answers. The two Scriptures I found were, "Hear, O Lord, when I cry with my voice; have mercy also upon me, and answer me." Psalms 27:7 and "Hear, O Lord, and have mercy upon me; Lord, be thou my helper." Psalms 30:10. I cried out to God many times. Why was I not getting any answers?

I closed my eyes and prayed, "Dear Heavenly Father, I come before You asking You to help me, just like the Scripture says. Please have mercy on me and help me through the hard decisions that I am being forced to make. I have been on a downward spiral for so long. I feel like I am about to hit bottom. You know I am scared to death. I cannot deny that my health is failing. I am falling deeper and deeper into despair. You are a mighty God and I need Your guidance in my life more than ever. Please give Chuck and me the strength to make the necessary decisions that we need to make. Our family is in Your hands. Amen."

19

FRIENDS FOREVER

I woke the following morning with tears streaming down my face. Chuck looked over at me and asked, "What in the world is wrong? Why are you crying?"

"I feel like the walls are closing in on me. I do not know what to do. My session yesterday with the psychiatrist really wore me out. She is deeply concerned about my well-being. I do not feel like myself at all. I am weepy all the time. I have no strength left. Everything I do is an effort," I said, trying to explain my feelings.

"What did the doctor say? I know you were terribly upset when you came home, but I did not want to ask you a bunch of questions. I felt when you wanted to talk, you would. Do you feel like talking?" Chuck asked.

"Yesterday I was feeling really down. I did not want to say much because I knew it would upset you," I said, trying to give him a reason why I said nothing the day before.

"Sharon, this is no time to pull any punches. You need to tell me what she said. I promise I won't get upset," he said. "Whatever happens we will deal with it. We have been through a lot together. Please don't shut me out now."

"She told me she talked to my other two doctors. All of them agreed that we should separate or get a divorce," I said, as I started to sob.

"Please calm down. I know where they're coming from," he said.

"What do you mean?"

"Sharon, I can see that you are not in good shape emotionally or physically, and you have not been for a long time. How do you think that makes me feel? Before you answer that, I can tell you it makes me feel pretty awful. I know I am the cause of your problems. I don't need a doctor to tell me that," he said.

"I don't know what to do anymore! My birthday is almost here. What do I have to celebrate?"

"I am going to call the doctor and go into see her. Right now, your health has to be number one. If we need to separate or get a divorce then that is something we might have to do," he said.

"You say that so nonchalantly, like it's no big deal!" I said, getting angry.

"It is a big deal! I do not take divorce lightly. I am not going to be the one to put you in an early grave either," he said, trying to express his feelings.

"Go ahead and call her. She wants to talk to you anyway. Maybe if you hear her view, it would be better than hearing things from me. I had better get up and see what the boys are doing."

"You have to know that they are also worried about you too."

"I do not want them to worry about me! They deserve better than that. I love them too much and would never do anything to hurt them. If we do what the doctors say and separate or get a divorce, don't you think that will hurt the boys?"

"Probably at first, but they are getting older and they will understand. If we have to divorce, then we will have to sit them down and talk to them. We have to make sure they understand that we love each other and we will always remain friends."

"I agree. We can ask the psychiatrist for guidance if that time comes," I said. "I'm hoping that I will start to feel better."

"Come over here and give me a kiss good morning. Let's get this day started."

Trying to calm down, I kissed him and lay there with my head on his shoulder. I did not want the boys to see me upset again. I was trying to rationalize everything, but it was hard to imagine my life without Chuck.

As I left our bedroom, I heard the key turn in the front door. Mother arrived to take the children to school and help me. Daddy, Nana, and Granddad continued to come over as well. They did not stay as long because they knew I needed my rest.

I eventually told Chuck that my family knew about his accidents. The next time they came over, he apologized profusely. Later, Mother told me that she felt Chuck was dealing with his own private hell. I agreed with her.

Chuck finally saw my psychiatrist. She told him what she felt was best for me. She also told Chuck that if I stayed in our marriage, I would pay a high price physically. Chuck agreed. It was hard on him to see me the way I was. He knew me to be a very strong woman that did just about everything. To watch me go downhill was weighing heavily on him. When Chuck came home, he told me it did him good to talk to my psychiatrist. It gave him a chance to get some things off his chest too.

A few days after my birthday, I passed out again during one of my attacks. Later, Chuck approached me and said, "God, I hate this! That's it! We either separate or get a divorce!"

"No way!" I yelled.

"You heard me! To see you in the bathroom for hours on end is hard enough. To see you pass out is awful. How do you think I feel?" Chuck asked, raising his voice.

"I don't know!" I yelled back at him.

"I feel guilty as hell!" Chuck said, yelling back at me.

"But we love each other!" I said, in a loud pleading tone.

"There is no doubt about that. Sometimes, loving somebody is letting him or her go. Maybe that is what we have to do," Chuck said.

I was afraid what direction my life was taking. I got to the point where it was becoming harder and harder to pray. I kept asking, "What was wrong with me?" I read my Bible, but I still could not find answers to my questions. It states, "I sought the Lord, and He heard me, and delivered me from all my fears." Psalms 34:4. "Why wasn't God delivering me?" I asked myself. I went to Him time after time. I pleaded with God to help me. I wanted God to heal me so I could get on with my life. How could a loving God allow this to happen?

A Psalm of David titled "Triumphant Faith" in the Bible states, "The Lord is my light and my salvation; whom shall I fear? The Lord is the strength of my life; of whom shall I be afraid?" Psalms 27:1. I did believe what the Scriptures said. Because I believed in my Heavenly Father and everything that He represents, I had to put my faith in Him even more. I had to trust that God knew what was best for me. As a human being, I kept trying to do things on my own instead of turning my life totally over to God. I had to try to figure out what God was trying to tell me. He was the only one that knew what my future held.

About a month later, someone at our church heard that Chuck, I, Rick, and Char were having problems. They started gossiping. The straw that broke the camel's back was when the pastor called our house one day. Chuck answered the phone. The pastor told Chuck that he heard I was pregnant by Rick and he wanted an explanation. Chuck was mad! He gave the pastor a piece of his mind, hung up the phone, and came to tell me immediately. I could not believe my ears when Chuck told me what the pastor said.

"The church has hurt me for the last time!" I yelled.

"We must keep our eyes on God. Forget the people," Chuck said. "God will take care of them in His own time."

"I have had it," I said. "To think the pastor thinks I'm pregnant with Rick's child is the most awful thing I've ever heard in my life!"

"Honey, you have to calm down!" Chuck said, raising his voice.

"I can't calm down. I am so angry. I could spit nails! If the pastor had taken some of his precious time to visit us, he would have seen just how sick I am. How can they say such horrible things about me?"

Chuck decided to call Rick and tell him what happened. After Chuck got through talking with Rick, I talked to Char. We were all pretty upset. We knew the truth and so did God. The four of us knew God loved us; that is all that mattered.

Later that evening, I had another attack. Both our families were going through some rough times. We needed the church more than ever, but nobody at the church was willing to be supportive towards any of us. Over the next few weeks, we got together with Rick and Char often. They needed us as much as we needed them.

One day after Rick, Char, and the girls left, I told Chuck that I had something I wanted to share with him.

"If we don't go to church, then the people might take that as a sign of guilt."

"You always feel guilty about everything. You are such a people pleaser. Any time you think somebody thinks poorly of you, you have a fit," he said.

"You know, I should put on the tightest dress I own and wheel right into that church and show everybody that I am not pregnant and prove them all wrong."

"You are one crazy lady!" Chuck said, laughing.

As the days went by, I was getting weaker and weaker. My weight had dropped below 90 pounds. My family was concerned and Chuck was beside himself with worry and guilt. The next time Chuck had an accident, he told me it was time for him to do some serious thinking.

A few days later, Chuck came to me and told me that he filed for a divorce.

"Why did you do that?" I asked, starting to cry.

"You cannot take care of this big house, two boys, and me with all my problems. You have tried for years. If something, God forbid, happened to you because of what I put you through, I would never forgive myself. Know I will always love you, but we can't live like this any longer," he said, with tears in his eyes. "Separating is not the answer. Divorce is the only way."

"I'm trying to understand all this, but it's hard. I can't imagine giving up all we have," I responded. "How are we ever going to explain this to David and Neil?"

"First, we have to talk to your parents. There is no way you can live on your own, right now. Then, we can talk to the boys. They will still be able to come over here to see me, go swimming, and see their friends. We are not going to have a nasty divorce. I will not stand for that!" Chuck said.

"I agree," I responded.

"If it is okay with you, I'll continue to live here. You can leave all your furniture here until you get better and when you are ready to find a place of your own," he suggested.

"That's fine."

"When you need your furniture, we can arrange to have it delivered to your new place. The divorce papers state that I will give you a cash settlement, plus alimony, and child support. Under no circumstances do I want you to go back to work. I want you to stay home with our boys. I have also bought you a car. The hand controls are being installed now, and the car should be delivered in a few days."

"That's pretty generous of you," I said, with a thankful heart.

"That is the least I can do," Chuck said. "I also contacted my cousin. She will be moving in with me. I will not be alone. If I need help, she will be right here. I do not want you worrying about me."

"Sounds like you have thought of everything," I said.

"Yes, I have," he responded. "I will not put you through anymore stress."

"I'll always love you," I said.

"And I you, but those two boys need you. You are no good to them in the condition you're in right now."

"I feel like such a failure!" I said, crying and reaching out to him.

As Chuck tried to comfort me, he said, "You did not fail anyone! You are too hard on yourself. I will always love you. I want the boys to know that. I'm not blaming you, and I hope you're not blaming me."

There was nothing more to discuss. We had said it all.

After Mother drove the boys to school, Chuck and I sat Mother down and told her everything. We asked her if the boys and I could move back home. She knew there was no way I could be on my own right now with two boys to care for. I needed time to heal both physically and emotionally.

Chuck and I acted like two very mature adults during this dreadful time. We decided to stay together until the boys' Christmas vacation. The day we had to talk to the boys and tell them what was going on was the hardest thing we ever had to do. To our amazement, they took the news rather well.

Later we told Rick and Char, and Chuck's family; other than that, nobody else knew. We spent long hours with my parents planning my move. I did not want them to make too many changes in their home. I was hopeful that eventually I would get better and could get a place of my own. They thought it best the boys come over first and that I should follow in a few days.

The day finally arrived for me to leave. I know we probably had the friendliest divorce in history. Thank God, my parents took the boys a few days earlier. This gave Chuck and me time to be alone and say our good-byes without the boys seeing all our emotions. Chuck and I were crying because we were upset that it had come to this. We loved each other. The feelings we expressed that day would stay with us forever.

"Just be happy, Sharon, and get healthy," Chuck said.

"Take care of yourself. Come see us as often as you want," I told him.

"You know I will. Remember the boys can come over here too. When I come over, I want to see some meat on those bones!" Chuck said, trying to lighten the mood.

"I'll be all right. Just wait. You'll see."

"You better get going. Everybody is waiting for you. Remember, friends forever. Nothing will ever change that," he said, kissing me.

"I feel the same way. When is your cousin coming?"

"She will be here later this evening. Please stop worrying. Now it is time for you to take care of yourself. I know in time you will be back to your old self again," he said.

"If anybody calls, tell them I will call them back when I feel better."

"I will," he replied.

"Gosh, Chuck, the house looks so bare without any Christmas decorations. I am so glad the folks put up a tree for the boys. Are you coming over for Christmas dinner?"

"I am not sure. It depends on how you are feeling."

"Thank you for your generosity in the divorce settlement."

"That's the least I could do, after all I put you through," Chuck responded.

Shedding more tears, we kissed and hugged each other knowing the love we had would never change.

"I guess it's time for me to go," I said.

"We can't put it off any longer," he said.

"Right now, I'm afraid my faith is faltering. Underneath, I know God is with us, but it is still hard for me to leave," I said. "Take good care of yourself. Promise me that."

"I will. Stop worrying. Be brave. Be brave for yourself, David, and Neil. They need their healthy mommy back."

"I'll try. I love you. Friends forever," I said.

"Yes," he said, "Friends forever."

When I left, I only drove a few blocks, pulled over onto the side of the road, and stopped the car. I sat there bawling like a baby. I could not believe I was on my way back home to my parents' house again. I could not figure out why God had given my boys and me so much, just to take it all away. Did I do something so terrible that God was punishing me? Maybe some day I would understand why all this happened to all of us.

20

ON THE ROAD TO RECOVERY

When I arrived at my parents' home, everybody was there waiting for me. As I wheeled into the house, Mother showed me what she and Daddy had done to make our stay as accommodating as possible. God proved His existence through my parents and the love they showed my children and me. They had such giving hearts and never complained. After spending some time with my family, I got ready for bed. I felt drained. I felt like a failure. I felt so much guilt for putting my boys through another divorce and disrupting my parents' home again. The only way now was up. I had to believe that, or I would fall deeper into despair.

I woke the following morning, to the sound of Mother knocking on my bedroom door. "How are you doing?" Mother asked, as she peeked in.

"I had a rough night. I could not stop crying, but eventually I fell off to sleep," I told her.

"Just remember that each day will get better. I wanted you to know, I called all three of your doctors to let them know you had moved home. Your regular doctor said that he wanted you to eat six small meals a day and get plenty of rest. In a week or so, he wants you to come into the office. He felt you made the right decision moving home."

"That was sweet of you to call my doctors," I said. "Where are the boys? Are they okay?"

"They are outside playing with Granddad. They had a good night. I told them after Christmas break they would be starting a new school. They seemed excited when I told them that they were going to be going to the same elementary school that you went to," she said, smiling. "Granddad or I will walk them to and from school because there are no crossing guards yet on the main boulevard. Your number one job right now is to get better."

"I will need to go down to the school to register them," I reminded her.

"We have time. I will go with you," Mother said.

"That would be great! How can I ever repay you and Daddy for all you have done? I can't believe I'm back living here again," I said, starting to tear up. "My life has been so screwed up. I do not know what to do anymore."

"I do not want to hear anything negative coming out of your mouth! Do you hear me? The only way you can repay us is by getting better. I am going to be your nursemaid for a while so you had better not give me any guff! My biggest goal is getting some meat on those bones. You look so pale and drawn. Anyone who looks at you can tell you're not well," she said.

"Did you tell my brother I moved home?" I asked her.

"As a matter of fact, I did. He called a few days before the boys moved in, to let us know he finished school. He received his Ph.D. He was glad all those years of schooling were behind him. Now he is waiting to hear about a teaching assignment. He seemed genuinely concerned about you. He told me he would call you in a few days. Now, my dear, it is time for breakfast. You have to get your buns out of bed. I'm not serving you breakfast in bed," she said, laughing.

"I'll be out in a second," I said, smiling back at her.

My main concern was my health and the well-being of my boys. Chuck called every day to see how we were doing. He reassured me that his cousin was taking good care of him. He did not want me to worry. I felt so relieved. I was trying to relay positive, emotional support to my boys. It was not easy. I had to deal with so many different emotions myself. However, I did not want my feelings of inadequacy, failure, and hurt to rub off on them. With the help of my parents, I felt I would succeed.

A few days later Chuck told me that Rick filed for divorce. I was not too surprised. I knew they were not happy and had not been for quite awhile. Chuck said their divorce was rather nasty. Rick spent his free time at Chuck's house. It was obvious these two men needed each other right now. They were both going through the loss of their families. I was glad they had each other.

As the days passed, bless her heart, Mother had her hands full caring for the boys and me. Nana and Granddad helped as much as they could, but they were getting older and could not do as much as they did years ago.

One morning, Nana and Granddad watched the boys so that Mother could go with me to see my doctor.

"As you get stronger physically, you will do better emotionally as well," my doctor said. "I want you to avoid stress as much as possible."

"I'm trying, but I feel terrible that I am going through another divorce. That kills me! I will do whatever it takes to get better. I am sick of being sick!" I told him.

"It is going to take time and a lot of hard work on your part. Your physical condition did not happen overnight. It has been coming on for a long time. I want you to set some goals for yourself. Small goals, one day at a time," he said.

"What about Sharon's diet?" Mother asked him.

"Continue as we discussed. Later, we will introduce new foods. Remember, this will be a slow process."

"Okay. I can handle that," Mother told the doctor.

"Sharon, you also need to take your medication like clockwork and stay on a bland diet," he instructed me.

"How much longer do I have to eat that awful tasting food?" I asked the doctor.

"There is no set time. Your body will tell you when you are ready to try new foods. We have to see how fast you progress. I want you to keep a diary of everything that goes into your mouth. Do not introduce a bunch of different foods all at once. If you do that, you won't know what food might be causing a problem," he explained.

"I desperately need to gain some weight. I look awful," I told him.

"Stop saying bad things about yourself! I mean it, Sharon!"

"Okay," I said.

"Do you think you will be able to handle the divorce?" He asked.

"I have my ups and downs, but I guess it could be worse. Chuck and I are staying in touch. It has been hard with the holidays, but I think we'll be okay," I said.

Then he asked, "And Chuck, how is he doing?"

"He is doing fine. His cousin moved in with him. At least he is not alone."

"The two of you should be commended for the way you've handled everything. I think you both made a hard, but wise decision."

"We know that now, but it wasn't easy."

"I've known you since 1952. You have been through a lot. I hope that soon you will be healthy and happy again. You can't put much over on me, so you'd better take care of yourself, or I'll sick my nurse on you," he said, laughing.

"I'll be good. Mother will see to that," I responded.

"Thanks for everything," Mother told him.

The day finally came to register David and Neil in their new elementary school. I went in to wake the boys. "Come on you two. We have to get you registered in school today," I said, tugging at their feet. "Today you start a brand new school and will make lots of new friends."

"I don't want to get up, Mommy, it's too early," Neil said.

"Me either. Can we sleep a little while longer?" David chimed in with a pleading look on his face.

"Don't give me those puppy dog eyes. You have to go to school. Ammy is making breakfast so come on," I said, as they slowly got out of bed.

Once we were done, the four of us drove to school. Registration was straightforward and the boys seemed excited. It did not take long to fill out the paperwork. Then we accompanied them to their classrooms and met their teachers. Their teachers were very nice. I told each of them that I had attended this school when I was a little girl. I also told them that my husband and I had just divorced. I asked both teachers to let me know if they felt the boys needed special attention. They wrote down my information and said they would call me if necessary.

As we drove home, I said, "Mother, I have put those boys through so much. I feel so bad about what I've done to them."

"I figured this would be a rough day for you. You know everything happens for a reason. David and Neil are fine. They have not said anything about their old bedroom or playroom. I thought they would miss the pool, but they haven't. They seem quite content."

"Maybe things are too new right now," I replied.

"Please remember what the doctor said. He does not want you thinking negative thoughts. He wants you to concentrate on getting better. The healthier you are, the better it will be for you and the boys," Mother said.

"I really want to get a place of my own that is close to you. I don't want to have to change the boys' school again."

"See what I mean, Sharon? You are worrying about something that is not even happening yet. Currently the boys and you have a place to live, so quit worrying. Just concentrate on today!" Mother said.

When we got home, Mother and I went to see Nana and Granddad. Mother told Granddad what time school got out so that they could walk the boys home. Mother wanted me to rest. Between eating and sleeping, I was hoping to feel better soon.

Later that morning, I called Chuck to tell him about the boys. "After being on vacation for two weeks, they didn't really want to get up," I told him.

He laughed, but was pleased to hear that the boys did fine. He said he would be by to see us in the next couple of days.

When Chuck came over to visit the boys and me, we had a chance to talk when the boys left to play with their schoolmates. Chuck started by saying, "I told you God had a plan for our lives. Being married just wasn't in the cards."

"That was hard for me to admit! I did not want to fail again," I said.

"You did not fail. My cousin is able-bodied. She has her hands full taking care of me, and she doesn't have two boys to look after."

"You're just saying that to make me feel better," I said.

"No, I'm not," he said. "Please take care of yourself. Tell the boys I said good-bye."

"I'm sorry they didn't stick around."

"That's okay. They need to be with their friends. Once the weather gets warmer, you'll have to bring them to the house so they can go swimming."

"I will," I said. "Oh, by the way, I gained ten pounds."

"That's great news. Keep up the good work!" Chuck said. "I'll call you in a few days."

One evening Mother and Daddy decided to go visit their friends. After the boys went to sleep, instead of watching TV, I decided to read my Bible. I was finally reaching out to God again. Usually I go to the book of Psalms for comfort, but that night I turned to Philippians chapter 4, divided into four sections. The second section titled, "The secret of the peace of God," caught my eyes. How wonderful it was for me to see those words. With all the turmoil in my life, I did need peace. In Philippians 4:4, it states, "Rejoice in the Lord always; and again I say, Rejoice." "After all I have gone through, how could I rejoice?" I thought. As I looked further down the page, I read, "Be anxious for nothing, but in everything, by prayer and supplication with thanksgiving, for your requests be made known unto God. And the peace of God, which passeth all understanding, shall keep your hearts and minds through Christ Jesus." Philippians 4:6-7. After reading that I thought to myself, "You must be kidding, God. Be anxious for nothing? I am anxious all the time!"

After going through so much, I finally feel safe and secure. Even though I had shut God out temporarily, I realized now that through it all, He was there. Every time I went through the valley and back on the mountaintop, I would give myself a reason why a certain life experience happened. Right or wrong, I would satisfy myself with my own answers. Right now God had a reason for what was happening to me even though I did not know what it was. I had to trust God for the outcome. I realized that I had only wanted pat answers. I had not wanted to wait on God. What a lesson I learned! God had me in His hands and knew what was best for me. He was going to take care of me in this valley and in His perfect timing. I would be back on that mountaintop again. Maybe God was trying to teach me patience. I put my Bible down, prayed, and called it a night.

Chuck continued to call me every day to see how I was doing. Occasionally, he came over to see the boys and me. On one such occasion, he noticed a change in me. This time he remarked, "It looks like you have gained more weight."

"I have," I said. "Thanks for noticing. I'm feeling much better."

"That's great news!" He said, with enthusiasm. "You will never know how guilty I felt seeing you so sick."

"It was hard on both of us. I have to believe that God has a reason for why we had to go through all this," I said.

"Sounds like you are on the right track. Have I told you, Rick and I have been spending a lot of time together?"

"Yes. You already told me the two of you go out and play pool."

"We're both kind of lost. I think it does us good to be able to talk to one another. Have you talked to Char?" Chuck asked.

"No, I haven't talked to anybody."

"Rick asked me about taking us out to lunch. What do you think?"

"I am not ready to socialize. Above all, I do not want to go to a restaurant yet. Maybe we can go later. Right now, I am concentrating on getting better. I am glad you and Rick have each other to talk to."

"If you don't mind, I'd like to take the boys for an ice cream cone."

"They'll enjoy that," I replied.

When the boys came into the house, Chuck asked them if they wanted to go get an ice cream.

"Sure," they both said. "Is it okay, Mommy?" David asked.

"Yes, but only one scoop. It's almost dinner time," I said.

David and Neil jumped into the back seat of Chuck's car and off they went, waving at me.

As each day passed, I could see God working in my life. I was improving physically. I was not as weepy as I was before. I even laughed from time to time. Gaining weight renewed my confidence. After six weeks, I was eating three meals a day.

With the boys in school and my health improving, my mother's workload lightened. Mother and I now had more time to spend together doing fun things. After shopping one day, Mother and I stopped for lunch. This was the first time I had been in restaurant since I had moved home.

"We sure have been having a lot of fun. You are a very determined person. I am so proud of you," Mother said. "You will rise above this and be even stronger."

"Sure," I sneered. "I just have to accept the fact that I'll never be happily married like you and Daddy or Nana and Granddad."

"You will some day!"

"You always say that. It is hard to be positive after failing so much."

"Please do not label yourself a failure. Never forget what I told you years ago. God does not give us more than we can handle," she said.

"God must think I'm stronger than I think I am," I replied. "When I was younger, I married able-bodied men. Then I waited a long time and finally married a handicapped man. I thought we would be married forever, but that did not happen either."

"Listen, someday things will work out for you!" Mother said, with conviction.

"I'm not going to hold my breath. I cannot see myself getting married again. Marriage causes too much heartache."

"Time will tell. Always remember, you did your best. That is all you can do."

"I want to say thank you for everything you have done. You are the best mother and nursemaid in the world. Because of all your help, I think I'm finally on the road to recovery."

21

TAKING IT SLOW AND EASY

After pondering what I had read in my Bible awhile back, I decided to visit Nana and Granddad and share what I had learned. I started very cautiously saying, "In the Bible it says we can find peace in all things, learn to rejoice during troubled times, and be anxious for nothing. That meant I had to turn my life around. I was doing the opposite of what I read in the Bible."

"You sure have had your share of problems," Granddad said.

"It also says to be thankful for everything. It is easy to be thankful when things are going good, but it is very difficult when things are not. As I look back, I can now see how God worked out many of my problems. For that, I am grateful. Things are not perfect, but I am learning," I said.

"Family is everything," Nana said. "Don't ever forget that! We will always be there for you and your children, just like we have been for our daughter and her family."

"Believe me, I won't forget. I thank God everyday for all of you."

"Sharon, I'm still waiting for my mother's letter. I cannot help, but be cynical about what you are saying," Nana said.

"I understand Nana. Please try to keep an open mind. Look how God has worked things out in my life. Even when I contracted polio, Mother blamed God; but God healed her over time. At different times, when I went to church, the church let me down, but God never did."

"I read that small booklet you gave me at Easter. It's in my Bible," Granddad said.

"If you have any questions, please ask me," I said.

"I will, but it's pretty straightforward. If you believe and ask Jesus to come into your heart, then you will go to heaven. Right?"

"That is the first step. After you accept Christ as your personal Savior, God will mold you into what He wants you to be. The best promise that God gives Christians is when we die; we'll be with Him in heaven," I said, with conviction.

"That's amazing, Sharon," Granddad said. "I don't go to church, but I do read my Bible and pray."

"God promises that when I die I will be able to leave my wheelchair behind and walk with Him. There will be no more pain or suffering either. As far as I'm concerned that's amazing!"

"I'm glad you have a strong faith," Granddad said.

"Many times throughout the years my faith has faltered, but God has always brought me back to Him," I responded.

Before I left, Granddad said, "Gee, I almost forgot. The other day I saw an article in the newspaper about Social Security Disability. You might be able to receive financial help due to your disability. It's worth checking into."

"I'll call Social Security and find out. Thanks for the heads-up," I said.

It was great to be able to spend time with my grandparents. They were both in their late seventies. I did not know how much longer they would be around. Life without them seemed impossible to comprehend. I was so thankful we were close.

Chuck and I still kept in touch regularly. One day when I called him, he said, "Rick's here. He just reminded me about that lunch date. I know before you were not up to it. How do you feel about it now?"

"I guess we could," I responded. "I'm doing a lot better. Come up with a date, time, and place, and let me know. I will meet you there."

"Great! I have to go. Rick and I are going to go play pool. I'll call you later."

A few days later, I went into the Social Security office to file a claim for disability. The woman taking applications helped me fill out forms and gave me additional paper work for my doctor to complete.

Two days later, I saw my doctor. He was very pleased with my progress. He could tell I was getting stronger and gaining weight. He said, "As long as you stay calm, the colitis should subside. You still might have bouts from time to time, but I think you are winning this battle. We can go a month now before I see you again. Make sure you get out of your wheelchair during the day to take pressure off the back of your legs."

"I will. Speaking of that, I have some forms with me for you to fill out. I applied for Social Security Disability."

My doctor took the forms and said, "My nurse will call you when I am done filling them out."

"Thank you so much for everything!"

After I got home, I phoned Chuck to tell him what the doctor said and about applying for Social Security Disability. "After getting such a good report from the doctor, do you think we can get back together again?"

"No," Chuck said. "Nothing has changed. I still have accidents. I will not put you through that again. I will always love you, but you need to find somebody that can take care of you and the boys."

"I'm not holding my breath. It's like you think there is a knight in shining armor out there just waiting to sweep me off my feet," I said, laughing.

"Maybe there is," Chuck replied.

"I wish our marriage would have worked."

"We did our best. At least we still are friends," Chuck said. "How about meeting me and Rick at noon, on Friday, at Palermo's for lunch?"

"I'll be there."

When we arrived at Palermo's, we spent time reminiscing. I could hear sadness in Rick's voice because he did not get to see his girls as often as he wanted. Going through divorce was hard on each of us. We could relate to each other's feelings. Chuck lightened the mood by telling me about some of the shenanigans that he and Rick had pulled playing pool. By the end of lunch the three of us were actually laughing. This was definitely good therapy for all of us. We promised to get together again.

Later that evening, before I turned off the light, I prayed. "Sweet Jesus, You never cease to amaze me. You are always there. You have seen me through my darkest hours. Please be with Chuck. I pray his future is bright. I want to pray for Rick too. He really misses his girls. We are all hurting in our own way. Please continue to heal our hurts. I also come before You to find me a place to move to. Amen."

As each day went by, I felt better and was able to do more. This helped my self-esteem and kept me from getting bored. Staying busy also helped me not to think as much. Mother and I did housework together, shopped, and enjoyed an occasional lunch date while the boys were in school. When my doctor's nurse called, Mother went with me to pick up the forms and then take them to Social Security.

Chuck told me numerous times that friends had called the house. I decided enough time had passed, so I started calling people back. I talked to some of my friends in the Wheelacade. I also called Marjorie, my girlfriend that led me to the Lord; Char, Rick's ex-wife; and Karen, my best friend from high school. Everybody seemed happy to hear from me. They were pleased to hear I was doing better. It was nice to catch up on what everybody had been doing. After talking to Karen, we decided to meet for lunch. During lunch, I was able to share my innermost thoughts with her. It was like old times. We promised to stay in touch.

One day Chuck called me when the boys were in school. He wanted to talk when he knew the boys would not interrupt me. He started by saying, "Has Rick called you?"

"No. Why?" I asked.

"As you know, Rick and I spend a lot of time together. One night after we came back to my place after playing pool, we talked for quite awhile. I suggested that Rick call you and take you out to lunch."

"You did what?" I replied, astonished by his remark.

"You heard me! I am dating and you should too."

"I did not know you were dating, but I guess it is none of my business anyway. I really do not think of Rick as a date. He is a friend. You know, I always put up a protective wall around myself. I do not want to be hurt again."

"Rick is a great guy!" Chuck responded. "You and Rick should get together. Who knows, maybe you will wind up marrying each other."

"You are out of line, Chuck," I said. "Besides, Rick is able-bodied."

"I know that would scare the daylights out of you because of the way Tom and Jim hurt you, but Rick would never treat you like that," Chuck said.

"I'm not dating, let alone thinking about getting married again," I told him. "I have other things on my mind like getting a place of my own."

"Have you found anything yet?"

"I have not even started looking, but I will soon. The boys and I really need more room. Finding a place of my own could be a challenge because I don't want the boys to have to change schools again."

"That's a good idea. When you find a place, let me know. We can work out the details about your furniture then," he said.

"I really appreciate everything you have done for me."

"I'm still going to encourage Rick to call you."

"Are you drinking?" I said, laughing.

"No!" Chuck said. "Once you move into your own place, I might move too. This place is too big. I'm thinking of moving to Arizona to be closer to my family or getting a place in Utah," he said. "My cousin cannot stay living here forever. She will probably go back to school in the fall."

"Utah?" I asked. "What's there?"

"Hunting, fishing, and good clean air," he said, laughing.

"The boys would be upset if you moved," I told him.

"If I have to move, then that's what I'll have to do. Time will tell what the future holds."

Rick eventually called me. Our conversations were light. Then one day, he asked me out to lunch. It was good to see him again. We had a nice lunch while we talked about everything in the world. Rick and I were like two lost souls. It was easy for us to talk to each other because we had been friends for so long. We could talk about anything, especially our day-to-day frustrations. The only difference was that I had the support of my family, but Rick did not.

When Rick took me home, the boys came in from school, right behind us. They were glad to see him, and so was Mother. David and Neil asked Rick about the girls. Rick promised that soon he would get the girls and bring them over to Chuck's house so that they could all go swimming. They were pleased to hear that. Mother asked Rick to stay for her famous spaghetti dinner, and he accepted her invitation.

After a few hours of good food, conversation, and reminiscing, Rick thanked Mother for asking him to stay. Then he headed back to the base.

After Rick left, Mother said, "Rick seems so lost without his family."

"Yes," I said. "It is sad things did not work out for him and Char. She told me that even though they were married a long time, she blamed their marriage for failing because he was gone so much aboard ship. At times, he was gone six or nine months. I don't know how women can be separated from their husbands that long."

"Me either. When your daddy is gone on a business trip, I miss him something awful," Mother said.

"I had better check on the boys, and get them ready for bed," I said.

One weekend Mother and Daddy took David and Neil to Waddell's Trailer Park. It did the four of them good to have time alone without me there to discipline the boys. Mother reminded me many times that it was their duty as grandparents to spoil their grandkids. While they were gone, I went over to Chuck's house for the first time since I had left. Chuck wanted me to go through some household items so that we could decide what I would take with me when I moved into my own place. I also had the chance to meet Chuck's cousin. I did not stay long. Being there brought back memories that made me sad.

As I drove back home, my thoughts went wild. I could not understand why I felt so uncomfortable in what used to be my home. Nothing made sense to me. Having Chuck's cousin living there made me feel like an outsider. Knowing Chuck was dating made me feel weird. I should not even care what Chuck did anymore, but I did. I wanted him to find happiness, or did I?

After getting ready for bed that night, I went to God in prayer. "Sweet Jesus, what is wrong with me? Being with Chuck at what used to be our home was hard. I know our marriage is over, Lord. I also have noticed that Chuck is not coming over as much as he did when we first separated. Maybe enough time has gone by, and now You are making it easier for us to be apart. I do not know! I have been taking it slow and easy for quite awhile. Please give me the guidance that I need to face my future. I feel lost. Please help me find my way. Amen."

22

THINGS ARE COMING TOGETHER

What I had been waiting for so long finally happened when I went to see my doctor. At the end of my appointment he said, "I am pleased to tell you that you won't have to come in to see me anymore unless you have a problem. Continue to be very careful with what you eat!"

"I am. Already I know I cannot eat anything fried, spicy, or with onions."

"That is why I had you make that list. Your body will tell you what is okay and what is not."

"I am really proud of you. Other than those cysts, I think you are doing remarkably well. I hope that you will not have anymore. If you do, come in right away. Did you weigh yourself at home on your special scale?"

"Yes, I did. I have gained 40 pounds! I can't believe it. I am now up to 127 pounds!"

"You look healthier than I have seen you in a long time."

"I have God and my family to thank for my recovery."

"By the way, did I ever give you a copy of the letter I wrote to Social Security?" He asked.

"No. Mother ran in and picked it up. The envelope was sealed."

"On your way out get a copy of the letter from my nurse," he said.

"Thank you for everything," I said. "I hope I hear from Social Security soon that I am approved."

"I don't know why you wouldn't be. No way can you sit eight hours a day at work. You wouldn't be able to get out of your wheelchair in a work environment like you do at home," he said, sharing his thoughts.

After I thanked him for everything, I got a copy of the letter. When I got into my car, I was too curious about what the letter said. Before I drove home, I read it. It stated that I was a post polio victim, confined to a wheelchair, that I had bouts of colitis, and had many cysts surgically removed from the back of my left thigh. In his professional opinion, there was no way I could work. This decision was in God's hands.

As I drove up to the house, I could see Mother, Nana, and Granddad sitting on the patio. As I approached them I shouted, "Wait until I show you what the doctor gave me."

"What is it?" Mother asked.

"It's a copy of the letter he wrote to Social Security," I said.

"Let me see it," Mother said, reaching for the letter.

After she read it, she gave it to Nana and Granddad to read.

"This letter sounds wonderful. Everything he said is true."

"If this doesn't do it, nothing will," Nana said.

"We'll keep our fingers crossed," Granddad said.

"The best news is I do not have to go back to see the doctor unless I have a problem. This has truly been a remarkable day. I've got to call Chuck."

When I called Chuck, I gave him an update on my progress and read the letter to him. He was hopeful things would work out for me.

"How are the boys?" Chuck asked. "I haven't been over that much."

"Is something wrong?" I asked.

"No. I really do not want to discuss anything at this time."

"You have my curiosity peaked, but I will leave it alone for now. Neil is still having problems with reading and math, but other than that he is doing okay," I said. "I wish school came as easy for Neil as it does for David."

"Things might change for Neil in time. I hate to cut you off, but I have to go," he said.

As I hung up the phone, my emotions were running wild again. Chuck seemed to be pulling back. Maybe it was because I was happy, but I also felt guilty.

That evening Rick called. During our conversation, I mentioned that Chuck was not calling as much and not coming over as often.

"I think Chuck's life is going in a different direction," Rick said. "Chuck told me that you knew he was dating."

"He did, I know he is, but I have this sickening feeling that he has found another woman; and, she will probably move away with him after I find a place of my own."

"You'll have to discuss things with Chuck. I do not want to get in the middle of this one," Rick said.

"I understand. I know you and Chuck are close. I had better get to bed. Take care of yourself. We'll talk again soon."

As the weeks went by Rick continued to call, and we started seeing each other more often. We seemed to be getting closer.

One day Rick and I took a drive out to the beach while the boys were in school. He parked his car by the cliffs overlooking La Jolla Coves. The sun was shining. It was a gorgeous day. We sat there watching the waves crashing along the shoreline. I told him this was where my family and I used to go when I was a little girl.

"I do not want you to think I am crazy, but Chuck and I have been talking. He thinks you and I should get married after our divorces are final. He has talked to me about this numerous times. He wants you to be happy. Above all, he wants you to have somebody that will take care of you."

"Oh, he does, does he?" I responded.

"Chuck thinks it's a great idea and I do too. Would you even consider marrying me?"

"We care for each other, but is it love? We have been friends for so long," I responded.

"I know I am falling in love with my best friend," he said.

"Love scares me," I said. "To top that off, you are in the military. That is a deal breaker for me because you're gone overseas for months."

"We could wait until after I get out of the military," he suggested.

"I honestly cannot commit right now. I hope you understand."

"I do. I just thought I would ask. I might not be seeing you for a while."

"Why?" I asked.

"Yesterday, I went in for another check up. The doctor decided I needed surgery on my left knee. I can't do my job because I can't climb ladders anymore. When you're aboard ship that's all you do. I will be checking into Balboa Naval Hospital to have my surgery. As yet, I do not know when it will be or how long I will be there."

"Let me know as soon as you know. I will come and see you while the boys are in school," I said.

"I know you said you could not commit to marriage, but will you be my girlfriend?"

"That is all it can be for now. We had better leave. My boys will be home soon," I told him.

"Sounds good to me, girlfriend," he said, teasing me as we shared our first kiss.

Later that night my thoughts went wild. Even though Rick and I were close, marriage seemed out of the question. First, he was able-bodied. I had been married to able-bodied men before and it did not work out. I knew I should not judge Rick like that, but it was hard not to. Another concern was Rick's family. They were all strict Southern Baptists. How would they ever accept my past? How would they accept my being disabled? I wondered why Chuck was encouraging Rick to marrying me. I was, after all, a handicapped woman. As far as I was concerned, Rick could have any woman he wanted. He was good-looking, 6' 5" tall, 275 pounds, and built like a football player. What could this man, who has been my friend for so long, want with me? Thoughts regarding sex made the hairs on the back of my neck curl! I had not been sexually active in years. I needed time to think.

When I went to bed that night, I kept tossing and turning. My mind was on overdrive. Before I would allow the devil to get a hold of me and tear me down, I looked up in my Bible the word "troubled" to see if I could find a Scripture to help me. I finally found, where it states, "We are troubled on every side, yet not distressed; we are perplexed, but not in despair; Persecuted, but not forsaken; cast down, but not destroyed." II Corinthians 4:8-9. I read that passage repeatedly. Through all my thoughts of feeling troubled, perplexed, persecuted, or cast down, the Bible stated that everything would be okay. It also spoke of not being distressed, not being in despair, not being forsaken, nor destroyed. Oh, what a mighty God I have. I placed my thoughts and feelings gently in God's hands and had to trust that He would work everything out. I chuckled to myself, as I remembered those words "Be anxious for nothing." This was going to be a true test for me. I finally went to sleep knowing that God was in control. Maybe Rick's pending surgery was God's way of putting a halt to rushing into something that we both would regret later. Only God knew what my future held.

One day I waited out front of our house for Granddad and the boys to walk home from school. When the boys ran up to me, David handed me a flier. It stated that after Easter they would have crossing guards on the main boulevard.

After entering the house, I told the boys that they would be walking to school all by themselves after Easter break.

"That is pretty cool," David said, and Neil agreed.

"Ammy and I are planning some fun activities while you are on vacation. Even better, Daddy Chuck is going to have you guys and Rick's girls over for a pool party," I added. "How does that sound?"

"Oh boy!" they shouted joyfully, as they continued on their way outside to play.

When I went into my room, there was a letter on the bed. I could feel my heart skip a beat. I noticed it was from Social Security. I opened it, thinking it was my award letter. Instead, I found another form enclosed for my doctor to fill in the surgical dates for my cyst removals. I had to have the form back to them within ten days.

Immediately I went out back and asked Mother, "Can you watch the boys for me for a little while?"

"Sure," she said. "What's up?"

"I just got a letter from Social Security. I have to take another form to my doctor. I will be back soon," I said, as I gave David and Neil a kiss good-bye.

About an hour later, I returned home and noticed that everyone was still sitting in the back yard. As I wheeled over to them, I announced, "I have some news! My doctor's nurse filled in the dates of my cyst removals and I took the completed form to the Social Security office. Everything is in order now. If all goes well, I will receive my first check in two months, maybe three."

"That's great news! Does this mean you'll start looking for your own place now?" Mother asked.

"Yes, I think I am ready. I really need a place of my own," I said. "With the money that I have in the bank, along with child support, I feel I can make it. Getting a disability check every month will be like icing on the cake."

Later that evening, Rick called to tell me that his surgery would be in about two weeks at five o'clock in the morning!"

"Boy, that's early! I don't think I'll be able to get down there that early, but I'll come as soon as I can," I said.

"Don't worry about coming that day. I will be out of it anyway. At least my surgery won't happen until after your boys and my girls go back to school," he said. "I was hoping I wouldn't have surgery until after the pool party at Chuck's house so that worked out great."

"We should all have a great time. I better get going. It's been a busy day. I love you. Take good care," I said.

"I love you too. Sweet dreams," he said, hanging up the phone.

God was working out all the details of my life. I was putting my faith and trust in God more everyday. As I continued to search God's word, I found a passage that states, "Brethren, I count not myself to have apprehended; but this one thing I do, forgetting those things which are behind, and reaching forth unto those things which are before, I press toward the mark for the prize of the high calling of God in Christ Jesus." Philippians 3:13-14. I felt God was telling me to press forward and that I would get the ultimate prize in the end.

Rick and I continued to see each other as time permitted and talked on the phone non-stop. When the boys got out for Easter break, we all met at Chuck's house the following day to have the pool party for the children. What a wonderful day we shared. It was so much fun for all of us to watch the children play. Chuck's cousin took off for the day, so it was just the seven of us. We also discussed Rick's upcoming surgery. Rick was nervous, so we tried to set his mind at ease. Chuck was still teasing Rick and me about getting married.

"Quit doing that!" I told Chuck. "I don't meddle in your love life, so stay out of mine."

"Okay, I will shut up. Let's send out for pizza," Chuck said.

"Sounds like a plan," I replied. "We all love pizza."

"How about it, Rick, can you and the girls stay?" Chuck asked.

"Yes, I told Char we would be making a day of it because I will not be able to see the girls for a while because of my surgery," he said.

"I'll call for pizza while you get the kids dried off," Chuck replied.

It was great having this time to visit and have the children together.

Starting on Monday, Mother and I took the boys to some fun places around town. Close by they had pony rides, carousel rides, and an amusement park. The area was great for my wheelchair because it was on asphalt. We also took the boys to the community swimming pool. Nana and Granddad came too because there were benches for them to sit on. I felt bad that Daddy had to work, but he assured me when the weekend came, everybody was going to the bay for the day.

On Sunday, as Daddy planned, we all went to Mission Bay. There was a grassy area, with a sidewalk and a three-foot block wall separating the grass from the beach. I could not swim, but I was close enough to watch the boys. Nana and Granddad always took their car just in case Nana got tired and needed to go home earlier than we did. After we set up our lawn chairs, blankets, and coolers, Mother, Daddy, Granddad, and the boys headed for the water. I longed to go swimming with them, but at my age, I would not let Daddy carry me any more. Nana and I would keep each other company.

After being at Mission Bay for quite a few hours, Daddy suggested, "Why don't we all go to the amusement park and let the boys ride on some rides."

In unison, David and Neil started yelling, "Yeah! Yeah!"

"I guess we could go for a little while," I replied.

"Count us out," Nana said. "Granddad and I are going home."

At the amusement park, it was fun watching David and Neil interact with my parents on the various rides. Their screaming and laughing brought joy to my heart.

Later that evening, I sat the boys down and told them how lucky they were to have two sets of grandparents that did such wonderful things with them and for them. Before they bathed and got ready for bed, I said, "I want the two of you to go into the living room and thank Ammy and Pappy for a wonderful day."

"Okay," they both said, running into the living room. They thanked Ammy and Pappy and gave each of them a hug and a kiss.

While I was getting ready for bed, Rick called. I told him everything we did. He was sorry he could not be with us, but he pulled weekend duty. He was glad I was able to have this day with everybody before the boys went back to school.

After I hopped in bed, the house was so quiet. Everybody was sound asleep, but I was wide-awake. I needed time with my God, so I prayed, "Sweet Jesus, thank you for the wonderful family I have. To be able to go to all these places this week has allowed me the joy of doing special things with my boys. Lord, are You opening up more doors for both my boys and me by placing Rick in my life? I know Rick loves me and I think I am falling in love with him too. Does my future include Rick? Please help me make the right decision. Be with Rick when he has surgery. Please be with David and Neil when they walk to school for the first time by themselves. Amen." After praying, I felt at peace. I knew, without a doubt, that God was in control and everything would work out. Finally, things were coming together for my boys and me. I lay my head on my pillow and fell sound asleep.

23

SOME NEW CHALLENGES TO FACE

The following morning I could see the sun poking through the slightly opened drapes. I figured I would get up early. I was both excited and skeptical about the boys walking to school for the first time using the crossing guards. As I rolled over in bed, I took my Bible from the nightstand and opened to a passage that God directed me to. I turned to the book of Thessalonians. There I read, "Rejoice evermore. Pray without ceasing. In everything give thanks; for this is the will of God in Christ Jesus concerning you." I Thessalonians 5:16-18. I noticed I was rejoicing more. I prayed every night and sometimes on and off during the day. Jesus was like an invisible friend, standing right beside me every minute of every day.

After I reflected some more, I went to wake up the boys. They looked so peaceful. I nudged each of them and said, "Good morning, David and Neil. It is time to get up on this glorious day. The sun is shining and you can walk to school with your friends."

"Mommy, I don't want to get up," Neil said. "It's too early."

"Ah, come on," David said, "It will be fun."

"Come on, let's go eat breakfast. Ammy is in the kitchen making pancakes," I said, motioning them to get out of bed.

After our normal morning routine, David and Neil were ready to leave. As I opened the front door, I could see children walking with no adults. Mother, the boys, and I walked out to the sidewalk and looked down the street. Sure enough, the crossing guards were there with their bright orange signs.

"Okay, you two," I said, giving each of them a hug. "This is your day to shine. You can finally walk to school with your friends. Ammy and I will stay right here and watch you walk all the way to school. Make sure to listen to the crossing guards. They will tell you when to cross the street. I love you."

"Okay," they both said, in unison.

Watching the boys walk those two blocks to school was bittersweet. They were getting older and gaining more independence. "Time goes by too quickly," I told Mother.

"It sure does," Mother replied. "It wasn't long ago when we were changing their diapers and now look at them."

Later that day, I took out my Bible again. As I flipped through some pages, I saw a notation that I had made in the margin: "Positive Thinking!" Those words caught my eye. In Philippians 4:8, it states, "Finally, brethren, whatever things are true, whatever things are honest, whatever things are just, whatever things are pure, whatever things are lovely, whatever things are of good report; if there be any virtue, and if there be any praise, think on these things." Once again, God was directing me to stay positive. After I read verse 8 in Philippians, I looked down to verse 13 where it states, "I can do all things through Christ, who strenghtheneth me." Philippians 4:13. I knew I had to claim this verse as a way to live for the rest of my life, but that was hard for me to do. I had to realize there would always be things that I will never be able to do because of my disability. I will never walk. I will never be able to do things as able-bodied people do. I could only do the best I could on any given day. As long as I did, God would be pleased with me. That was all that mattered.

My thoughts were interrupted when I heard the back door open and Mother hollered, "Sharon where are you?"

"I'm in the bedroom," I yelled back.

Mother responded, "I went for a walk and saw a 'For Rent' sign out in front of a house right up the street. I took down the phone number so you could call."

"I'll call right away and see when we can take a look at it."

After talking to the property owner, I went back into the living room and told Mother that I had made an appointment to see the rental house in one hour. We would meet the owner in back because there were no steps there. "Do you want to come with me?" I asked.

"Sure, I do! I would not miss this for the world. You have wanted a place of your own for a long time. This just might be it. Think positive," she said.

"I sure hope the rent isn't too high," I said. "I didn't think to ask."

Finally, the time came for us to leave and see the house. We met the property owner and went inside. As we entered, I could feel my heart starting to pound. The place was cute and big enough for the boys and me. Down one side of the house was a living room, dining room, kitchen, and laundry room. Down the other side were two huge bedrooms and one bathroom. The rent was inexpensive too. With a little bit of paint and some cleaning it would work perfectly for the three of us. I asked the property owner if she could hold the house for a few hours. I wanted my boys to see it before I signed anything. The owner agreed to meet us after dinner.

After we ate, we all went to the rental. While Daddy and Granddad checked out various things, Mother and I took Nana and the boys throughout the house. The boys' eyes got huge when I showed them what would be their bedroom. The room was so big that it not only would accommodate their twin beds and each of their dressers, but also left remaining space to make one end of the room into a play area. The longer I was there, the more I knew this was going to be our new home. Knowing the boys were excited warmed my heart.

The property owner said I could take occupancy right away. Since we were willing to do some painting and cleaning, she said that she would give me the keys now, and I would not have to pay rent until the first of the month. At that moment, I knew God found this place for the three of us.

After I signed the necessary papers, we said our good-byes and went back to my parents' house. There we gathered on the patio to share our thoughts on how perfect this rental place was going to be for the boys and me. We would only be four houses away!

"Do you think all the painting will be done by the first of next month?" I asked Daddy.

"I see no reason why not."

"I'm going to go in and call Chuck," I said.

I told Chuck the good news, and he was willing to do whatever I needed to make this move go smoothly.

Later, when Rick called, I told him the news. He was happy for us too. "I'm bummed that I won't be able to help because of my surgery," Rick said to me, apologetically.

"Don't worry, I have plenty of help. I want you to take care of yourself and get this surgery behind you, so you can get on with your life," I said.

"Do you think we can get together for dinner tomorrow night?" He asked. "That will probably be the last time we can go out for a while."

"I'll let you know if Mother can watch the boys. If she can, I'll take you up to see my new place," I said, before saying goodnight.

After a long day, my heart was so full that I could hardly stand it. To try to calm down I prayed, "Sweet Jesus, my prayers have been answered. I am so thankful. Please relax my body and mind. This new house is perfect and the boys will not have to change schools. You are such a mighty God. Thank you for Chuck and his willingness to help me. Thank you for Rick's compassion for me and my boys. Please be with Rick as he faces surgery on his knee. You are in control of everything. I have to believe that everything will work out for all of us. Amen."

The following evening Rick and I did go to dinner and went to see my new place. Later, we discussed his knee surgery. Rick made me promise not to run back and forth to the hospital everyday. He wanted me to concentrate on moving and taking care of the boys and me. He reassured me that everything would be fine.

As promised, Chuck went up to the hospital the morning of Rick's surgery. He called me later to tell me everything went fine. He told me Rick would not be able to call because there are no phones by the patients' beds.

"Thank you for calling. I am glad everything went well. Next time you go, please tell Rick I'll come to see him in a couple of days."

"I will give Rick your message. Take care of yourself and do not overdo. I know you are anxious to get into your new place. When you're ready, I'll call my friends to help get your furniture moved," Chuck said.

"I better get going. I have a date."

"Another date," I said, laughing. "I hope these gals are treating you okay."

On that note, I said, "good-bye."

While the boys were in school, I had a chance to go see Rick. He was running a temperature and did not look good. I asked him about his knee and he said he thought it was fine. He was waiting for the doctor to check it in the next few days when they removed the wire stitches. I was concerned about Rick's temperature. I prayed that everything would be okay.

I waited a few days and went back to the hospital only to find Rick in severe emotional distress.

"What in the world is going on?" I asked him. "You look awful."

"As you know I had a fever and then it went even higher," he said. "My knee was also swelling. When the doctor came in to remove the ace wrap, the stitches fell out onto the bed along with all this goop that was oozing from my knee. It made me sick to my stomach. The doctor told me gangrene had set in."

"Gangrene!" I said, astonished. "You should have had Chuck call me."

"I didn't want you to worry. That's not the worst of it," he said, starting to choke up. "They might have to amputate my leg. The doctor is hoping that they can get rid of all the infection with surgery, but there is no guarantee. I just signed the papers. Surgery is tonight."

"Oh, my God, Rick." I said, starting to choke up.

Just then, Rick's doctor came over to the two of us, introduced himself to me, and discussed everything about the surgery. I sat there watching as the doctor literally drew a line across Rick's leg where they might have to amputate. I thought I would die inside. No wonder Rick was a wreck. Now I was too.

"Why did this happen?" I asked the doctor angrily. "How could you let this happen? Rick said that he had a fever for days, but nobody checked his incision."

"Sometimes infections just happen when you are in a hospital," the doctor replied. "We have some 50 patients on this ward and we do not have the staff to attend to each and every patient 24/7."

"That is no excuse!" I yelled at him.

"I know you're upset, but this isn't helping Rick. You have got to calm down!" He said, putting his hand on my shoulder. "Rick's surgery is at 8 o'clock this evening. You are more than welcome to wait and see how he does."

Just the thought of Rick having to have his leg amputated made me tremble. Instantly, my body tightened up. The fear of my colitis resurfacing scared me to death. I felt helpless. I did not know how my body would react. I tried hard to force myself to relax. I started taking slow deep breaths and took some medication from my purse.

"Honey," Rick said. "Everything is going to be okay. Just say an extra prayer for me. I am in God's hands."

"I've got to call Mother and see if she can watch the boys, so I can stay here," I told him, before I wheeled to the nearest phone.

When I returned to Rick's room, I told Rick that Mother had agreed to take care of David and Neil.

"That's great. I would tell you to go home, but I really need you here with me right now."

A few hours later, the nurse came for Rick and said, "Sharon, follow us and I will show you where you can wait. The doctor will talk to you after he is done."

"Thank you. I beg you, please take good care of Rick and make sure they do everything they can to save his leg," I pleaded with her.

"The doctor will do his best. You can go in that room over there," she said, motioning me to the surgical waiting room.

As I sat there in that room, I could not stop crying. I realized just how much I loved this man. He meant the world to me.

A little before midnight, the doctor came to talk to me. "I'm pleased to tell you that we were able to save Rick's leg."

"Thank God!" I said.

"Rick will have to go through another surgery in a week or so to remove the drainage tubes that we put in. After that, he will undergo lengthy physical therapy. He will have to stay in the hospital for six to eight weeks," the doctor said. "We left the knee open so it will heal from the inside out. It will take time for the knee to close."

"Thank you, for everything," I said, as he left to go be with Rick.

After what seemed like an eternity, the doctor came back and told me I could see Rick in recovery. He warned me that Rick was still groggy.

As I went into his cubicle, Rick exclaimed, "Sharon, they did not take my leg!"

"I am so relieved. If I could dance, I would!" I replied.

"I knew God wouldn't let that happen," Rick said.

"I prayed for hours while the doctor was operating on you. God answered our prayers. You will be just fine!"

"Thank you so much for being here," he said. "I love you."

"I love you too," I said, hiking up on the arm of my wheelchair so that I could reach Rick to give him a kiss good-bye.

It was in the wee hours of the morning before I got home. Mother was sitting in the dining room waiting for me. As I came in, she reached out to me with her arms opened wide. I went directly to her and started crying. "This has been such an awful day. The surgery seemed to take forever. Praise God, the doctor was able to save Rick's leg."

"I'm so glad everything worked out. I think you have deep feelings for this man. Maybe more than you're willing to admit," she said.

"I realized today, just how much I do love Rick, but I do not know what to do. Rick's being in the military really bothers me. To be apart for months on end will cause me too much stress. I am so afraid of my colitis returning."

"Don't start worrying about that. Moving is going to take enough of your energy. Remember, Sharon, Rick is an able-bodied man. You have to think long and hard about that," she said. "Get to bed. I'll take care of the boys and get them off to school in the morning."

"Thank you, I don't know what I'd do without you," I said, as I finally headed to bed.

When I got up, I was still tired. I decided to stay home. I called Chuck and some of my friends that knew Rick to tell them about the infection. Chuck said he would go to the hospital later that day. I asked him to tell Rick that I would come the following day. I needed today to regroup and make some phone calls regarding my move.

The following day, I returned to the hospital. I thought Rick would be doing better. Instead, he was in a terrible frame of mind. He could not move his leg. He was scared to death. His doctor was with him when I arrived and said, "There is nothing wrong with Rick's leg, Sharon. He just will not move it! You've got to find a way to get through to him."

I stayed with Rick for a few hours. He tried to move his leg numerous times, but nothing happened. It had been a long day, so I decided the best thing was for me to leave, go home, and relax. As I drove home, I wondered why Rick could not move his leg. If he does not improve, he could have a permanent disability. Could he handle that? Could I? I did not know what to think.

Two days later, I returned to the hospital. Rick was no better.

"What in the world is wrong with you?" I asked him. "I thought you would be moving your leg by now!"

"I've been trying, but nothing is happening," Rick said.

"That's just an excuse. I have known you for years and I have never seen you like this before."

"You act like I'm not trying, but I am," he responded.

"Well, you must not be trying hard enough," I said, angrily. "Awhile back you talked to me about getting married, and I told you I needed time to think. Do you remember?"

"Yes. Why?" Rick asked.

Not answering him, I wheeled to the end of his hospital bed, picked up his left foot, and held it up.

"What are you doing?" Rick asked, raising himself up on his elbows.

"I will marry you if you start moving your leg up and down. If you don't, I'm leaving and you won't see me until you do," I told him.

"You don't mean that," he said, rather startled by my comment.

"Oh, yes, I do," I said. "I'm sick of coming here and seeing you this way."

I saw his face wrench with pain as he tried to hold that leg up. My arm was getting tired. When I quit holding his leg, it fell back down on the bed.

"Let me try again," he said. "I think I can do it."

Again, I held his leg up and it fell. At that point, I was getting scared. "Come on, Rick, you can do it," I said, encouraging him.

Then, all of a sudden, Rick lifted his leg! Then he started moving it up and down! With tears in my eyes, I hollered, "I knew you could do it!"

I noticed Rick was getting weepy too. I did not know who was more excited, him or me. I went to the side of his bed. We held hands knowing that everything would be okay.

"I'm going to hold you to your promise that you'll marry me," he told me. "Don't tell your folks though until I have a chance to talk to them first."

"Okay," I responded.

When the nurse came over to change Rick's bandage, I told her to tell the doctor that Rick started moving his leg. She was pleased. Then Rick said, "Sharon said she would marry me if I moved my leg and I did."

"Congratulations! I'll ask the doctor to come to the ward as soon as he can," she said, leaving us alone after she changed Rick's bandage.

"This is a big load off my mind," I told him.

"Yours and mine too," he said. "Are you sure you want to marry me?"

"Yes, I am sure. I have always cared about you. When I was sitting in that waiting room during your second surgery, I realized just how much I really do love you," I told him.

"If this surgery brought us together, then I'm glad I had it done."

"Your doctor said you're going to be here for quite awhile. I hope you will understand that I cannot come every day. I have a lot to do so that I can move. The house is almost ready," I said.

"I told you to come only a couple times a week. Now that I am doing better, you should take a few days off and not come at all."

"I'd better get home. I can't wait to tell Mother, Daddy, Nana, and Granddad the good news. I'll call Chuck and Karen too," I told him. "Take care of yourself."

"Give me a kiss," Rick said, as he reached for me to come closer.

I kissed Rick and said, "I'll see you in a few days."

As I was wheeling through the ward, Rick's doctor came towards me and gave me a big thumbs up. "The nurse just told me that Rick is moving his leg," he said. "Now we can remove the drainage tubes and physical therapy can begin."

Driving home, I felt overwhelmed with joy. I gave God all the credit for what transpired today. I felt that my future with Rick looked promising. I felt very proud of myself. I had gone through many emotions lately and faced some new challenges as well. Not getting sick during this stressful time gave me great hope.

24

MANY CHANGES ON THE HORIZON

Over the next few weeks, there was so much to do. Between taking care of my boys and working on my new place, I had my hands full. Added to that, I had to get my phone installed and purchase some appliances. Mother and I also made trips over to Chuck's house to pick up small items. In my spare time, I also visited Rick; he was progressing nicely. He was continuing to move his leg, and he was back to his jovial self again. He knew I was busy and encouraged me not to worry about him. He always said, "When I really needed you, you were there. Now you should concentrate on yourself."

The night before my move, I could hardly sleep. I was so excited. I finally felt I could handle having my own place, even though I was a handicapped, single mother. The more things I could do for myself, the better I felt. I knew my own limitations. Living on a schedule helped me.

Moving day finally arrived. First, I drove over to Chuck's house. Once his friends loaded up the U-Haul, we were off to my new place. David, Neil, and the rest of my family were anxiously waiting for us. After the truck was unloaded and my furniture set in place, we ordered pizza. I wanted everything to be perfect, but realized that would take time. "So what if there are boxes everywhere," I thought to myself, "As long as the boys and I have a place to sleep and eat that was all that matters."

After everybody left, the boys took their showers and got ready for bed. They were getting older and wanted to do more for themselves. That was a big help to me. I sat between their twin beds that first night and told them what a powerful God we have and how God provided so much for us as a family.

"I know you guys have had to deal with a lot because I have been sick. You are both very special. God really answered our prayers with this house. Now let's say our prayers and thank God for His blessings."

With that said, we bowed our heads and the three of us prayed in our own special way. When I listened to David and Neil pray, I could hear their innermost thoughts and feelings. First, they thanked God that they lived in a larger house, and that their bedroom was big enough to play in. Next, they were glad that they did not have to change schools. Finally, they were relieved that they still lived close to their grandparents. They asked God to watch over their mommy and their grandparents. This gave me tremendous comfort. Their contentment was an answer to my prayers. I always marveled at how well David and Neil adjusted to change in their young lives.

As soon as the boys were sound asleep, I went through my entire home. I looked in every closet and cubbyhole. Being alone, I needed to put everything within my reach. I did not have Mother or Daddy here to reach things up high. I wanted to pinch myself. I could not believe I actually had a place to call my own to raise my boys. I felt that I had accomplished something great. Even if it killed me, I would do whatever it took to prove to everybody that I could take care of my boys and myself. There was that perfectionism coming back, but I did not care. I was going to strive to have the best-kept house on the block and the best-behaved children in the neighborhood. With God's help, I could do whatever I set my mind to.

Before turning off the lights, I opened my Bible. I read, "Peace I leave with you, my peace I give unto you; not as the world giveth, give I unto you. Let not your heart be troubled neither let it be afraid." John 14:27. Oh, what a promise that was. I was going to place myself, Rick, my boys, and my new home in God's hands to claim the peace that God promised me through His word.

The next couple of days I felt like I was playing house. I would get myself ready, get the boys up and off to school, and mess around the house. One morning I heard a knock on my front door. As I opened it, Mother handed me an envelope and said, "I guess you forgot to change your address at the post office."

"I never even gave it a thought. What do you have?"

"It's a letter from Social Security. I thought you'd want it as soon as possible," she said, as she came into the house.

When I opened the letter, I started yelling, "Yes! This is my award letter and retroactive check!"

"I'm so happy for you," Mother said.

"The letter states that I will receive a check on the third of each month. Now I can get rid of my gas-guzzling car and get an economical one. With this check and trading in my car I should be able to pay cash."

"I'll tell Daddy about your disability check. Maybe this weekend he can go with you and see if you can find a car."

"That would be great," I told her. "Right now I have to go see Rick."

"Say hello to him," Mother said, as she kissed me good-bye.

When I arrived at the hospital, I told Rick all my good news. After I was done, Rick said, "I have some really good news too. I'm getting out of the military."

"You're what? When did that happen?" I asked, with enthusiasm.

"The military is discharging me on a medical discharge due to the severe damage done to my knee. They feel I will not be able to perform my duties anymore because I have a disease that eats cartilage from the knees, and it will continue to get worse."

"You mentioned knees, but you only had surgery on one knee. Does the doctor think your other knee will have problems too?"

"Yes. The doctor told me this disease progresses slowly. Right now, the right knee isn't that bad, but the doctor said I will definitely need surgery on my right knee in the future."

"I cannot believe this prognosis, Rick, but I am so glad you are getting out of the military," I said.

"I knew you would be thrilled about that news," Rick said. "Just remember, I won't be getting out for a while."

"Is a medical discharge going to hurt you finding a job?" I asked, concerned.

"I hope not, but it doesn't matter. I will have to cross that bridge when I come to it," he responded. "Not to change the subject, but how is Chuck doing? He hasn't been around for a while."

"The last time I saw him was on the day I moved into my new place. I guess he has been busy with his new girlfriend," I said.

"As soon as I can, I'm going to call my folks and tell them about the medical discharge. I will also tell them we are dating and what a support you have been to me during my surgeries," Rick said.

"Do you think telling them about us is wise? Your folks might not like to hear you are dating a handicapped woman," I said.

"I know you worry how people feel, but if they do not like it, tough," Rick said.

"You know I love you deeply. Honey, I'd better get home before the boys get out of school. I'll come back in a few days," I said, as we kissed each other good-bye.

A few days later Rick surprised me by calling the house right after the boys left for school. He was finally able to use a wheelchair because the doctor removed the drainage tubes. That meant he could get out of bed, use the phone, and start additional physical therapy. He also told me he called his parents and told them about the boys and me. They were not happy that he was dating a divorced woman who was confined to a wheelchair and who had two children. Rick hoped that in time they would change their minds and accept me.

Over the next month or so, things kept falling into place. I was able to purchase another used car and have hand controls installed. David and Neil loved our home and spent a lot of time in their bedroom/playroom. I had the house so well organized that I had more time to visit Rick and spend with my family and friends. Life was good. I was anxious for Rick to get out of the hospital and see my new home now that it was all finished. We were hoping he would improve enough to get a pass to spend some time away from the hospital. The doctor told Rick that his knee would never be the same, but that he should be able to function all right.

Chuck and I stayed in touch, but our lives were definitely going in different directions. He continued to call me to see how the boys and I were doing, but he was not coming over as much. He told me that his girlfriend moved in and his cousin moved back to Arizona. Then he told me that he put the house on the market and planned to move. He wanted out of California, and said that he and his girlfriend were getting married. I was concerned about how the boys would take the news.

Rick spent hours in physical therapy and was doing remarkably well. He was out of the wheelchair and using crutches now. Weeks later, all his hard work paid off because he was able to get a pass and leave the hospital for four hours. He told me he wanted to see my new home, the boys, and my parents to talk to them about our getting married. With that in mind, one evening he came over to my house for dinner. After dinner, while the boys were playing in their bedroom, Rick asked my parents if we could go talk in the living room away from the boys' listening ears.

"We sure have had a lovely evening. I have to admit I had an ulterior motive asking Sharon to invite you to join us," he said. "I would like to ask for your daughter's hand in marriage," Rick said, smiling as he reached for my hand.

"You must have a hole in your head," Daddy said, to Rick, "but if you want to marry her, then who am I to say no. I just hope you know what her track record is with able-bodied men."

"Daddy, what a mean thing to say," I told him, as tears filled my eyes.

"Well that's how I feel. I'm sorry, Sharon, but I can't see any reason why Rick would want to marry you," he said. "You're a fantastic woman, but you're handicapped. You need to be with somebody of your own kind."

"I was married to a man in a wheelchair. Look what that got me!" I reminded him.

"Bill and Helene," Rick said, "Sharon and I have talked, for many hours about marriage and all the pros and cons. Sharon is a very strong woman and she is the type of woman I want to marry. However, she will not consent to being my wife without your blessing."

I just glowed when Rick said those words to my parents.

"What do you think, Helene?" Daddy asked Mother.

"I figured this was coming. It is obvious that Sharon has deep feelings for Rick, and they have been friends for years," she said. "Rick seems genuinely to love our daughter, or else he wouldn't be asking us for her hand in marriage."

"Rick," Daddy said, "I respect you for asking us, but as one man to another I would think long and hard before you jump into something that you might not be able to handle years down the road."

"I know exactly what I'm getting into, Bill. Above all, I love your daughter. I will treat her with nothing but dignity and respect. I will take care of her in every way possible," Rick said. "You and Helene can count on that."

"I guess that's all any parent can ask," Mother responded.

"I guess you're right, Helene," Daddy said.

"Do whatever makes you happy," Mother said, and Daddy agreed.

With much relief, I said, "Rick's got to get back to the hospital and I've got to get the boys ready for bed. Let's call it a day."

"Fine with me," Daddy said, getting off the couch.

"Let's say goodnight to the boys before we leave," Mother said, motioning to Daddy to go into the boys' bedroom with her.

After my parents left the room, Rick and I talked briefly. We were both shocked at what Daddy said, and Rick knew I was hurt. They did give us their blessing in a roundabout way, so we had to be thankful for that.

"I had better get back to the hospital. The more I improve, the longer I can stay out. I'm going to go say good-bye to the boys."

Just then, Mother and Daddy came out of the boys' bedroom.

"We're going to head home," Mother said, as she and Daddy gave me a kiss goodnight and said good-bye to Rick.

When Rick came out of the boys' bedroom, he came over to me, put his arms around me, and kissed me.

"Please take it easy driving back to the hospital," I said. "Call me when you get there if you can."

"I will. Please do not dwell on what your dad said. God will work everything out. Our parents will eventually accept the fact that we love each other."

"Okay. Now get out of here, so I can tend to the boys," I said, smiling.

Once Rick left and the boys were asleep, I had time to think about what had transpired earlier. I was still in shock. I felt so confused. Doubts filled my mind as I thought to myself, "Could Daddy be right? Was Rick blind to my being handicapped? That could not be true! Rick has known me for years and has always accepted my being in a wheelchair. I knew that friendship or dating was different from marriage. Could I make this marriage work? My relationship with Rick seemed right. Was I just kidding myself?"

After getting ready for bed, I grabbed my Bible to find some answers. I knew that was the only way I would find peace. I opened my Bible and read, "Be, therefore, not anxious about tomorrow; for tomorrow will be anxious for the things of itself. Sufficient unto the day is its own evil." Matthew 6:34. I took this verse to mean that I should not worry. As I continued reading, I came across another verse that stated, "Come unto me, all ye that labor and are heavy laden, and I will give you rest." Matthew 11:28. There it was! God was telling me that He would give me rest. I closed my Bible, said a prayer, and went to sleep.

Finally, Rick was able to leave the hospital and move into the barracks. Rick was anxious to get out of the military, but the doctor said that would not happen until his physical therapy was over and that could take months.

For years, Rick knew all there was to know about me. Then one evening, he filled me in on some more details about his past. According to Rick, his family was not as close as mine was. His family owned a chicken ranch. Even though they had four generations living in one house, the main objective of his family was working the ranch and going to church. Rick felt he had a strong, Christian upbringing, but left home at an early age to attend the New Mexico Military Academy in Roswell, New Mexico and later joined the service.

Rick's parents were still upset that Rick got a divorce. I did not totally understand everything that the Bible said about divorce, but I hoped that Rick's parents could still love him. As far as I was concerned, being a Christian meant loving somebody through his or her hardships and forgiving them their transgressions. I prayed that Rick's parents would eventually come around. My parents raised me to treat people the way I would like to be treated. In the Scripture it states, "Therefore, all things whatever ye would that men should do to you, do ye even so to them; for this is the law and the prophets." Matthew 7:12. Reading this verse really touched me. I prayed that I would never judge anybody the way people had judged Rick and me. Forgiveness is very powerful because it sets you free. I know first hand because of my previous marriages. That is not saying it is easy. It is not! Rick, like I, had times when he enjoyed going to church and times he did not. We loved God, read our Bibles, and prayed. God's closeness never left our hearts. I tried to keep my eyes on God and forget what people said or did to us. That was all I could do for now. We knew our parents felt our marriage would never last. It was up to us to prove them wrong.

When David and Neil got out of school for the summer, we planned many activities to do together. As Rick improved, he was able to spend more time with us and his girls. We enjoyed watching TV, playing table games, and taking day trips. We also took the four children to the community swimming pool. Rick and I made an effort to spend as much time with my parents and grandparents as well. We invited them to dinner at least once a week. I felt the more time my family spent with Rick, the more they would see what a genuinely kind and caring man, he was. They would also be able to witness, first hand, how attentive he was towards the boys and me. Rick's knee was continuing to improve. The more he could do, the more he enjoyed helping everyone.

One day, Mother came over to my house to visit, and we started talking.

"Rick has such a giving heart," Mother said. "You are truly blessed."

"You are so right, Mother," I said. "God has given me a gift, bringing Rick into my life."

"I'm starting to agree with you, Sharon," Mother said. "He treats you like a queen, but there are times I am jealous of him."

"Why?" I asked her, astonished by her admission.

"All your life you have needed me, and now you don't need me as much. Rick helps you and the boys in areas where I used to help you," she said.

"I would think that that would make you happy," I responded.

"It does. I just do not feel needed as much anymore. That's not your problem; it's mine," Mother said.

"Mother, you are needed. I just do not have to come to you for everything like I used to. That does not mean that I don't need you because I do," I said, giving her a hug.

"You are the sweetest daughter. I am so lucky we are close."

One night, Daddy, Nana, Granddad, and I were all on the patio and we started talking about Rick. Mother said, "We wanted you to know that all of us can see that Rick is such a caring man."

"I'm glad you all noticed that. Rick and I have tried very hard to include all of you in our activities just for that reason," I said. "If we had stayed to ourselves, then all of you would never have known how wonderful he is."

"Do you think you'll be getting married soon?" She asked.

"Yes, we probably will. We were going to wait until Rick got out of the military, but I don't think we will," I replied. "Rick has built up enough vacation time, so we can get married and go on a honeymoon. Afterwards, he can move in with me and hopefully find a job."

That night as I lay in my bed, tears of joy filled my eyes. I was so thankful for all of God's blessings. Every day I felt a deeper connection to Rick. I never would have dreamed that he would be in my life now and in my future as well. It amazed me how God was working in my life. My biggest desire was to do the best I could and be a witness to those around me, showing everyone that with God all things are possible.

One day Chuck called me after our divorce was final. He said that the house sold and he would be moving. He had planned to marry soon and move to Utah. He wished Rick and me all the best with our pending marriage. I wished him all the best too.

"As each of us begins our new lives, I want you to know that I'm going to back off being David and Neil's father," he said.

"Why? They love you. I do not understand."

"They do not need two fathers telling them what to do. Rick will be in their lives daily when you get married. I do not want them pulled between their loyalty to me and to him. I have seen kids go off the deep end because of that. I won't be a part of it."

"I'm trying to understand, but this comes as quite a shock!" I said.

"I'm not dead! I will call them from time to time and send cards, but I want you to know, right here and now, that I will never allow Rick to adopt them. I already discussed this with Rick. I love my boys and they will be able to get benefits through me for their college education. This is something I want to give them. When the boys are older, maybe I will come back for a visit. Then they can make their own decision if they want me in their lives. If they want to call me that would be great, but do not encourage them. I want it to be their choice," Chuck said.

"I might not agree with your thinking, but I'll accept it," I said, in response. "I will be forever grateful to you for giving our boys the opportunity to have a college education."

After I hung up the phone, I started to shake. Trying to accept change was hard for me. Maybe it was easier for Chuck to stay out of my boys' lives because he was not their biological father. I decided not to tell David or Neil what Chuck had said. If they asked questions, I would deal with them later. I sat there thinking again about the verse that says, "In everything give thanks." I was learning daily that this was hard to do sometimes. My main desire now was to give my boys as normal a home life as I possibly could. With God's help, Rick, and my family by my side, I could achieve anything.

25

OUR LIFE TOGETHER BEGINS

Now that our divorces were final, Rick and I decided not to wait to get married. Because Rick had made great strides in physical therapy, his doctor felt he could take off for two weeks. We were thankful because we wanted to go to Canada for our honeymoon. Later, we shared our news with my family. This time they seemed genuinely happy for us, even Daddy. When Rick called his parents, they still did not approve, but wished us well. I phoned my brother and my friends to tell them too. Everyone seemed happy for me. Unfortunately, my brother and Margaret would not be able to attend our wedding. They were busy packing and getting ready to move to Pittsburgh, Pennsylvania. Neil accepted a job at the University of Pittsburgh as an assistant professor of math. I was very proud of him and all that he had accomplished. I knew after he moved, it would be a long time before I would see him again. He promised to visit us before they left. I was holding him to that promise.

Before our wedding, I spent many nights playing mind games. My thoughts were on overdrive. I looked forward to getting married and leaving on our honeymoon, but I was nervous. Being a wife in every sense of the word scared me. Even though Rick and I discussed this, I could still feel my body tighten. I also realized I had not been that far away from my family since I went to Texas with my first husband. In order to get from Washington State to Canada we would be using ferries to cross the waterways; I had never done that before. Meeting Rick's parents and his grandmother who lived in Washington State made me anxious. I was glad his sister was living in the East; that would be one less person for me to impress. More than anything, I wanted Rick's family to know how deeply I loved their son and to accept me as his wife. Staying in one hotel after another as we traveled the interstate North and then driving along the coastline part of the way home would present many challenges. I tried desperately to think positive. It brought me some comfort knowing Rick would be there to help me. We would be sharing new memories together.

Rick and I decided on a small wedding in my parents' home. The only people present were my immediate family, our friends Dan and Joan who stood up for us, the minister; and, of course, David and Neil. After saying our vows, we walked two blocks to Palermo's, our local Italian restaurant. We ate pizza, drank wine, and ate cake. Mother and Daddy agreed to watch the boys and take them on a trip to the Colorado River.

After our informal reception at Palermo's, we hit the road for ten days. As each day passed, we knew this was where God wanted us to be. We were very much in love. I believe our relationship was even more special because we had been friends for so long and fell in love slowly. Rick was so attentive towards me in every way. He wanted this trip to be memorable. When I faced challenges along the way, he was right there to help me. He often said, "My goal in life is your well-being and happiness." I cherished those words. Rick showed me daily that he meant every word that he said. I felt like a queen!

Our trip was truly in God's country. Everything kept getting greener the further North we traveled. I was in awe. When we arrived at Rick's parents, I was nervous; however, in a short time, I felt more relaxed. They could visibly tell Rick was happy. I reassured them I was going to do my best to keep him that way. That evening Rick's parents took us to the Space Needle in Seattle for dinner. The restaurant rotated 360 degrees while we ate. The view was magnificent. I never saw anything so spectacular in my life. I was grateful we could spend time with Rick's parents and grandmother. It gave all of them a chance as well to see Rick's progress after his surgery.

One evening, we were relaxing in our hotel room. Before going on to our final stop in Canada, Rick said, "You seem more relaxed. I know you were anxious about making this trip."

"I can't remember being so relaxed, having so much fun, and seeing so much. I know you have been all over the United States and abroad, but I have not. If I never go on another vacation, at least I have this one to remember for years to come."

"Believe me, this will not be our last vacation. I will see to that," Rick replied.

"There have been many obstacles on this trip because of my wheelchair, but with your help, I have conquered all of them. I would have never been able to make this trip without you," I said, sharing my feelings.

"Please know I enjoy helping you and taking care of you," he said, coming closer to put his arms around me. "Making this trip has opened both our eyes to the problems we will have traveling, but we will continue to travel. Later, we can go places with the children."

"I appreciate everything you do for me. I do not know how handicapped couples travel with so many barriers. You are able-bodied, so when I have a problem you can help me.

Chuck and I only went on one vacation; and, my parents had to go with us because we needed help."

"Another thing we need to discuss is going back to church," Rick said.

"I want to be darn good and sure before I step foot in church again after the fiasco we went through at the church we attended."

"Whenever you're ready, let me know," Rick said.

"After what happened, it might be hard for me even to go back to church. I am thankful I did not lose my faith through that big mess," I responded.

"We were all hurt," Rick said, "but that is in the past."

"I know I am a stronger person because of it, and my relationship with God has grown," I said.

"Now that we are married and starting our new life together, we need to keep our priorities straight."

"What do you mean?" I asked him.

"I was brought up to put God first, your spouse second, and your family third. I believe if we keep things in that order, our family will be able to get through whatever comes our way," he explained.

"Do you think God approves of us getting married?" I asked him. "We both have been divorced; I more times than you."

"Yes, I do. We went to God in prayer and asked for forgiveness. That is what the Bible says to do. I know without a doubt that God has forgiven us and brought us together in the process. I'm very grateful you are a part of my life," Rick said.

"I'm grateful you are a part of mine too."

We finally went to sleep, knowing we had to leave early in the morning.

After leaving Canada, we headed home along the coastline. The evenings were warm with a slight breeze coming off the ocean. The sky was blue mixed with white clouds. Seagulls were flying overhead squealing while looking for fresh fish to catch and eat. One place we went to that was extra special was an underground water aquarium. At another place, we actually fed deer in an enclosed sanctuary. Leaving the coastline and coming into Northern California, we stopped at the Redwoods. The trees were huge! My mouth hung open in utter amazement. Rick kept saying, "Close your mouth, you're going to catch a fly." I took hundreds of pictures and gathered memorabilia throughout our trip. I wanted to make a scrapbook when we returned home. Our trip was a time of joy, growing, and getting to know each other on a deeper level.

On our last day, while Rick was in the shower, I sat in my wheelchair with my feet up on the bed. I felt like the luckiest woman in the world. To have found a husband like Rick was a gift from God. He was a quiet man, yet he showed so much strength. I felt that as long as Rick was by my side, I would be okay. He made me feel safe and secure. Even though I missed my boys and was anxious to see them, I did not want this time with Rick to end. Knowing we only had a five-hour drive ahead of us, we left late that morning. The closer we got to home, the more I was amazed at how dry Southern California looked. The hills were mostly brown with an occasional tree here and there.

When we pulled up to my parents' home, everybody was sitting on the patio. David and Neil spotted our car and came running over to us shouting, "They're home!"

"Hi you two," I said, reaching out to give them a kiss. "Did you have fun on your vacation?"

"We sure did," David said.

"Yes," Neil said, "but it was hot!"

"Did you have fun?" David asked us.

"We did indeed. If you move out of the way, Rick can get my wheelchair out, and we can go over to the patio and talk."

After I transferred into my wheelchair, Rick said, "Come here you two and give me a hug."

Everybody was glad to see that we made it home safely. We asked the boys to tell us about their vacation first. They told us they had a great time and spent hours swimming in the river. They kept saying how hot it was. They were so cute. Then it was our turn.

"I still can't believe how beautiful God's country is," I told everybody. "I hope some day, when you boys are older, we can go back to Washington on vacation. Then you can see for yourselves how beautiful and green it is."

I took out a map that I had marked with a yellow highlighter showing the route we took up to Victoria, Canada and the route we took home. Everybody enjoyed hearing about the places we saw, as I pointed to various locations on the map. I told them that as soon as I had the pictures developed, I would share them. We ended our evening ordering pizza. Now it was time to face reality and get into the mode of every day living.

The four of us left and went home. After getting the boys tucked in, we gathered by their beds and prayed. We asked God to be with all of us as we adjusted to each other as a family unit. I think it did David and Neil a world of good to see their mommy happy. Later, Rick and I prayed for guidance as parents and for Rick to find a job when he got out of the military. We knew we had to trust God daily for whatever our future held.

A short time later, my brother and his family came for a three-day visit before they moved to Pittsburgh. We were happy to all be together. Even though it was a brief visit, it was better than no visit at all. When we waved good-bye as they drove away, I could feel a tear roll down my cheek. Rick put his arm around my shoulder to comfort me. Mother was crying and Daddy tried to comfort her as well.

"Helene, they will be fine," Nana said.

"They will be back again or you and Bill can fly out to see them," Granddad added.

A few hours later, we ordered pizza. I guess pizza was my family's comfort food. We sure ate a lot of it.

A month or so later Mother called to let me know that the house directly across the street from hers was going up for rent. Mother told me the house had a fireplace in the living room, a separate dining room, and a huge kitchen. It also included two large bedrooms, one bathroom, a laundry room, and a sunroom. The home sat on a level lot and included a one-car garage. As soon as I got off the phone, I called the property owner. She agreed to meet us later.

When Rick got home, he, the boys, Mother, Daddy, and I met the property owner at the house. There was natural wood throughout; it was clean and freshly painted. There was only one step up onto the front porch and one step into the house. The back door had a couple of steps, but with the property owner's consent, Rick could pour a ramp. Once the owner agreed to the ramp, we signed a month-to-month rental agreement that same night. Rick was excited that he would finally have a garage where he could "putts," as he called it.

Because our new home was only four houses away, it did not take long to get everything moved. Now we had four generations living in a row. Nana and Granddad lived in the little house behind my parents' home, and now Rick, the boys, and I lived across the street from my parents. One day Rick left early to go to the base to finish the last of his therapy and start filling out paperwork for his discharge. After getting the boys off to school, I called Mother to see if she was done with her housework.

As I wheeled across the street to visit her, I thought, "How convenient is this? I can visit my family and not have to use my car."

"Mother," I hollered, opening the back door. "Do you have any coffee left?"

"I sure do," she said, as she poured me a cup.

"Let's go in the dining room. We can sit by the table and talk."

"You sure seem happy," Mother said.

"I really am, Mother. I have not felt this good in a long time. Rick loves doing things for David, Neil, and me. The other day Neil's bike broke and he could not wait until Rick got home. He knew Rick would fix it. Another time something happened to my wheelchair and he fixed that too. I feel so safe and secure because I know Rick is here for me and he is so willing to help. I remember awhile back when you felt I did not need you as much anymore. Please, never feel that way. I need you in a different way now. You are my mother, my friend, and my confidant. We have a bond that will never be broken," I said.

"I'm so glad you came over. It does my heart good to see you happy for a change. Knowing Rick is there for you and the boys makes me feel good. I do not have to worry about you anymore. I prayed for that for a very long time," she said.

"I really believe that God brought Rick and me together. We are planning to spend the rest of our lives together. Rick told me on our honeymoon that divorce would never be an option. He said if we ever have a problem that we will turn to God. As long as we live by that principle, then we should be together for years, just like you and Daddy and

Nana and Granddad. This is always what I had hoped to be God's answer to my biggest prayer," I said.

After the two of us visited, we went over to Nana's house to see how she was doing. As we went through the patio area, Granddad was in his garden pulling weeds, and he stopped to wave. Nana was glad to see us. She was having more rough days. This concerned all of us. At times, Nana's back pain was almost unbearable. Mother was doing all the laundry now. Mother considered it a privilege to be able to help her parents after all they did for her. After Mother and I spent precious time with Nana, I had to leave. The boys would be getting out of school soon.

On the way back to my house, once again I felt blessed to have such a strong family bond. Rick often remarked how close we all were. He too was starting to develop a special bond with Daddy. For me that was another prayer that God had answered. Daddy's son, my brother, was so far away now that I felt that Rick was helping fill that void in Daddy's heart.

Rick occasionally brought up the subject about going back to church, but he never pushed. I talked to my girlfriend Karen, about going back to church. I knew when the time was right I would go with her and her family. For now, I was so happy I did not want to do anything to jeopardize that. Rick, the boys, and I were doing so well and occasionally Rick's girls would come over. If we all went to church, then I would have four children to get ready. That seemed like a monumental task for me to handle. I knew I was making excuses not to go to church, but I did not care.

Later that evening while Rick was watching TV and the boys were asleep, I went into our bedroom to pray. "Oh Sweet Jesus," I prayed. "I just read 'call unto me,' so I am doing just that. Please guide me as I make a decision about attending church. I feel so torn. I do not know what to do. I lay all these requests at Your feet. Knowing You will direct me, Amen."

After I finished praying, I went into the living room. Rick motioned for me to sit next to him on the couch. As I cuddled beside him, I said, "We are so blessed. I can't believe we have barely started our life together and we have moved already. Each day I thank God for our many blessings."

"God knows exactly what we need. This house is wonderful. I pray we can stay here for a long time. I think it is time to stop for the day. What do you say?" He asked.

"That sounds like a great idea," I said, giving Rick a kiss.

"Come on," he said, with a big grin on his face. "It's time for the two of us to hit the sack."

26

TESTING MY ENDURANCE

I was doing everything in my power to embrace happiness. I tried to keep a positive attitude and count my blessings on a daily basis. One of those blessings was when Rick walked off the military base for the last time. He received an honorable discharge with a medical disability. He would never have to be gone for months again.

When Rick started looking for employment, many companies would not hire him because of his medical discharge. He finally applied at the Naval Aviation Repair Facility (NARF) because it was a Federal Civil Service job. NARF had great benefits and gave preference to veterans. Rick wanted to go through their apprenticeship program. This four-year course guaranteed employment when the program was completed. Not only would Rick have retirement benefits, but also full health insurance. This meant a lot to a young married couple with children. NARF put Rick's name on a waiting list; there were no job openings at the time. As a last resort, Rick accepted a night custodial job at a local school. The only downfall was he had to work nights. This was not what he wanted, but we were thankful he found a job. We continued to pray that a job at NARF would open soon.

Once again, it was time to celebrate Christmas. Rick and I were like two little kids decorating our new home. David and Neil, along with Mother, Daddy, Nana, and Granddad could sense our joy while they helped trim our tree. Our family traditions came back in to play too. To be able to share this time with Rick by my side made it even more special. Char agreed to allow the girls to share Christmas with us too.

Right after the holidays, I received a note from Neil's teacher telling me he was having a difficult time concentrating and was falling behind academically. Neil's teacher suggested that a doctor evaluate him. After going to the doctor and having a barrage of tests run, he told us Neil was hyperactive and dyslexic. Now we finally knew why school was so difficult for Neil. Our doctor told us some children outgrow these conditions. Neil's doctor prescribed medication for him to take. In a very short time, we noticed a big improvement, and Neil seemed happier. This did my heart good.

In the spring of 1971, I found a large lump in my right breast. The fear I faced during this time was insurmountable. My heart pounded when Rick and I went to see my doctor. The doctor said I would need the lump removed and a biopsy performed. As tears rolled down my cheeks, Rick put his arm around my shoulder to console me. My doctor was the sweetest man. He delivered both my boys and showed a lot of empathy towards me for years. I could tell he dreaded telling me that I would need surgery. While waiting for the day of my surgery, I cried out to God daily. I could not figure out why God would add one more ordeal for me to go through. I thought, "Have I not been through enough? Was my being disabled and facing challenges every day, not enough?" In the Bible, God says, I will not forsake you. I felt He was and my faith faltered. Rick had enough faith for both of us and prayed for me daily. Rick's strength during this time counteracted my every weakness. I do not know what I would have done without him and my family. After having the surgery, I learned the mass was not malignant. I was able to relax, pick myself up, and settle down emotionally. Rick and I thanked God for bringing me through this dark time.

A few days after my surgery, after the boys left for school and Rick was still sleeping, I retrieved my Bible and hopped from my wheelchair onto the couch. I needed to find the Scripture that Rick kept telling me about during my cancer scare. Rick always said, "God would not forsake us." Finally, there it was! "Let your manner of life be without covetousness, and be content with such things as ye have; for he hath said, I will never leave thee, nor forsake thee. So that we may boldly say, The Lord is my helper, and I will not fear what man shall do unto me." Hebrews 13:5-6. Why my faith had not carried me through this cancer scare was beyond me. Instead, I had allowed the devil to place me in deep despair. I looked for more answers and came across another Scripture that stated, "Humble yourselves, therefore, under the mighty hand of God, that he may exalt you in due time, Casting all your care upon him; for he careth for you. Be sober, be vigilant, because your adversary, the devil, like a roaring lion walketh about, seeking whom he may devour; Whom resist steadfast in the faith, knowing that the same afflictions are accomplished in your brethren that are in the world." I Peter 5:6-9. I kept reading and rereading those Scriptures. I realized God had not forsaken me; God was always there. I was the one who had pushed God away. I felt guilty for having allowed the devil to regain a foothold in my life.

A month or so later I started feeling tired and weepy. When this happened before, I assumed it was stress. Right now, however, I was not feeling stressed. My doctor always told me to listen to my body. I knew something was not right. I needed to see my doctor. After he examined me, he told me I was pregnant! I could not believe my ears. I was so excited! Finally, I would have my husband by my side throughout my pregnancy and the birth of our baby. I could hardly wait to tell Rick.

On the way home, the devil was right there putting doubts in my mind. I started asking myself, "Was Rick going to leave me like Tom and Jim did? That could not happen! Did I even dare tell Rick? I had to. I was too excited not to." I tried desperately to turn off those negative thoughts. Rick told me we would never get divorced; we were one in the eyes of God. I had to believe his words. I prayed that when I told Rick the news, he would be excited too. After going through a deep valley of despair during my cancer scare, I felt God was saying, "I am here to pick you up and bring an abundance of joy back into your life."

One morning, while in bed I took Rick's hand and placed it on my stomach. Smiling from ear to ear, I said, "We're pregnant!"

Rick sat up instantly, looked at me, and said, "Are you sure?"

"Yes, I went to the doctor. He confirmed it. He was happy for us, but not about my getting pregnant because of the phlebitis and toxemia during my other pregnancies. Remember I told you that?"

"Yes, I remember. We have been really careful," Rick said.

"I guess we weren't careful enough. I truly feel if God did not want me to get pregnant, I would not be. This must be God's plan."

"I'm so excited. You have made me the happiest man in the world," he said, hugging and kissing me. "I can't wait to tell everyone the news. You are going to have to take really good care of yourself."

"I am so blessed to be able to share this miracle with you."

"I'll be with you every step of the way. With God's help, we will get through this. We had better get our day started. If we stay in bed much longer, we might be here longer than we planned," he said, with a grin.

"I know what you mean," I said, laughing.

As we got out of bed, Rick blurted out, "I'll start breakfast. I want to spoil you rotten."

"That is music to my ears," I replied, joyfully.

I could not wait to tell everyone our news.

After breakfast, Rick called his parents. Later we walked across the street and told my family and the boys. Everyone was thrilled. They could tell we were ecstatic. Typical for their age, David and Neil acted as if it were no big deal.

We discussed moving into a larger home, but we really could not afford to. Shortly after that, the owner came by to tell us that we would have to move in 90 days. She informed us they were tearing down the entire block and putting up condominiums. Even though finances were tight, we felt that God was opening a new door, so our faith, once again, was tested. With Rick's G. I. Bill, we could purchase a home with no down payment. Could we find a home in less than 90 days that was wheelchair accessible? We would have to start looking soon.

Rick continued to call NARF. Each time he called, they told him his name was higher on the list. He was encouraged, especially with a baby on the way. Neil was doing much better in school, and David was very protective of him. As they got older, their interests were still very different. David loved sports; Neil loved music and art. This was great because there was no sibling rivalry. Rick's girls still came over from time to time. When we told them about the baby, they giggled saying they wanted a sister.

Months later, Chuck called. He wanted an update on how we were all doing. I told him about the boys, our move, and my cancer scare. I also mentioned that I was pregnant. He wished us the best with the pregnancy, and told me life in Utah was the best move he ever made. He loved the area, his new home, and he had remarried. He told me that he still was not going to interfere with raising the boys.

A few weeks after I had talked to Chuck, I went into a downward spiral. I started bleeding profusely. Rick and I were frightened. Rick called the doctor's office, and the doctor told Rick to take me immediately to the emergency room. Rick called Mother to let her know what was happening, and she offered to watch the boys.

Shortly after arriving at the hospital, I lost our baby and had to have a D and C performed. When I woke up, the doctor told me our baby was a boy. I was heartbroken!

When Rick came into the recovery room, tears were streaming down my face, as I blurted out, "Our baby boy is gone! I can't believe I lost him! I can't believe this has happened to us. I am so sorry! I feel like I let you down! I am such a failure!"

"It is not your fault!" He said, trying to console me.

"I don't understand why God allowed me to get pregnant, experience so much joy, and then take our baby from us?" I yelled.

"I don't have any answers, Honey. Just know I love you!"

We both sat there crying and hanging onto each other. We could not speak. Rick and I were beside ourselves with grief. How would I ever be able to handle this loss? How would Rick?

For weeks, I could hardly get out of bed. I do not think I ever cried so much in my life. Rick tried to comfort me. Mother, Daddy, Nana, and Granddad tried too, but nothing anyone said or did helped.

I continued to see my doctor because my bleeding would not stop. My doctor felt I needed to have a partial hysterectomy as soon he could schedule one. After just losing our baby, now I had to deal with another surgery. Why God had allowed all this to happen haunted me. I knew one thing for sure: happiness in my life did not last. I had no answer as to why.

My surgery went as planned. I stayed in the hospital for five days. Mother watched the boys while Rick was at work or at the hospital. I was not very good company. I felt I was falling into a deep dark hole, and I did not have a clue on how to get out.

After I was home for a few days, I talked to Rick.

"All I keep doing is asking God why? I just don't understand," I said, crying.

"Sharon, we'll probably never know the answers, but we must keep the faith that God knows what He is doing."

"Nothing makes sense to me. It's as if I can't be happy for any length of time. I read encouraging verses in the Bible, yet nothing changes."

"I don't know what to say or how to comfort you," Rick said.

"Nobody can," I said. "My incision hurts something awful. I feel drained emotionally, physically, and spiritually. I wonder if I'll ever feel like myself again."

"You will. Just give it time," Rick said, trying to comfort me, yet again.

"I know this sounds crazy, but I am afraid to be happy. I'll just have the rug pulled out from under me again."

"You can't think like that!" Rick said, sternly. "God wants you to be happy. God wants us to be happy."

"From your mouth to God's ears," I replied.

Rick turned the light out, wrapped his arms around me, and we finally fell off to sleep.

For days, I felt empty inside. I would never be able to have another baby. I felt I would never be a complete woman again due to my hysterectomy. Emotionally, I was still mourning the loss of our son and physically, I was still in a lot of pain from my surgery. I used my stomach muscles to do everything. Daily, I screamed out to God wanting answers! Once again, I felt God had forsaken me.

Rick did everything he knew to help me get through this terrible time, as did my entire family. My mood swings were all over the place. I knew I was not easy to be around, but I did not know what to do. Going through all of these emotions was bad enough, and we still had to find a place to live.

One evening Rick came to me, and said, "I'm here for you. Remember it says in Galatians 6:2 that we are to 'Bear ye one another's burdens, and so fulfill the law of Christ,' and that is what I'm trying to do. I am here to help you get through this very rough time. Do not get me wrong, I hurt too seeing you go through all this, but we have to go on. God would not want us to be sad everyday. Through these life experiences, God wants us to grow. It also says in the Bible that God will not give us more than we can bear."

"I read that and it is a crock! God must think I am stronger than I think I am," I said, bitterly. "I'm trying to keep my faith, but it is hard to do right now."

"I know it is; however, with God's help, we will get through this."

Later that same evening, we received a phone call from the property owner. She told us that we could stay in our home longer. She said the new buyer was going to start tearing down houses on the other end of the block first. Our home would be one of the last to go. I felt so relieved. I still needed time to recuperate before moving. Because of this reprieve, we decided to take time to relax, enjoy what was left of the summer, and spend time with

David, Neil, and Rick's girls. When the children played together, it helped lift my spirits. Their laughter filled our home.

Because of everything I had been through, I realized I was not praying or opening my Bible. At times, I felt guilty, but not guilty enough to change my ways. Because of Rick's insistence, we finally started reading the Bible together again. I believe, in the back of my mind, I knew God was there, but Rick had to keep reminding me. I had blamed God for the loss of our son. My mood changed from day to day. Some days, I loved God with all my heart and soul. Then on other days, I was so angry with God I wanted to spit. I would have a pity-party one day and on other days I felt happy and peaceful. Those mixed feelings scared me to death.

As time passed, with Rick's help, I started to accept God's will rather than blame God for what happened. I noticed I was starting to lean on God more. I learned that when your mind is in accordance with God, your physical well-being would be too. After not being able to pray or read my Bible without Rick, I decided tonight was the night. On my own, I read, "Cast thy burden upon the Lord, and he shall sustain thee; he shall never suffer the righteous to be moved." Psalms 55:22. Then I prayed, "Lord, I come before You asking for forgiveness for not praying and reading my Bible the way I used to. It has been a long time since I came before You without Rick. You have tested our endurance and I am coming before You now, casting my burdens upon You. I am placing my health, Rick's job, our move, and our family in Your hands. I have one other request: Please take care of our son in heaven until we get there. Amen." After praying, I felt God's presence stronger than ever and fell into a deep sleep.

God knew I had a lot on my mind. It was also hard with Rick working nights. Our family time was limited during the week, but we tried to make up for it on the weekends. Right now, my stamina was low, so we limited ourselves to playing board games, watching TV, and taking an occasional day trip to Waddell's Trailer Park. Mother and Daddy had purchased a trailer and parked it on site. That was great for me. It allowed me a place to lie down if I needed to. Nana and Granddad went occasionally too. We could drive to Waddell's in 45 minutes, spend a few hours, and still be home early.

I tried a new approach to my Bible reading. I decided to pick a Scripture and then ponder it throughout the day. I was hoping with this new approach that God would help me be that happy person I loved so much. One afternoon I read, "Trust in the Lord with all thine heart, and lean not unto thine own understanding. In all thy ways acknowledge him, and he shall direct thy path." Proverbs 3:5-6. Learning to trust God with all my heart was not easy, but God knew I was trying. That was all I could do right now.

On another day, I read a Scripture that seemed to speak right to me. It said, "And he said unto me, My grace is sufficient for thee; for my strength is made perfect in weakness. Most gladly, therefore, will I rather glory in my infirmities, that the power of Christ may rest upon me." II Corinthians 12:9. God was telling me that even though I was not totally myself yet, He was there and His strength was all I needed. Reading, "My strength is made perfect in weakness" was teaching me a vital lesson. I was determined to try to apply that verse to my life on a daily basis. Through this new approach, I could tell God was healing me.

Shortly after the boys went back to school, we contacted a realtor. We gave her the price we could afford and a list of what we needed for my special needs. Within a few days, Rick got a call from NARF to come in for an interview. We were beside ourselves with anticipation. The night before, we prayed harder than ever. We did not sleep much either. We were too excited. Getting this job would be paramount for our buying a home and having health benefits. In Luke 18:27 it states, "And he said, The things which are impossible with men are possible with God." We had to hang onto that Scripture for dear life and trust God for the outcome.

When Rick came home, he was smiling from ear to ear and said, "I've been accepted into the apprenticeship program! It lasts four years. I will work during the day, but I will also have class four nights a week for two hours. That will be a challenge, but with God's help, we will manage. I start in two weeks."

"I'm so proud of you. I knew things would work out. Now we can buy a house. I am going to call Mother, Daddy, Nana, and Granddad and invite them over for dinner tonight so that way we can tell them and the boys the good news."

That evening we shared a wonderful dinner. My family was thrilled when Rick told them the news, and everyone congratulated him. After my family left, Rick called his parents. They were planning to come down for a visit, but Rick asked them to wait, until we moved.

A few weeks later, the realtor called and told me she thought she found the perfect house. It was located in Spring Valley about ten minutes from where we lived in La Mesa. We would no longer have four generations living in a row, but that was okay. It was time for me to spread my wings again.

As soon as Rick got home from work that Friday, we left the boys with Mother and drove to Spring Valley. As we entered the house, we could tell it was perfect. The house had three bedrooms, two-baths, and included a family room with a brick fireplace. The back yard was huge with lush green lawn and trees. The boys would finally have separate bedrooms and Rick would have a two-car garage. The only drawback was that the laundry was in the garage. An added bonus was that the elementary school was only about 300 feet away. That meant the boys could walk to school. If there were something going on at school, I could wheel down the street and not have to use my car.

We asked the realtor if we could bring our family over the following morning before we made an offer. She agreed. After taking one more look around, we left and headed to my parents. Everybody was in the back yard. As I opened the gate, I said, "We found a house! We would like all of you to take a look at it tomorrow morning." We agreed to meet after breakfast. When we told David and Neil that they would have separate bedrooms, they were ecstatic. After the boys went to bed, Rick and I prayed, "Sweet Jesus, thank you for finding this beautiful home for us. We give You all the credit! We ask for Your guidance as we make a major decision as to whether we buy this house or not. Please help us. Amen."

The following morning, we all went to the new house. Everybody loved it and said it was perfect for my special needs. When we finished, Rick and I followed the realtor back to her office and the boys went to their grandparents' house. The realtor wrote up our offer and said she would present it to the seller and get back to us. We wanted to close escrow as soon as possible, so we could paint and carpet while the house was empty. Everything went like clockwork. We thanked God daily for providing us with this beautiful home and for giving all of us the strength to get everything done before the boys got out of school for Christmas break.

Our moving day finally arrived. Rick rented a truck, loaded it, and away we went. We truly believed that God found this house for us, and we planned to stay for many years. My entire family was with us that day. Everyone was so happy for Rick, the boys, and me. After unloading the truck and piling boxes throughout the house, we took a break. We found the nearest pizza place, and ordered in pizza. After we ate, Mother and I made the beds and found enough supplies so that we could take showers later. It was wonderful to have four generations in our new home that first day.

With Christmas right around the corner, we planned a family tree trimming party. When my parents and grandparents arrived, the boys anxiously wanted them to see their bedrooms. We still had things to do in the house and furnish our family room, but there was no rush. As I handed out Christmas ornaments to hang on the tree, we sang Christmas carols to music playing on the stereo while we drank hot chocolate.

A few days before Christmas, Rick and I surprised my parents with a small gathering of family and friends to celebrate their 30th wedding anniversary. When Mother and Daddy walked in, they were surprised and Mother started crying. After all my parents did for us, this was the least we could do for them. To see them so happy made for a wonderful evening.

Five days later, we all gathered for Christmas. This Christmas was extra special because it was in our very own home. I made a ham dinner with all the trimmings. We shared the day opening presents, eating, and spending precious time together. After dinner, Daddy made a toast, "We wish you happiness for many years to come." Everybody raised their glasses and said, "Amen to that." The following day Char brought Rick's girls over so we could celebrate Christmas with them too.

Before the children went back to school, we took them to Balboa Park to see the Nativity. As I sat there, contemplating the birth of Christ, I thought how thankful I was to have such a loving God. With God's help, Rick by my side, and my family there to encourage me, how could I not get through everything that we did? Through every challenge, God was teaching me to lean on Him. In the Bible, it states, "For we through the Spirit wait for the hope of righteousness by faith." Galatians 5:5. Every day God was testing my endurance. Daily, I learned more about God's enabling love.

27

FACING LIFE'S CHALLENGES

After celebrating the New Year, I registered David and Neil in Avondale Elementary School. With the boys gone and Rick at work, I had plenty of time to get my chores and errands done. I also had time to visit my family. I never wanted to give up the closeness we shared. Being a few miles apart somehow made me feel more independent. I do not know why I felt I had to prove to them I could manage on my own, but I did. We made it a point to get together, at least once a week. I also stayed in touch with my girlfriends. Due to Rick's heavy work and school schedules, we could not get together with couples as much as we would have liked to.

Every day when David and Neil came home, they enjoyed sharing what happened at school with me. Sometimes David and Neil's friends would come to our house after school. Having separate bedrooms was a bonus. When Neil's friends came over, they would listen to music in his room. When David's friends came over, they would visit in his room or go outside and play basketball in our driveway or throw a ball in the back yard. How dull my life would have been if both boys had liked the same things. I had the best of both worlds.

Dinner was always at five o'clock. This allowed Rick time to get home, relax, spend time with the boys and me, eat dinner, and head off to college. Rick took extra classes so that he could graduate in three years, rather than four. With weekdays full and only weekends free, Rick missed the boys and they missed him. I had to remind them, as well as myself, that this schedule would not last forever.

Rick's parents finally came for a visit. It was good to see them. They liked our new home. I will never forget the day when Rick's mother pulled me aside and said, "You are the best thing that has ever happened to our son."

As a tear rolled down my cheek, I said, "Lucille, you don't know how happy I am to hear you say that."

"I can tell you love Rick and he adores you. He has really changed. He has more confidence in himself and is genuinely happy. I haven't seen him like this in years."

"He has been my rock. He is always there for my boys, my family, and me. He is also very attentive to his girls. He has a lot of love to give. He just doesn't seem to show his emotions outwardly."

"That's probably because our family did not show emotion," she said.

"Each family is different."

"We could tell that Rick was upset when we did not give him our blessing to marry you," Lucille admitted.

"I know he wanted your blessing, but you were not ready to give it."

"We were upset Rick had divorced. We were so against that, but now we changed our minds," Lucille said, with conviction.

"I am thrilled that your feelings have changed."

Rick's parents stayed for a few days. They had the opportunity to meet my parents and grandparents and visit their granddaughters. They were very polite to David and Neil, but I hoped that some day they would develop the same close connection they had with Rick's girls.

After George and Lucille left, I had a lot of time to think about some of the things she told me about Rick. I finally realized it was because of Rick's upbringing that he did not show emotion as openly as I did. There is a saying that goes, "You live what you learn." Rick was also carrying around a lot of emotional baggage from serving three tours of duty in Vietnam. Whenever I asked Rick what happened over there, he only said he witnessed things that nobody should ever have to witness in one's lifetime. Maybe, in time, he would open up more. Even though Rick had trouble showing emotion, there was not one thing that Rick would not do for my boys, my family, his girls, or me. That spoke volumes!

Joining two families has many challenges because each brings different viewpoints into a new family unit. One evening when I discussed Rick's childhood with him, he admitted to this day his father had never said he loved him. As I reflected back on my own childhood, Mother and Nana were more affectionate. Daddy and Granddad did not display their emotions as often. Daddy and Granddad provided for their families. They showed how much they cared by what they did. Back then, a woman's place was in the home, caring for her husband and children. Each member of the family had a role to play and each performed it well.

In the summer of 1972, while the boys were still on summer break, we decided to take a five-day vacation to Anaheim, California about two hours north of San Diego. Anaheim had many tourist attractions, including Disneyland and Knott's Berry Farm. I was excited, but still felt apprehensive when I left home. Some days I did pretty well, especially when

I went to a familiar place. Going far away, I felt fearful of the unknown. I read in the Scripture, "For God hath not given us the spirit of fear, but of power, and of love, and of a sound mind." II Timothy 1:7. I knew what God wanted, but I also knew there were things I would never be able to do sitting in this wheelchair.

Before leaving on vacation, I was on the phone for days trying to find a place that could accommodate my wheelchair. Because my wheelchair was small, I could manage in the main bedroom area. At some motels, the problem was entering the bathroom. In most cases, the door was too narrow. I would always bring my special stool to use, just in case. Bathing in an unfamiliar environment was also dangerous if there were no grab bars to hold onto. When I asked my handicapped friends how they managed, most said they did not travel because it was too hard.

The night before we left, Rick and I prayed that God would be with us. We knew we would face challenges. We did on our honeymoon, but then it was just the two of us. Our prayers did not make me less apprehensive, but I had to put my fears aside and trust that as long as God and Rick were with us, we all would have a good time. When we finally left, I did not know who was more excited, the boys or Rick or me.

Without exception, at every tourist attraction, there were barriers. There were steep hills that I could not push up, or on which I could lose control of my wheelchair going down. There were public bathrooms I could not use because my wheelchair could not fit inside the stall. This meant that I would go most of the day with nothing to eat or drink. The fear of having to use the bathroom and not be able to frightened the daylights out of me. If I did by chance find a bathroom I could use, I could not close the stall door for privacy. Then there were the rides. It hurt me to watch David, Neil, and Rick go on the rides without me, but I thanked God that Rick was there so my boys could enjoy themselves. I prayed that someday people would realize that those of us who are disabled just wanted to have fun like everybody else.

One bonus at some amusement parks was when we did not have to wait in long lines. As we entered Disneyland, the greeter handed me a list of six rides that I could go on in my wheelchair. Because I was in a wheelchair, the attendant would take us to the front of the line. This thrilled the boys, but it upset those standing in line. People would make snide remarks, give us dirty looks, and were rude. I did not want to embarrass my children, or I would have said something nasty back at them. I had to let their narrow-minded attitudes roll off my back, but it was hard. I was determined not to let their insensitive remarks hurt me.

That evening after we got back to the hotel, Rick and I explained to David and Neil that many people have never been around a person with a disability. These people did not understand what I had to go through. I told them if somebody said something or gave us dirty looks, they were to hold their heads up high and not get into a confrontation. Both David and Neil were very protective of me, just like my brother was so many years ago.

During those five days, we conquered as many barriers as we could and had a wonderful time. At the end of our vacation, we were ready to go home. On our way home, I thought, "What would I do without Rick?" I would have to stay home. With two active boys to keep up with, plus helping me, Rick looked tired at the end of each day, but he never complained. Rick always had such a loving and caring spirit. It was good for David and Neil to see how attentive Rick was to me too. They could see first hand how they should treat their wives when they got married. When we arrived home, we thanked God for being with us and allowing us to share this precious time together as a family.

Once we were unpacked, ate dinner, and said good night to the boys, Rick and I had time to talk about our vacation.

"Sharon, you didn't say much all the way home."

"I had a lot on my mind," I replied, "but I want you to know how thankful I am for all your help. It is obvious that I could never have taken a vacation without you."

"I enjoy helping you and I always will," Rick replied.

"After this vacation I realized even more so, why many of our disabled friends don't travel. It's not easy out there. At least our houses are accessible so that we can get together from time to time."

"We can always see somebody that has it worse off than we do," Rick said.

"I am so thankful that we had this opportunity to do something special with the boys. You will never know how much I love and appreciate you. What would I have done without you?" I said, expressing my gratitude.

"That's really sweet of you to say, but you would do just fine. Look, at all you did and went through before I came into your life. You are stronger than you think. Let's call it a day and get ready for bed," he said, reaching out to push me down the hall to our bedroom.

After experiencing so many obstacles as a handicapped person, on vacation, I happened upon a book written by Alfred Katz and Knute Martin titled, A HANDBOOK OF SERVICES FOR THE HANDICAPPED. In it the co-authors stated, "Although many people in modern society suffer from psychological tensions and difficulties, it is widely recognized that being physically disabled imposes some extra challenges. The sufferer and his or her next intimates, in the first instance the immediate family are affected not only by the general pressures of complex social forces, but by the particular and special tasks of making an adaptation to social life that will maximize the capacities and abilities of people with disabilities. Overcoming the stigmatizing, negative effects of stereotyping and discrimination sometimes presents particular problems of attaining and maintaining mental health through the development of a positive self-image. Much modern thinking has concluded that the barriers of effective functioning of people with disabilities come from negative social arrangements and attitudes that the person with disabilities comes to internalize through his or her life experiences." [7] When I read that, it was as if a light bulb went off in my head. Every word was true about how I felt daily. We, the disabled, just wanted to be able to maneuver in an able-bodied world without problems all the time.

It was easy for me to attend a parent/teacher conference, a PTA meeting, David's basketball games or Neil's art exhibits because they were all on level ground with easy access. It was far different when David played baseball or had a track meet. I could not maneuver through dirt or gravel. I had to sit in my car and use binoculars to watch my son's games. If an able-bodied person invited me to their home, I would always have to ask if there were steps. If there were, I could not accept their invitation. Some houses had no steps, but I could not use the bathroom. Every time I left my home, I had to ask questions. When we went as a family to a local concert or sporting event, I had my special place to sit and my family had theirs. It made me cry inside when I realized our family and other families with a disabled person could not even sit together. Unable to support myself on my own two feet alienated me from the rest of the world in many ways. Many times, I prayed silently, "God give me the strength to accept what I cannot change."

Going to the doctor or the mall was easy, except for the problem with parking. If I parked too close to another car, I could not open my car door wide enough to get my wheelchair in or out of the back seat. Other times, when I went to leave, another car parked too close to me. I would then have to wait for that person to come out to move their car. Once I waited 45 minutes. After that, I only parked in end parking spaces. I did not care how long I had to drive around to find one. It was worth not having to deal with the frustration of not being able to get into my car when I was ready to leave.

Other disabled people with vans equipped with a wheelchair lift needed at least eight feet clearance to exit or enter their van. I had a dream that one day Rick and I would be able to purchase a van with a lift. I would insist on having a portable potty inside. I could then actually leave home and never have to clean or worry about being able to use a public bathroom ever again.

I tried to laugh at some of these predicaments. One such incident happened when I went to the bank. When I took my wheelchair out of the back seat of my car, it got away from me. As my wheelchair rolled away from my car, I was horrified! Cars were slamming on their brakes trying to avoid hitting it. I could tell by the looks on drivers' faces, they wondered where the wheelchair came from. I sat in my car, waving my arms and yelling for somebody to catch my wheelchair. After what seemed like forever, a man stopped his car, got out, and grabbed it. As he looked around, he saw me waving at him yelling, "It's my wheelchair. Can you please bring it to me?" When he did, I told him what happened. The two of us started laughing. Afterwards, I had to admit it was funny. When I saw my wheelchair take off for parts unknown, my eyes got as big as silver dollars; I was scared to death my wheelchair would be damaged. Wheelchairs are not cheap!

Things would not change until around 1974. Another quote from, A HANDBOOK OF SERVICES FOR THE HANDICAPPED foretold, "New possibilities for services, housing and the removal of architectural barriers were opened through the Rehabilitation Act of 1973, The Housing and Community Development Act of 1974, The Rehabilitation Act Amendments of 1974, and The Social Services Amendments of 1974. All this legislation signalized an increased consciousness of human rights and needs. Academic and professional groups produced studies of principles and specific programs leading to the barrier free environment for the disabled. Taking their cue from the federal legislation, a number of states also studied the problem and produced reports that analyzed every phase of the environment - civil rights, architecture, transportation, street mobility - as it affects the disabled." [8] Handicapped people had been waiting years to live an easier life free of barriers.

Being handicapped all my life was hard enough, but as my children got older and I became more involved in their various activities, I had to face more challenges than I had ever encountered before. When Rick was gone, Mother used to go with me; but, as her parents aged, she was spending more time now with them. With Mother busy and Rick gone long hours at work and school, I had to do more things by myself outside my home. At times, I was frightened and could feel my body tense-up like a rubber band stretched to its limit. I still had to keep my stress down in order to keep my colitis under control.

Because of my faith, I figured that everything would work out. Mother used to say, "You can do whatever you set your mind to." I found that not to be true. Many times my mind wanted to do something, but my disability kept me from it. My daily prayer was, "Sweet Jesus, teach me to cope."

My home was my sanctuary. I felt peaceful there because I could do just about everything, except reach high things. Rick felt I was very competent and had accomplished more than most considering my disability. I told Rick that the Scripture says, "I can do all things through Christ," but I knew that not to be true for me. I will never be able to walk again; that was a given. My only alternative was to have enough faith to get through whatever happened in my life.

As my children got older, I asked them about my capability as a mother, especially if I could not attend one of their events. They were always encouraging. They assured me it was okay. They understood and loved me just the way I was. I will never forget the day, David said, "You are the best mom in the world. Maybe you sit down to do everything, but you manage to get the job done."

As the years passed, I learned to make some definite changes in my attitude. I had to force myself to be thankful for what I could do and quit worrying about the things I could not. My psychiatrist told me years ago, "You are what you think." What a true statement.

Because the boys were in school and Rick was at work, I had more time to do Bible study. In the Bible, there are many places where it talks about the mind. The following Scriptures really touched my heart. In Matthew 22:37-38 it states, "Jesus said unto him, Thou shalt love the Lord, thy God, with all thy heart, and with all thy soul, and with all thy mind. This is the first and great commandment." In Romans 8:6, it states, "For to be carnally minded is death, but to be spiritually minded is life and peace." Finally, in Colossians 3:2 it states, "Set your affection on things above, not on things on the earth." As I read these passages, I knew God was speaking to me. I had control over my thoughts, my attitude, my happiness, my sadness, and my anger. By being more positive, I would be a happier wife, mother, daughter, sister, and granddaughter. I knew God would always be there. Through every challenge, I would try to keep a healthy mind and continue the best way I could.

28

COMING TO TERMS WITH LIFE

A few weeks later, I called my friend Karen. I told her I was perplexed about my attitude. I told her I felt I was doing better, but there was still something missing in my life. During our conversation Karen blurted out, "Why don't you, Rick, and the boys meet us at church on Sunday? You are always talking about God and His influence in your life. Why not put those words into action?"

I was a little shocked, but said, "I'm going to take you up on that. Rick has wanted us to go back to church for years. Now that we have been married three years, I think we have waited long enough."

"Church starts at 11 o'clock," Karen said. "Can I expect to see you there?"

"Yes, I can't wait to tell Rick. We'll see you on Sunday."

Later that night, I told Rick about my conversation with Karen. He was ecstatic. This was going to be a new beginning for our family.

The following Sunday we met Karen and her family. We all enjoyed church so much that we went every Sunday after that. With great anticipation every Saturday night, I would get the boys' clothes and Bibles out, along with mine. On Sundays, old traditions resurfaced. While the boys and I got ready, Rick cooked pancakes and eggs. After church, we visited Mother, Daddy, Nana, and Granddad. Sometimes Mother fixed dinner; other times we ordered pizza. Going back to church was an answer to our prayers. We felt very comfortable at our new church; less than 100 people attended. On December 9, 1973, Rick and I rededicated our lives to Jesus Christ. David and Neil accepted Christ into their hearts that same day. This day was even more special because it was Nana's birthday. I could hardly wait to get over to my parents' house and to tell Mother, Daddy, Nana, and Granddad our news and celebrate Nana's birthday.

Were things perfect in our home because we attended church? No! Rick was still gone long hours going through the apprenticeship program. I still had challenges to face when I left the house. I still had occasional bouts with colitis and had more cysts removed. The boys would still argue from time to time; and, when the four children were together, we really had our hands full. God never promised life without turmoil; God only promised that He would be there, and He was.

Eventually Rick's hard work paid off. He graduated from the apprenticeship program at NARF in three years with honors. We were so proud of him. We were all excited that Rick could finally spend more time at home. Now we could attend evening functions at church. Rick also started coaching David's Little League team. As a family, we enjoyed going to his games. When I went to the games, Rick would lean me back on my wheelchair's rear wheels and push me through the dirt or gravel. I no longer had to sit in my car and use binoculars to watch the games. David also played basketball. There were also times when things were not good. Rick still had knee problems and had to undergo more surgeries. One time he was in a long leg cast for six weeks. With him on crutches and me in a wheelchair, we made quite the pair. With God's help, we worked things out.

One day when I went shopping, there were a couple of parking spaces marked with a wheelchair symbol on the pavement. I could not believe my eyes. When I went into the store, I asked the clerk what happened, and she explained that those parking spaces were marked for handicapped people to park in. The spaces were closer to the entrance of the store and wider, allowing wheelchair users more room to get in and out of their cars. I thanked the clerk for the information, did my shopping, and left. On the way home, I thanked God for answering my prayers. I thought to myself, all good things come to those who wait. As soon as I got home, I called Mother and Nana and told them the good news. Later, when the boys and Rick got home, I told them as well. I wanted to shout this news from the rooftop. After dinner, I called some of my handicap friends. They noticed the changes too. Oh what a glorious time this was!

A few days a week, Mother and I would drive around town with a notepad listing the places with easy access. We started checking out bathrooms as well. As my list grew longer, I could tell I was not as fearful when I left the house. For years, I had nothing to eat or drink before leaving the house. Now I could finally drink a cup of coffee in the morning, and not worry what I would do if the "urge" hit. How great it was to see my community becoming more aware of people with disabilities.

A few months later, however, I noticed able-bodied people using handicapped parking spaces. I thought, "Of all the parking spaces available to them, why did they use a handicap spot?" When I went to use a public bathroom, able-bodied people were using the one marked for the disabled. If they had six stalls to choose from and I only had one, why would they use the only one I could use? Witnessing this kind of abuse of the new laws implemented for the disabled made my blood boil!

Over the next few years, we had many celebrations as well as times of great sorrow. In 1976, my grandparents celebrated their 60th wedding anniversary. What a witness they were to everybody who knew them. They were there for each other through the good and the bad and shared a bond like no other couple I knew, except for my parents. Shortly after celebrating their anniversary, Nana fell and broke her hip. During that time, I saw more of that special bond that my grandparents shared. Because Nana was a large woman, Granddad could not care for her at home. She went to a rehabilitation center after leaving the hospital. Granddad missed her so much; he spent many nights at the center sleeping next to her bed on a cot. He often said how lonely it was at home without her; he was counting the days until Nana could return home.

A few months later in 1977, Mother came by my house one morning while the boys were in school. Before Mother uttered a word, I knew something was wrong. Mother started sobbing and said, "Sharon, Granddad passed away. I found him in his chair when I went over to fix him breakfast. I cannot believe my daddy is gone! I don't know how I will ever be able to tell my mother."

"I knew Nana and Granddad were getting older, but I am shocked," I said, with tears in my eyes.

"When I found him he had the Four Spiritual Law booklet you gave him in one hand and his Bible in the other. He looked so peaceful. I know my dad had a good life, but I'm going to miss him something awful," Mother said.

I got out of my wheelchair and sat next to my mother on the couch. We sat there crying and holding each other trying to comprehend the loss of a dear family member. No words could express our thoughts that day. Our only consolation was that Granddad had lived a long life. He was 86 years old. I am glad I had the chance to witness to Granddad about God. I knew I would see him in heaven. Years ago, Mother, Daddy, Nana, and Granddad decided they did not want to have a service. They all chose cremation; they wanted their ashes spread at sea off Point Loma, California. I did not know how my mother would be able to cope with Granddad's death because they were so close. As always in God's perfect timing, Daddy retired a few months later. This meant Mother would have Daddy's round-the-clock support, while trying to accept her father's death and the possibility of caring for her mother at home.

As time went on, Rick and I had one physical problem on top of the other. I had more cysts removed. After scheduling my 17th cyst surgery, I finally found a doctor that pulled the skin, back and forth, over this deep hole that formed on the back of my left thigh. This provided me with some padding. Rick, on the other hand, had two more knee surgeries and one elbow surgery. Sometimes, I did not know if I should even get up in the morning. Our classic joke was, "Who is taking care of whom today?" We were also thankful we were members of a small church. The parishioners provided us with help and prayer when we needed it.

One day in 1978, my brother, Neil, and his family flew to California for a visit. Neil wanted to share some fantastic news with his entire family in person. Neil finally made full professorship at the University of Pittsburgh. His goal now was to become the next Administrative Assistant to the Dean at the University of Pittsburgh, followed by Director of Management Information and Policy Analysis, Data Administrator. Neil had always set high goals for himself; and, so far, he accomplished each one of them. Because miles continued to separate us, we stayed as close as we could by talking on the phone and by getting together for occasional visits.

Shortly following Neil and his family's visit, Rick's oldest daughter talked to us about moving in with us. We were thrilled. We knew we could not have the boys share a room, so Rick decided to take half of our patio and add a fourth bedroom with a door leading off our family room. It took some doing, but when it was finished, we purchased some bedroom furniture and Rick's daughter moved into David's old bedroom. David, being the oldest, moved into the new bedroom. After being the only female in our home for so long, having another female in the house was a joy.

In September of 1978, David came home from high school and asked if he could change churches.

"All my friends go to Skyline Wesleyan Church," he said. "It is only a few blocks from our house. It would be cool if I could start going there. What do you think?"

"When Rick gets home we can have a family meeting," I replied.

"Sounds good," David said, before leaving for his part-time job.

After having our family meeting, we decided we all should start attending Skyline Wesleyan Church. Skyline was larger and had a great youth program. We felt this would be beneficial to our children. Five months later, much to our delight, our senior pastor, Orval C. Butcher, baptized David. That same evening, Rick and I rededicated our lives to Jesus Christ again. At the altar of the church, Rick knelt down next to me and held my hand while Pastor Butcher prayed over us. Warm tears of joy filled my eyes as I thanked God again for bringing Rick into my life.

Pastor Butcher was not the normal pastor. He was more of a shepherd. He cared deeply for every member of his church. He was always there for anyone no matter what time of day or night. He always referred to his congregation as his "flock" and took good care of everyone.

When I went to church or Sunday school, there was literature passed out. If it were something special, I filed it away. One day, I found a sheet that I had torn out of a POWER FOR LIVING pamphlet titled, "I've Been Thinking" by Joyce Landorf. In the middle of a long list of statements she wrote, "Being a Christian Means…Releasing your children into God's hands from the moment they are born, and trusting Him with their lives." [9] These words really hit home. God was telling me to release my boys and trust Him. On that day, I did not realize how profound those words would be.

One day I was sitting on the couch in my living room when I saw a Sheriff's car pull up out in front of our home. I could not figure out who it was. Then I noticed it was Chuck. Years went by with no contact from him and now he was at my house! I yelled for the boys to come into the living room as I hopped off the couch into my wheelchair. As the boys approached me, I pointed out the front window and said, "Look! Chuck's here!"

"What is he doing in a Sheriff's car?" David asked.

"I don't know," I said, bewildered. "Your guess is as good as mine."

"I can't believe Daddy Chuck is here," Neil said, as he went running out the front door to greet him.

David went out front for a short time and came back in the house to shower and get ready for work.

I finally went outside and invited Chuck to come in the house. Neil went ahead of us to hold the front door open. On our way in, I leaned over to Chuck, and whispered, "You could have given me some warning."

"I was in the neighborhood," Chuck said, laughing.

As Neil, Chuck, and I sat in the living room, I said, "It's been a long time since we've seen you. "What are you doing driving a Sheriff's car?"

"Even though I am disabled, the State of Utah said I could be a Sheriff. I drive around and if I see something suspicious, I radio the office."

Neil excused himself for a minute and went into his bedroom. David was still getting ready for work.

"A lot has happened, since we last spoke. I got a divorce and so did my brother. He moved in with me. Because the boys are in high school now, I thought the time was right to come back and see them."

"You still should have called me," I said.

Before Chuck could respond, Neil came back into the living room. "Can we go some place?" Neil asked Chuck.

"What do you think, Sharon? I would like to take the boys to dinner."

"Neil can go, but David has to work tonight. He has a part-time job."

Chuck and Neil left right after David did. I sat there still in shock, watching the clock, and waiting for Rick to come home so that I could tell him what had happened.

After a couple of hours, Chuck dropped Neil off out front. When Neil came into the house, he told me Chuck would call me in a few days. Then Neil dropped a bombshell! He told Rick and me that he wanted to move to Utah with Chuck and finish high school there. When Neil said that, my heart dropped and my stomach turned into a knot. I told him that Rick and I would need time to think, talk to Chuck, and come to a decision that we all agreed would be in his best interest.

Rick and I talked and prayed for days. We knew Neil still struggled in school. Maybe this was the answer. Neil would be living in a rural town with less peer pressure. The only question was how could I let him go? I kept hearing the words I read awhile back, "Release your children into God's hands." I always felt that nobody could ever take my boys from me and now Chuck was doing what I had feared the most.

A few days later, Chuck finally called. Later, I told Neil it was okay for him to move to Utah, but he had to promise me that he would stay in school and graduate. Chuck assured me Neil could visit us whenever he wanted. I felt that Neil's education took priority over my feelings.

While we were packing, I put on that happy face, but when Chuck and Neil drove off, I broke down. Rick did everything to comfort me, but nothing worked. Once again, I hung onto God for dear life. Neil promised he would call as soon as he arrived at Chuck's house.

Rick knew it would take most of the day for Neil and Chuck to get to Utah. While David was at work, and Rick's daughter was with a friend, we took off for the beach. We parked on top of a cliff overlooking Ocean Beach. We would be celebrating our tenth wedding anniversary soon.

"I can't believe everything we've been through," I told Rick.

"We've had our share of challenges. That's for sure."

"Watching Neil leave, was really hard," I said, with tears rolling down my face. "After all, he is my baby."

"There comes the time that we have to let our kids go," Rick said. "Soon, they will all graduate from high school and start lives of their own. What are you going to do then?"

"Don't go there," I told him. "I want to hang onto the children as long as I can."

"I'm serious, Sharon," Rick said. "Pretty soon you'll be alone. You have done your job as a mother and even a stepmother. Part of that job is training them so they can leave and go out on their own."

"I want them to grow up and have lives of their own, but that does not make it easy when they actually leave."

"You're probably like most mothers that stay at home full-time. I think it's harder for you to let go."

"You're probably right. The majority of my life I have been a mother, so when they leave home, my life will change drastically."

"Think of these times as milestones," Rick said. "Pretty soon all the kids will graduate. Some will go off to college. Some will get married and have children. Later we will be grandparents."

"I am starting to feel old," I said, laughing.

"Well, I have accomplished what I set out to do; make you laugh," Rick said, as he leaned over, put his arm around my shoulder, and gave me a kiss. "Want to go grab a bite to eat?"

"That's a great idea," I said, smiling, "I don't feel like cooking."

After Rick and I got home, Neil called. He arrived safely.

"More than anything I want your blessing, Mom," he said.

"Neil, I want you to know that we both love you very much. As long as you are happy and do well in school, that is all that matters. Getting your education is number one. Rick and I will pray for you every day."

"Thanks, Mom. I needed to hear that."

After I hung up the phone, I went to bed. Lying alongside Rick always made me feel safe and secure. He was my rock and always seemed to know just what to do or say to help me through the rough times. Before turning the light off, we prayed to God to grant us peace with our decision to let Neil go, and we asked God to watch over him.

For days, after Neil left, I had mixed feelings. Every morning I would go into his room and sit by his bed asking myself what seemed like a hundred questions. I could not understand why God allowed Chuck to be out of my boys' lives for so long, and then come back and take Neil away with him. I felt like Chuck slapped me in the face! Nothing made sense to me. "Had this been part of God's plan all along?" I thought. If God accepted me with all of my problems, then I must show that same kind of acceptance to my children and stepchildren. God loved all of our children right where they were and our family had to show that same kind of love. We could not just love them when they did what we thought they should do. We had to love them when they were going through their own struggles as well.

Christmas of 1979 was rough. It was the first Christmas Granddad was not with us; Neil was in Utah; and Rick's oldest daughter moved out to go back and live with her mother. We were sad to see her go, but I totally understood the closeness between a daughter and her mother. Rick and I had to let her go. Nana, diabetic and confined to a wheelchair, was now living in a convalescent facility. My parents could no longer care for her at home. On Christmas day, my parents arranged for Nana to leave the facility so she could spend the day with us. My feelings were all over the place that day. We celebrated the birth of Jesus and were thankful for those there with us, but we were also trying to cope with the loss of those who were not.

29

ACCEPTING GOD'S PLAN

Over the last few years, our home had always been buzzing with teenagers. Now that was changing. David was the only teenager living at home, but he was going to school and working part-time. Rick's girls came over occasionally and Neil came home from Utah when his schedule allowed. I was spending more days by myself.

After the New Year, David went to church camp with a bunch of high school friends. While he was gone, the parents of one of the girls, who also went to church camp, approached Rick and me and asked us if their daughter could move in with us. We had known their daughter for about two years because she attended Skyline Wesleyan Church. Her parents explained they were alcoholics and wanted to keep their daughter away from their lifestyle. How could we say no? We originally added the fourth bedroom for Rick's oldest daughter; now it was going to work for another girl. Once again, it was nice having another female in the house. We referred to her as our foster daughter. We had a lot of fun together.

In the spring, Rick had additional surgeries on both his knees. We were also planning a graduation party. In the summer of 1980, David and our foster daughter graduated from high school. We had a huge party for both of them, including family and friends. I could not believe both David and our foster daughter would be starting college in the fall. I was glad David chose to live at home. Our foster daughter decided to move out and live in the dorm on campus because she received a scholarship to attend Point Loma Christian College. As parents, we did not know what the future held, but we did know that God made all parents a promise. As stated in the Bible, "Train up a child in the way he should go and, when he is old, he will not depart from it." Proverbs 22:6. Over the next few years, more of our children would start working part-time, graduate from high school, and become adults. They would be making their own choices. They had to learn from some of their mistakes, and we had to give them the chance to do so. All we could do is love them unconditionally.

Shortly after the graduation party, Mother and Daddy invited us to their house to celebrate our 10th wedding anniversary. After spending a few hours eating pizza and playing cards, Daddy suggested that he and Rick buy a 17-foot Bayliner boat. We were thrilled and took him up on his offer. Rick and Daddy loved to fish, and the kids would be able to waterski. Anything that kept our family close was well worth the expense.

My life was changing again. By nine o'clock in the morning, I finished my housework. That left many hours to fill with other things. The children were busier than ever and Mother and Daddy started traveling. While they were gone, I took care of their mail and paid their bills. I would also visit Nana regularly, trying to lift her spirits and talk to her about God. Nana seemed to enjoy my visits, as did the other three women that shared a room with her at the convalescent home. None of Nana's roommates had family close by. I thought how lonely they must feel. Maybe this was where God wanted me to be right now. To be there for my nana and my parents made me feel good. I felt it was about time I did things for them after all they had done for me.

I tried to get the family together when Neil came home for visits. Sometimes it worked out; sometimes it did not. I am glad Daddy and Rick purchased the boat. Every Wednesday, except in the winter, I would pack a dinner. As soon as Rick got home, he would hook up the boat to our mini-van and we would head to Mission Bay. When we arrived, Rick would carry me from the van, and gently place me in the boat. Then I would crawl, literally, to the driver's seat, start the engine, and back the boat off the trailer while Rick parked the van. As soon as any of our children arrived with their friends, Rick would drive the boat and I would "flag" while they water-skied. Later, Rick would carry me from the boat to the grassy area so that we could enjoy our evening meal. Sometimes Mother and Daddy would join us too. I could never have done all those things without Rick. He helped me create memories. I felt blessed!

With only David living at home, this was the perfect time to reconnect with old friends. In addition, when Mother and Daddy were home from traveling, Rick and I would meet them at Waddell's Trailer Park. When Daddy and Rick fished, Mother and I would go shopping. God was helping me as I tried to rediscover myself and look to the future with new hopes, dreams, and goals. Part of that was also letting my children fulfill their hopes, dreams, and goals too. I knew in time, I would be more peaceful, because in Psalms 7:1 it states, "O Lord my God, in thee do I put my trust..."

With God's grace, I finally realized my job raising my children was almost finished. Once I was at peace with that, I still had to deal with my feelings of being disabled. Even though my confinement to a wheelchair for most of my life made finding ways to overcome barriers difficult, but not impossible, there were still limitations that I could not change and that was hard to accept. I knew I was not alone. My handicapped friends felt the same way.

We all had our good days and bad days. I felt like the woman at the well described in John chapter 4 in the Bible. Jesus accepted her right where she was, and I knew Jesus accepted me right where I was too. I was the one who had to learn to accept my life. God was still molding me.

I filled some empty hours reading inspirational books written by Christian women. Each woman went through trials. Each one conquered her struggles because of her relationship with God. I remember my own past. There were times I would hang onto God for dear life when things were going bad, but when things were going good, I would release God and take matters into my own hands. Sitting in my living room one day, I figured that was my problem. I was only giving God part of myself instead of giving God all of me. I knew life would be a learning process, but I could not understand why I had to go through so much. I still wanted perfection in my life. I had to realize that I would never be perfect. Only God was perfect!

Colleen Townsend Evans wrote a book titled, A NEW JOY. It is a book written about the Beatitudes addressed specifically to woman. She refers to the humble woman, the sorrowing woman, the gentle woman, the fulfilled woman, and the suffering woman. Towards the end of the book she says "Happy is the woman who is used by the Lord to warm and enliven the human spirit...and whose life becomes her daily witness to His immeasurable goodness." [10] I wanted God to use me in any capacity that He could. As I sat there, I realized that the more I absorbed God into my life, the better off I would be. He was going to have to provide me with His strength. Then I would not shatter emotionally every time something went wrong. I did not know what God had planned for my future; however, with God's help, I knew I would get through it.

In 1981, my beloved Nana passed away in her sleep at the age of 84. I was thankful that my parents, Rick, and I went to visit her the day before she died. I felt blessed to have both my grandparents in my life for so long. Nana's death was hard for me. I did not know for sure if she was a Christian. I decided to talk to Pastor Butcher one day and he said, "Sharon, you're going to drive yourself crazy. You never know a person's heart at the time of their death. You witnessed to her for years. Sometimes that is all you can do. Then you must release your pain and trust God for the results." After we talked, we prayed together. Pastor Butcher always knew the right words to comfort me. He pointed me to Psalms 107:13, "Then they cried unto the Lord in their trouble, and he saved them out of their distresses." What a comfort that verse was to me.

I was so thankful for Pastor Butcher. He was always there when I needed him. After 27 years of ministering at Skyline Wesleyan Church, it was time for him to retire in 1981. To say Pastor Butcher was a mighty man for God is an understatement. Some 150 of Skyline's members went into Christian service. Forty-eight dedicated their lives to work with missions under his great leadership. When Skyline first opened its doors there were about 175 in attendance. When Pastor Butcher retired, the average attendance was 1,100 per Sunday. The church gave Pastor Butcher a great send-off, listing the many accomplishments that he made in our community and for his flock. It was heart wrenching to see him leave.

It took a very special man to take over when Pastor Butcher left. That man was Dr. John Maxwell, who became our senior pastor. The transition was wonderful. Our new pastor was a young man and a dynamic speaker. Everybody loved him. This transition went so well because Pastor Butcher gave Pastor Maxwell his blessings and encouraged his flock to make him feel welcome. Pastor Butcher said, "John Maxwell is on fire for Jesus." Every Sunday, you could see that was true.

In December of 1981, Rick had to have surgery again on both knees. The surgeon had to remove cartilage from time to time from both knee joints. Medical science was improving, so now the surgeon would perform Rick's surgery arthroscopically. By making four small incisions, Rick recovered more quickly. In most cases, once surgery was over, Rick was able to walk out of the hospital.

Rick's daughters finally graduated from high school. We were so proud of them. Rick's oldest daughter could have graduated in January, but waited for her sister so they could graduate together in June. That brought back memories when I waited for my brother. I must say, at the girls' graduation, they were the most beautiful girls there. Both planned to work after graduation; neither planned to attend college. My son, Neil, still struggled in school, but he was determined to get his high school diploma, no matter how long it took.

My son, David, moved out of our home in July of 1982. He rented from Mother and Daddy the house that Nana and Granddad had lived in. Our house was so quiet now you could hear a pin drop. Mother warned me about the empty nest syndrome. She was right. No longer were their children running in and out. I would always be my boys' mother, but I took on a different role now. Then I realized Rick's lifestyle did not change. He still got up early and went to work five days a week. I was the one whose life had changed. How I longed for the comings and goings of my children and their friends. I looked forward to Wednesdays even more now when the children would meet us at Mission Bay to water-ski.

In the fall of 1982, Rick came home from work and told me he would have to start traveling. I was disappointed to learn Rick would be gone one week a month to check government laboratories all over the world. This meant I would be by myself even more. I knew Rick had no choice. Every night I prayed and asked God, "What in the world was I going to do?" I knew I could not live with this empty feeling. I had to find a purpose in my life, but I did not know what to do. Then it hit me; maybe I should go back to work. I went to see my doctor. He said, "After having 17 cysts removed on the back of your left thigh, I feel you should not go back to work. Remember, in a work environment you will not be able to get out of your wheelchair as you do at home. Sitting in one position all day will only aggravate the situation." I did not like hearing what he had to say, but I had to agree with him.

I tried to change my attitude and consider this time a blessing. I would be able to spend more time with Rick in the evenings and weekends. For years, we gave ourselves to our children and others. Even though our children were all grown up now, I still had Rick who needed and appreciated me. Now would be the perfect time to concentrate on each other more. It was nice to share Saturdays together and not worry about getting home to fix dinner. We still enjoyed special times with our children and my parents. I knew I did not handle change well, but with God's help, I was learning. There was nothing in the Bible that said life was going to be a "bowl of cherries." My mind always reflected on Job in the Bible whenever I felt like having a pity-party. Job went through one trial after another; yet, Job knew God was by his side. I knew that to be true. Each day I would learn another lesson about my life as God continued to mold me.

In between our daily challenges, both Rick and I still endured more surgeries. By 1983 between Rick and me, we had more surgeries than anybody we knew. Then the bottom fell out again. I started having pain in both hands. I figured it was from overuse pushing my wheelchair for so many years. Then a burning sensation started waking me up in the middle of the night. My hands were my life, so I went to see a hand specialist immediately. He ran a bunch of tests on both hands and told me I had carpal tunnel in both wrists and needed surgery. He was adamant that I have the right hand done as soon as possible, but I could wait on the left hand because it was not as bad. In the meantime, I had to wear braces on both my hands, when I slept at night, to help the blood flow better.

Driving home from the doctor's office, I wanted to cry. I wondered how I would manage getting around my home. I did not have the use of my legs; and, now according to the doctor, I would not have the use of one hand for approximately eight weeks. I was scared to death. Transferring was going to be difficult and driving a car was out of the question. I would be housebound! I also thought about Rick. Obviously, I would need help or I would have to go to a rehabilitation center. As I pulled into the driveway, I started laughing. This too must be part of God's plan when Chuck came into my life. For years, I saw how Chuck managed with only the use of one hand. Because of our marriage, I knew ways Chuck compensated for his loss. At that very moment, I was so glad that I had my children when I was young. The thought of going through this surgery while caring for them would have been next to impossible.

When I got home, I called Mother. She could not believe my news. I reminded her that Rick was gone one week a month. The fear of totally being alone after my surgery, while Rick was gone, frightened me. Mother said she and Daddy could move in and take care of me when Rick was gone. Once again, my parents were right there willing to help. When Rick came home, I told him what the doctor and my parents said. He felt so bad that I had to have another surgery. He told me he would talk to his boss and see if they could cancel his business trips during my recuperation period. As tears streamed down my face, I thanked Rick for always being there for me and being so understanding. Rick reminded me of all the times I was there for him when he had surgery and said, "That's what husbands and wives do. They are there for each other in sickness and in health."

"We've really had our share of surgeries," I said. "Maybe these two hand surgeries will be the end for a while."

I had to wait two months before the doctor could get me on his schedule. This would give me plenty of time to practice getting around the house with one hand and getting organized. With everything in order, I knew I would feel better. To keep my mind off my upcoming hand surgery, I read a book written by Joni Eareckson, titled JONI. This book told of her struggle as a quadriplegic confined to a wheelchair. When I finished reading the detailed account of her accident and rehabilitation, my attitude changed. Here is a woman who would never be able to do many of the daily tasks that we take for granted. This would last a lifetime for Joni; I only had to worry about a minor inconvenience for eight weeks. With God's help and my family, I was going to get through this.

Before my hand surgery, I had my yearly check up on my spine. The news was not good. My spine was curving at a more rapid pace. This alarmed my orthopedic specialist. He felt I would need major back surgery in the near future. He told me not to worry, but to come in every six months instead of once a year. To look at me I appeared straight sitting in my wheelchair. I was not leaning to one side like some of my friends who had curvatures. The doctor showed me the x-rays and explained that I had a double curve. One curvature was side to side and the other was front to back. I appeared straight, but my body was shrinking from my neck to my hips. He said that eventually there would be no room for my vital organs, and my curvature could become life threatening. I had to put this out of my mind for now. My hand surgery had to take priority. In the spring of 1983, my hand surgery was over. I breathed a sigh of relief. With the support of my God, Rick, and those around me, my recuperation went relatively well. It was not easy, but God taught me endurance and my faith grew even stronger.

Almost a year later, I received a notice in the mail that the Wheelacade was going to have a reunion hosted by Red and Marene at a local park. I called right away to RSVP. When Marene answered the phone, I told her Rick and I would be attending. I also told her I joined the Post Polio Network (PPN) of San Diego County. This group consisted of post polio victims who were fighting for the rights of the disabled. They were also checking ongoing research regarding post polio syndrome. I encouraged her to talk to Red and see if they could join.

The Wheelacade reunion was on a beautiful sunny day in the summer of 1984. We visited for hours, ate, and even danced some square dance routines. Many members brought their children who got a kick out of watching their parents dance. Some polio victims now had post polio syndrome. They were scared to death. Some were experiencing abnormal fatigue, muscle weakness, headaches, and severe pain. Some that walked on crutches for years were now using wheelchairs full-time. Many saw their futures changing.

Going backwards made some have a complete attitude change; they felt cheated. One of the Wheelacade members brought in a news article, from the SAN DIEGO UNION that stated, "It strikes some polio victims 25 to 30 years after they initially contracted the disease. Its cause is unknown, and there is no known cure." [11]

I have been handicapped for 35 years. I felt lucky that my disability had not changed that much, except for my hands and my spine. I did not consider either was post polio syndrome. Before leaving, I announced to the group that Red and Marene had joined PPN of San Diego County. I asked others to do the same. We needed all the help we could get to continue the research regarding this terrible dilemma all of us might face in the years to come.

Later that night, I thought once again how easy it is to rejoice when things are going good. I learned it all comes down to choices. I could accept God's plan for my life, or condemn God for allowing things to happen to me. That was reaffirmed when I read "And not only so, but we glory in tribulations also, knowing that tribulation worketh patience; And patience, experience; and experience, hope; and hope maketh not ashamed because the love of God is shed abroad in our hearts by the Holy Spirit who is given unto us." Roman 5:3-5.

30

AN ATTITUDE ADJUSTMENT

Whenever I picked up a newspaper, there was something written about a person with a disability. Handicapped people were coming out of the woodwork and talking about their lives. The more accessibility people with disabilities had, the easier it was for them to leave their homes. I also noticed able-bodied people were starting to understand what people with disabilities had to deal with.

A friend of mine gave me a book she felt would be of interest to me. The book titled, JOB HUNTING FOR THE DISABLED. Attracting my attention was a passage that said, "We are all familiar with the great ones in history who, despite their handicapping conditions, achieved national and international recognition. Helen Keller, of course, comes immediately to mind, as does Franklin Delanor Roosevelt, our thirty-second president, crippled with polio. It is now believed that both Albert Einstein and Abraham Lincoln suffered from handicapping conditions; Einstein from learning disabilities, Lincoln from depression. When Beethoven was profoundly deaf, he wrote his most sublime music. The late Nelson Rockefeller, former New York State governor, had dyslexia, a problem affecting his ability to read." [12]

The same book also stated, "You're in the news almost daily. Authors use you as subjects for their award-winning books, plays and films. You're Terry Wiles playing yourself as a thalidomide victim in a TV dramatization. You're acting in 'Children of a Lesser God.' You're a Vietnam veteran in 'Coming Home.' Who are you? America's newest and one of its most vocal minorities - the disabled. You make up about 12% of the population, and your voice is being heard through the land as you vie for your place in work and leisure activities." [13]

After I finished reading this book, a light bulb went off in my head. Most books I had read were Christian books. I thought to myself, "What in the world, was God telling me now?" If I could not work outside my home, then writing would fill the many hours when I was alone. If other people with disabilities told their stories, then I could too. Maybe telling others about the challenges I faced would serve as a witness to how powerful God was in my life and could be in theirs.

For years, I kept journals/diaries of my innermost thoughts. Mother suggested I do this when I was only nine years old. I also kept yearly calendars with concise notes. I took hundreds of pictures and had them neatly kept in photo albums. I also saved notes from sermons, seminars, and books. There had to be a reason why I did this. I asked myself, "Could I write a book?" I prayed and asked God for guidance. I knew reliving my past would be hurtful. Maybe I could finally let go of some of the pain I still felt. I knew some wounds were still very raw, even after all these years. I knew I could not sit for eight hours all day in a work environment, so this seemed perfect. I could type for a while, lie down, proofread my work, and type some more. I prayed daily and looked at my electric typewriter as thoughts went through my mind. "Why did God give me such power in my hands? I could type over 120 wpm." I had to tell my story! I felt God was telling me to push forward.

I phoned Mother and told her about my idea. She was excited. I asked her if she would gather up all my polio information that she had saved and bring it over to my house the following day. When Rick came home, I told him my thoughts, and asked him if he would be embarrassed if I told my story. Rick said, "I would not be the least bit embarrassed. I am very proud of you. I think writing your story would heal you from past hurts and help others to learn about people with disabilities." With Rick's words of encouragement, I knew this was the right thing for me to do.

When Mother came over, we went through her box of various things that she saved from my polio years. While taking notes and reminiscing, we spent a lot of time crying which was therapeutic for both of us. It was hard for Mother to relive painful memories, but she did. Because of my mother, I was able to reconstruct the first nine years of my life that I still did not remember. God must have known years ago that both she and I needed to keep all this stuff. Without it, I would have never been able to write my book. During this time, Mother and I shared an even deeper bond than we already had.

After being with Mother for a few days, it was time to start typing. I went to the local stationery store and bought reams of paper. When I got home, I sat at my electric typewriter and started banging out one word at a time. Hours whizzed by and pretty soon Rick was home from work. This was a new adventure. Each day I would get up early, do my housework, take a shower, put myself together, and work on my book. My fingers were flying across the keys of my typewriter. As I finished each chapter, I read it, changed it, and retyped it repeatedly until I was satisfied. Pages started stacking up on my table. Maybe no one, besides my mother and Rick, would ever read my book, but I did not care. I believed with every inch of my being that God was using this writing to heal me. As I read each journal and put my thoughts and feelings into my book, I tossed my journals and diaries into the trash. I was giving each phase of my life to God. As I read every prayer, every comment, every thought, every feeling, I could see how God worked for years molding me into the person I was. The older I got, I learned how important it is to love; not just saying the words, but also expressing love daily to those around me.

While writing, I never cried so hard or laughed aloud so much. I could see God's remarkable power in a complete new way. I also had a new appreciation for my family. The love that my parents and grandparents showed me was truly my gift from God. I finally found something to fill my days during the week. Each day, when Rick came home from work he was in awe. My attitude changed; I had found a purpose again. When Rick saw my journals, diaries, and notes in the trash, I told him that was the "let go and let God" pile. Mother encouraged me to keep writing. As she read each chapter, she would cry or laugh aloud saying, "Oh, I remember when that happened." My book was already healing two souls: Mother and me.

After Rick had two additional knee surgeries and I had my left hand operated on, it was time to rejoice. In May of 1985, Neil graduated from high school in Utah. It took him longer to accomplish his goal, but he did it! We could not have been prouder. We found comfort in the Bible, where it states, "Even the youths shall faint and be weary, and the young men shall utterly fall, But they that wait upon the Lord shall renew their strength; they shall mount up with wings like eagles; they shall run, and not be weary; and they shall walk, and not faint." Isaiah 40:30-31. What a mighty God we have. Neil later attended college.

For the first time, in a long time, I was genuinely happy. I quit waiting for the other shoe to drop as I had for so long. I was thankful for every day. That same year Rick and I celebrated 15 years of marriage. We took a trip to Las Vegas and then up to Utah to see Neil. Rick and I were as close today as we were the day we got married. We had been blessed with many good days and conquered many challenges. Through it all, He was there.

Shortly after our anniversary, Rick's oldest daughter married her high school sweetheart. Tears of joy filled my eyes as I watched Rick walk his daughter down the aisle in the church that day. She glowed in her beautiful wedding gown that we had purchased for her. Afterwards, at the reception, tears flowed again as I watched Rick dance with his daughter. She had tears in her eyes too.

After coming home, I said to Rick, "One child down and three to go."

"This was a very emotional day," Rick said.

"To see you walk your daughter down the aisle and then dance with her at the reception was extraordinary. I too will never forget this day."

Shortly after, Rick flew to Washington State to celebrate his parents' 50th wedding anniversary. I wanted to go, but Rick's parents moved into a new house that had a flight of stairs leading to their front door. Because of Rick's recent knee surgeries, I did not want him pulling me up and down those stairs in my wheelchair. I reassured Rick that I would not be upset. I reminded him that I just saw his parents at the wedding. This would be the perfect time for me to finish writing my book.

When I finally finished my book, I felt very proud of myself. This book had served its purpose in three major ways: God healed me from many hurts. God helped me to forgive others and myself. God helped me accept the mistakes I made and not feel guilty anymore. I put my book in a box and put it on a shelf in my closet. Later that night, while I was doing my Bible study, I read, "His lord said unto him, Well done, thou good and faithful servant; thou hast been faithful over a few things, I will make thee ruler over many things. Enter thou into the joy of thy lord." Matthew 25:21.

After Rick and I ate dinner, I told him that I had finished my book and put it away in the closet. Rick said, "I am very proud of you. As long as you feel good, that is all that matters. You are definitely a changed person. Do you remember the plaque I gave you on our 10th wedding anniversary?"

"Yes, of course. It still hangs on the wall in our bedroom."

"Let's go look at it and read it together," Rick suggested, "because that is what I have been telling you for years. I am glad that you are finally starting to believe it yourself."

The plaque reads:

> BELIEVE ME
> YOU ARE A TRUE FIND,
> A JOY IN SOMEBODY'S HEART.
> YOU ARE A JEWEL, UNIQUE AND PRICELESS.
> I DON'T CARE HOW YOU FEEL.
> BELIEVE ME,
> GOD DON'T MAKE NO JUNK!

(Distributed by Ogunquit, Costa Mesa, California)

Toward the end of 1985, Rick talked to me about starting a consulting business that we could run out of the house. Some men at work broached Rick about running golf tournaments. Because I finished my book, Rick felt that I could help by calling golf courses in the San Diego area to book tournaments and to set-up T-times. Before we started, Rick needed to get a business license, buy a computer, and teach me how to use it. He also made it clear to the men that we would run their tournaments, but not on Sundays because we went to church. We met some great men and even had the opportunity to witness to some of them about our faith. There is no greater joy than leading a soul to Christ and watching them grow in their faith. My life was moving now in yet another direction. As long as I felt I had a purpose in life, I was content.

A few months later, David received his Bachelor of Science Degree in Business, with an emphasis in Finance, from San Diego State University. We gave him a huge graduation party, including family and friends. Chuck and Neil came from Utah. Chuck reminded me how important his government benefits were in helping pay for David's education. Now, all our children had achieved the goals they had set for their education. We were very proud of all of them.

One evening, Rick got a brainstorm and shared it with me. "I would like to take the front two bedrooms and bathroom and convert that area into a huge master bedroom suite with a walk-in closet. Then we could use our old bedroom as an office and the back bedroom for guests."

"Sounds like a great idea. It would give us more room too when I have to have back surgery. Remember, the doctor said that I might have to use a hospital bed for a while after I come home."

"So, I guess the question is should we do it?" Rick asked.

"It is up to you. You will be doing all the work. How long will it take?"

"Not long. I think I can handle it in a relatively short period of time."

"If you want to do it, let's go for it."

In between working at NARF, working on the new room, and running golf tournaments, Rick was extremely busy. He even added some new clients to the business. I enjoyed helping him as much as I could. Staying busy and feeling needed kept my attitude in check. God was making sure that with my newfound attitude I would start to feel better about myself and continue to grow in my faith.

In October of 1986, Rick's oldest daughter gave birth to his first grandchild, a girl. I was in the delivery room with her when she gave birth because her mother was stuck on a houseboat on Lake Mead in Nevada and unable to get back in time. I never witnessed anything so beautiful in my life.

Not long after that, Mother and Daddy went to see the doctor. Daddy was acting strange for quite a few years and was starting to forget things. When Mother later told us that Daddy had Alzheimer's, we were in shock. "How could this happen to my daddy?" I thought. The news was heart wrenching. Along with our help, Mother became Daddy's caregiver. As we watched Daddy decline, we wanted to have my parents and their children together one last time. This meant I would have to fly to Pittsburgh, Pennsylvania, along with Rick and my parents, to be with my brother and his family. I was afraid to fly. I heard horror stories from my friends at the Wheelacade. One incident involved both Red and Marene who were both in wheelchairs. They flew to Chicago; their wheelchairs landed in New York City. For three days, they had to rent wheelchairs until theirs arrived. There was nothing more frightening than to have your "legs" taken away, even temporarily. Knowing this was scary enough.

Then when I called the airline, they informed me that I could not use the bathroom while we were in flight for six hours! They said they would help me to my seat and put my wheelchair in the baggage compartment. The thought of having my "legs" taken away caused me a lot of stress, but I was determined to go.

The morning of our flight, I could feel my insides shaking because I knew I could not use the bathroom on the plane. This seemed so unfair. I was terrified that my colitis would kick in. To try to help the situation, I had nothing to eat or drink for 24 hours prior to boarding the plane. I felt like I was preparing for major surgery instead of taking a joyful trip to see my brother and his family. No matter what it took, we had to get Mother, Daddy, and their twins together.

When the plane landed, my heart soared as the flight attendant actually brought me my very own wheelchair. To have my wheelchair and me both land at the same airport, no less, was an answer to a prayer. Nothing pleased me more than getting off the plane that day. After being on the plane for over six hours, the very first thing I did was wheel at a high rate of speed to the closest bathroom!

As we left the airport, the anticipation of seeing my brother consumed me. I was so excited! When we finally arrived at their house, my brother and his family ran out to greet us. To see my brother and his family again was a joy. My nephews were all grown-up. It did not seem possible so many years had passed by so quickly. Knowing he still worked full-time at the University, I laughed when I saw my brother sitting on top of his tractor farming his land. "Was this my brother?" I thought. I could not believe my eyes. We spent five wonderful days together.

Mother and Daddy flew back to San Diego ahead of us. We stayed on because Rick had some meetings in Washington, DC. Once his meetings were over, we traveled through 13 eastern States. We saw many places of interest. For a woman like me, who only traveled through eight States and Canada, this trip was quite an experience. We actually drove through New Jersey, where I was born, but nothing jogged my memory. To be able to go up inside the Statue of Liberty astounded me. To drive through Hershey, Pennsylvania and smell chocolate throughout the entire town made my mouth water. We also traveled through the Amish country. To see people riding in black horse-drawn buggies down the streets was like traveling back in time. To drive through Washington, DC and see the Capital and the various monuments to past Presidents amazed me. To drive by Arlington National Cemetery and many of the other monuments around the Capital gave me a real sense of history.

Because of my disability, we experienced many challenges on this trip. I understood what my disabled friends meant when they said, "Back East is not very wheelchair friendly." That was an understatement. Nevertheless, I did not want to go home. I knew I had to board a plane to do so. When we landed in San Diego, I told Rick I would never fly again. He understood. Not being able to use the bathroom was the worst. All I could pray for was that the airlines would make changes in the future to make it easier for disabled passengers to fly.

After arriving home and recovering from jet lag, I heard Pastor John Maxwell wrote a book titled, YOUR ATTITUDE: KEY TO SUCCESS. In the book, Pastor Maxwell did not just talk about problems, but gave distinct solutions on how we could change our attitude. Pastor Maxwell wrote, "Many intelligent adults...are restrained in thoughts, actions and results. They never move further than the boundaries of their self-imposed limitations." [14] Pastor Maxwell also wrote, "Accepting failure in the positive sense becomes effective when you believe that the right to fail is as important as the right to succeed." [15] Those words, "right to fail" and "right to succeed" hit me hard. I always thought I could not fail; and, if I did, then there was something wrong with me. It was my attitude that needed changing. Finally, yet importantly, he wrote, "It is impossible to succeed without suffering." [16] That last statement was so true in my life. I suffered plenty, but God was faithful and brought me through everything I had to endure. Emotionally, physically, and spiritually I was growing. By the sheer grace of God, my attitude was changing; and, I was becoming a happier, healthier woman. Daily I prayed, from Psalms 51:10, "Create in me a clean heart, O God, and renew a right spirit within me."

31

THE EXPECTED HAPPENS

Right after we came home from back East, I faced a crisis. The curvature of my spine became life threatening. My orthopedic surgeon told me I needed surgery right away. Putting myself totally in God's hands, I had the eight-hour surgery. My orthopedic surgeon inserted a 3/8" metal rod that went from just above my shoulders to my hips. I grew four inches. For one year, I would have to wear an orthopaedic brace made out of hard plastic that went from above my breasts to my crotch. We knew this was going to be a rough year. I was trying to keep my attitude in check. At times that was hard. We were so thankful that Rick had converted the front two bedrooms into a master suite. I had to use a hospital bed, so at least we were in the same bedroom. Rick was by my side, every step of the way. I could not drive for a year. The first month was hard until I found new ways to care for myself in the brace. Rick's boss allowed him to work at home, so I would not be alone for the first six weeks.

Seven weeks after my surgery, I managed to get fully dressed. I had a wedding to attend. David was getting married. His fiancée was a gem and came from a large, close-knit family. She had a son from a previous marriage, so Rick and I became instant step-grandparents. To witness my first-born marry was thrilling. At David's wedding, Mother and Daddy were sitting with us, and Mother remarked, "It seems like yesterday we brought David home from the hospital and look at him now!"

"I feel the same way. He is all grown up, and looks so happy dancing with his wife."

"You will never forget this day," Mother said.

Two years later, my youngest son, Neil called to tell us he had eloped with a woman he met in Utah. She had two children, a boy and a girl, from a previous marriage. This meant we had more step-grandchildren. Neil and his wife had planned a small reception to give all of us the opportunity to meet her and her children. Our family was definitely expanding. Rick and I felt a special bond with all our new family members.

A few months later, Neil called to tell me his wife was expecting. I was going to be a grandmother. I was thrilled! I needed some happiness in my life. This could not have happened at a better time. Over the past couple of years, Daddy's mind was deteriorating. My heart was broken daily watching Daddy slowly withdraw. Rick and I continued to help Mother. We eventually talked Mother into getting a live-in nurse/housekeeper to help her. Mother was beside herself with sadness. Some days Daddy did not know who she was and often told her to leave saying, "You better leave before my wife gets home." It was hard to watch Daddy brush his mustache instead of his teeth with a toothbrush. At times, he would start to eat a paper plate rather than the pizza on top of it. Many of my parents' friends stopped visiting. Just when my mother needed them the most, they stayed away and eventually they stopped calling. Knowing Daddy was not going to be with us much longer, my brother flew to California to spend as much time with us as he could.

These marriages and my brother's visit helped bring joy into months of sadness. If it were not for God, I do not know what we would have done. In May of 1990, Neil called to tell us his wife gave birth to a baby girl. As soon as we could, Rick and I drove to Utah to see my granddaughter. Two weeks later Rick's oldest daughter gave birth to another child, a boy.

I praised God that we traveled when we did. A few months later, I felt like somebody stabbed me in the back with a knife. I called Rick at work and he came home immediately and took me to the emergency room. After taking x-rays, my orthopedic surgeon said the 3/8" metal rod broke inside of me. I needed emergency surgery. I could not believe this was happening. I had only been out of my brace for nine months. After surgery, the doctor told me the fusion looked good, except between my shoulder blades. When he took out the broken rod, he put in two rods about three inches long between my shoulders. I was glad I did not have to wear a brace again. I could not thank God enough for having Rick by my side. I do not know what I would have done without him.

One afternoon, I went to our bedroom to read my Bible. For whatever reason, I thanked God that Chuck and I got divorced. Physically, Chuck was going downhill. Even though Chuck and his new wife lived in Utah, Chuck spent many months in the Long Beach Veteran's Hospital in Long Beach, California. His diabetes got so bad that he had to have multiple amputations; eventually both of his legs were gone. With all our physical problems, there would have been no way for us to take care of each other. I thanked God for all the decisions He made on my behalf. Chuck and I stayed close talking on the phone. He had recently married a nurse that he had met at the hospital. Later, I read in my Bible, "For I know the thoughts that I think toward you, saith the Lord, thoughts of peace, and not of evil, to give you an expected end." Jeremiah 29:11. God knew because of our disabilities,

Chuck and I would need help. God in His wisdom brought special people into our lives, not only as our spouses, but as our caregivers too.

A few months later, I called my son, Neil. I told him Pappy was failing; I wanted the family together. Within a few days, Neil and his family arrived. This visit was joyous and sad at the same time. I still remember my daddy looking down into his great-granddaughter's eyes and saying "Ah" with a big smile on his face. It was one of those treasured memories only God supplies when you need it the most.

A month later, we had to move Daddy into an Alzheimer's care facility. Keeping him at home was too hard on Mother, emotionally and physically. Daddy was a big man: 6'2" tall, 200 pounds. I was scared to death, caring for Daddy would kill my mother. I told her if she did not slow down, I would be burying her before Daddy. Mother, Rick, and I visited Daddy daily. On one visit, I noticed that when Daddy saw me, his eyes lit-up. Then he pointed to his wheelchair and then to mine. It was as if he were saying, "I'm in a wheelchair now just like you." To see my daddy like this was heart breaking. Being in a wheelchair was nothing compared to Daddy losing his memory. I would not want to change places with him for anything. Daddy's quality of life was gone. He needed to be with Jesus. Daddy only lasted four months. Two weeks before Thanksgiving, he passed away at the age of 75. This was hard for our family; but, in a sense, it was a blessing. To this day, I thank God that my daddy did not suffer. To say my mother was beside herself with grief was an understatement. Nothing either Rick or I did or said comforted her. She was like a lost puppy. Ever since Daddy retired, they were rarely apart except on Wednesdays when Daddy played golf and Mother cleaned house. Mother thanked Rick and me for helping her. We told her we were glad we could be there for her. Once again, I felt another family member was on vacation; respecting Daddy wishes, we never had a service. After seeing her mother and her husband in a "home," Mother feared that would happen to her. Rick and I promised her we would never let that happen.

Rick came home from work one day and said, "Sharon, you are not going to believe this! The government has asked me to relocate to Washington DC. They gave me two options: I can either relocate or take an early retirement."

"I was in Washington, DC when we visited my brother. I cannot imagine living there in a wheelchair, especially during the winter," I replied.

After much prayer and discussion, Rick opted for the latter.

Five years ago, God knew this was going to happen when Rick started the small business. Now Rick could expand the business and work out of the house. Every evening, during our prayer time, we thanked God for watching over us. When we did not know what our future held, God did!

When Rick retired, he set his own hours. We were able to travel more, and Mother went with us on every trip. People called us "The Three Musketeers." Traveling was good for us. The loss of Granddad, Nana, and then Daddy still weighed heavily on our hearts.

I loved seeing new and different places. By now, we had traveled through 27 States. Rick said many times "Sharon, I want you to see as much as possible before you die. I know we will have challenges along the way, but with the Americans with Disabilities Act of 1990 (ADA), things should start getting easier for every person with a disability." No matter what obstacles we faced, we were determined not to let them stop us from traveling. We came across many motels who advertised wheelchair accessibility, but when we got there, they were not. No matter how many times I would ask questions when making reservations, it did not seem to matter. I soon learned many managers had no concept about what people confined to wheelchairs needed. I had to laugh one day. I had called to make a reservation and asked, "Are there grab bars in the shower and by the toilet?" The girl responded by saying, "What are those?" That was my first clue not to stay there.

Even though Rick never advertised, he kept adding clients to his small business. Rick handled many clients' accounts that raised money for various charities around San Diego. After three years, he had over 40 clients. One of his clients was Marie Chapian, a well-known Christian author and speaker. We filled her book and tape orders. Marie planned to write a book called MOTHERS AND DAUGHTERS. She interviewed Mother and me for one of the chapters called "Heaven's Special Child." This chapter told about our special bond. We were in awe when Marie handed each of us an autographed copy of her book.

A couple of years later, the three of us, Mother, Rick, and, I decided to leave California and move to Las Vegas, Nevada. We figured if we sold Mother's two houses, our house, and the business, we could pool our money together and buy one home big enough for all of us. Mother hated living by herself. We often took trips to Las Vegas, and we all liked it there. It seemed like a good choice because we would be located between California and Utah, so we could visit our children and grandchildren. After looking at all the pros and cons, we contacted a realtor.

We made a trip to Las Vegas and found the ideal house; it was 3,000 square feet. The builder was willing to make changes for my special needs. He also agreed to take the front two bedrooms and one bath and make that area into a mother-in-law's quarters with a mini-kitchen. Mother would also have her own private entrance. Mother was thrilled. We thanked God for directing us to this house and builder. We made an offer, left, and went home. Within three months, we moved to Las Vegas and started a new adventure.

One month after moving, Rick's youngest daughter got married. God blessed each of our children with wonderful spouses. All four of our children were married now and all, but one, had children. They had their spouses to lean on now. Our children knew we were there for them if they needed us.

In August of 1992, my brother came to Las Vegas for a visit. It was good to see him. It was during this visit he told us that he had filed for divorce. We were shocked and saddened by his news. Rick and I knew first hand what going through a divorce meant. The day my brother Neil left, I told him, "You have got to come back and go swimming in our new pool. It should be done in a couple of months."

"I will. I had a great time. I promise to keep in touch," Neil said to Mother and me, as he hopped into Rick's car, so Rick could drive him to the airport.

After my brother's visit, Mother, Rick, and I continued to travel. Throughout Nevada there were many museums and ghost towns. We also made occasional trips to California and Utah to see family and friends. Coming home was a treat because our in-ground pool and spa were finished. Our back yard looked like a show place with desert landscaping and many palm trees. We all loved to swim and to sit for hours in the spa. Even though Mother still missed Daddy, she was doing much better. Our main objective was keeping Mother busy so that she had less time to think. When our children visited, they, along with their children, enjoyed swimming and sharing in family barbecues.

In November of 1992, Mother and I were out shopping when suddenly she felt dizzy. She went to the car to lie down while I checked us out of the store. When we got home, I told Rick we needed to take Mother to a doctor, but she put up quite a fuss. She vowed when she was 65 years old, she would never go back to another doctor. She did not want to know if something was wrong. After a lot of prodding, I finally convinced Mother to let me call a doctor. After the initial visit, the doctor admitted Mother into the hospital for tests. After the test results were in, the doctor told us that Mother had pancreatic cancer. He gave her only three to six months to live. We were devastated. We had only moved here four months ago. We were having so much fun. How could I ever face losing my mother? We were soul mates. I knew nobody who had a mother/daughter relationship as close as ours. After hearing the diagnosis, Mother and I hugged each other and cried for hours. I assured her that we would take her home. We could see the relief on her face. Before we left the hospital, we spoke to a Hospice representative to gain knowledge about what we were facing. The doctor also arranged to have nurses come to our home three times a week.

Once we got everything in order, Mother came home. I called my brother, but he said that after just being here, he did not want to come back. He wanted to remember Mother the way she was. He promised to come back next summer. It was hard for Rick and me to watch Mother go downhill. Mother always took such great pride in her appearance. I think that was a throwback to her modeling days. Every day she would put her makeup on and was fully dressed. She was the most beautiful Mother in the world. Now she looked different; she appeared drawn and jaundice. All we could hope for was she would not suffer long. Mother felt embarrassed because we had to care for all her personal needs. I reminded her of all the years that she had taken care of me. Now it was my turn to take care of her. The doctor prescribed morphine patches for her terrible pain. David, Neil, and their families came to see their Ammy during Christmas. They knew this would be their last Christmas with her. This was much different from the Christmas celebrations we celebrated in the past.

A few days after Mother turned 75, in January of 1993, Hospice told us Mother would not last much longer. The next three weeks broke my heart. Seeing my mother like this, who cared for me throughout my childhood and into my adulthood, was killing me. To watch her lay in her hospital bed, in her bedroom, waiting for God to take her home was almost too much for Rick and me to bear. I was so thankful Rick was with me. Mother was not going to leave this earth peacefully; she was going to fight right up to the end.

One day, Mother said, "I don't want to leave you, Sharon."

"Mother, it is okay. Rick is here. He'll take care of me," I responded, with tears streaming down my face.

Rick added, "Helene, I will take care of your daughter forever."

"Hear that?" I asked. "Rick will take care of me. He always has. You have to go be with Daddy. He is waiting for you in heaven. Nana and Granddad are waiting too. You told me there is no pain in heaven. You will be at peace. You will be with your loved ones, and later I will join you."

"But I don't want to leave you!" Mother said, raising her voice, hanging onto my arm.

"I don't want you to go either. You are everything to me. You have been there with me through thick and thin. If I had my way, you'd be with me forever." With those words, my mother fell off to sleep.

For three days, I never left my mother's side. She hung onto my arm not wanting me to leave. When my dear sweet mother took her last breath, I was holding her gently in my arms. She was gone. She was at peace. She would be with our Lord. She would suffer no more. Mother was there when I came into this world; and, thankfully, I was able to keep my promise and be with her when she left. At that moment, I totally fell apart! I had been strong for her, but now every emotion that I had held inside for weeks came rushing to the surface. As the funeral attendant wheeled her body out, I cried hysterically. I could not stop! My body shook from head to toe. It was the worst thing that ever happened to me. Granddad, Nana, and Daddy were gone and now Mother. "What in the world am I going to do?" I cried out while Rick tried to console me. Rick called Hospice and two people came over right away. They tried to comfort me, but nobody could. Rick told them that Mother and I had a special bond because of my disability. He was right.

That afternoon, I called David and Neil to let them know Ammy passed away. They came as soon as they found sitters for their children. Seeing my boys helped. I also called my brother. My mother's ashes were scattered at sea off Port Loma, California, where Granddad, Nana, and Daddy's ashes were scattered as well. Now Mother was with her parents and her husband. I never had the chance to go to a funeral service for Mother, Daddy, Nana or Granddad. That left me feeling empty inside. My only consolation was I knew I would see them again in heaven.

After the boys and their wives left, I felt numb for weeks. My colitis kicked in with a vengeance. I was a mess both physically and emotionally. I wanted out of this house. Why

God took my mother so soon after we moved here, I would never understand. Hospice counseled me and told me this was not the time to move or make any major decisions; I needed time to grieve.

As each day passed, I was getting sicker. That brought back all those horrible memories that I had when Chuck and I were married. I finally gave in and went to see my doctor. He referred me to an internist. After running tests, the internist said I no longer had colitis; instead, I had Irritable Bowel Syndrome (IBS). He said that I probably had IBS for years because IBS mostly kicks in under stress or eating the wrong foods.

The first Mother's Day after my mother's death, I was sick again for two weeks. This time, I knew why, but I could do nothing to bring my mother back. I wondered if I would ever be the same again. I tackled each day the best way I could. I missed all my family members, but the loss of my mother was the hardest.

One evening, I talked at length with Rick. I felt so guilty being sick again. He told me it was not my fault; I was going through a rough time. He knew, as I did, that getting over the death of my mother would take years. I had to find a way to accept what I could not change. I had to learn to go on without my mother. That was going to be my hardest lesson to learn. That night, I prayed, "Lord Jesus, please be with me. I am so far down. I need You more than ever. Losing my mother has taken its toll on me. I pray that You will help me accept this terrible loss. Please take care of my family for me in heaven. Amen."

32

LIFE GOES ON

After losing Mother, it took me weeks to calm my insides down and get my emotions in check. I had been through a lot in my life, but this was the worst. My mood swings were all over the place. One day, Rick came to me and said, "I know the loss of your mother has hit you hard, but life goes on. Helene would not want you sitting around the house everyday thinking about her and making yourself sick. We cannot bring your mother back. Now that you are feeling better, we need to start traveling again."

"I know you're right, but I have been so afraid to leave the house. Now that my IBS seems somewhat better, I would like to try. Traveling might help me."

We traveled to California and Utah to see our children and grandchildren, and Rick's parents in Washington State. We also traveled to Texas to see my friend Connie and her husband from the Wheelacade. It did me good to get away, but I always knew when I returned home that Mother would not be there. That was still hard to accept.

A few months later, we finally heard some good news. Rick's youngest daughter and her husband were now proud parents of their first child, a girl. We were thrilled!

In September 1993, David called to let us know that he and his family were leaving California and moving to Washington State. He received a job opportunity he could not pass up. I was very proud of David, but sad he would be moving so far away. Trying to lift my spirits, Rick told me to look at David's move as a perfect excuse for us to travel more now to see him.

Later that same year, Rick's parents decided to move to Las Vegas. Rick's mother had suffered a stroke. The wet weather in Washington State and the flight of stairs leading to their home made it harder for Lucille to manage. Their move to Las Vegas was an answer to our prayers. Once they moved, we had more opportunities to see Rick's girls and their families when they came to visit their grandparents.

Just when things were settling down, the bottom fell out again. We received a call in the middle of the night from Rick's dad. Lucille was on her way to the emergency room; she had suffered another stroke. By the time Rick and his father, George, arrived at the hospital, Lucille had lapsed into a coma. Ten days later, she was gone. Rick lost his mother 13 months after I lost mine. We were so thankful Rick's dad lived close by after suffering this terrible loss.

Over the next few years, our home felt like a motel. We had so much company. Everybody stayed in my mother's quarters. We enjoyed visiting, swimming, and going to shows on the Las Vegas Strip. My disabled friends loved staying with us because our home was wheelchair accessible. Our house was better equipped than most motels. Having people around helped Rick and me too. One night, I was sitting in our spa thinking about Mother. It was as though, at that very moment, Mother was reassuring me that we had made the right decision moving here. This same feeling returned to me when my son, Neil, and his wife decided to sell their home in Utah and move to Las Vegas. Neil lived with us for six weeks. Once their house in Utah sold, his family would move in with us until they found a place to rent in Las Vegas.

Shortly after Neil and his family found their own place, Rick and I had to have more surgeries. Rick continued having knee surgeries and a shoulder scoped. I had three shoulder surgeries for rotator cuff tears. These shoulder surgeries were not difficult, but the physical therapy that followed was grueling and painful. It took six months to get the use of my shoulders back after each surgery. To save my shoulders, we finally did what my doctor had recommended. We bought two wheelchairs: a lightweight one to use in the house and an electric one to use when I went out. I had to learn new ways of doing things. I could no longer "hop" up on the arm of my wheelchair to reach high things; I used a grabber now. We also had to purchase a van with a side lift. I would never be able to fold-up my wheelchair and put it in the back seat of my car again.

My brother continued to come to Las Vegas, but now he would bring his girlfriend. Every time they came, we would get up early, eat breakfast, pack a lunch, and go to Lake Mead to water-ski. Since I could not water-ski, Neil bought a huge inner tube to pull me behind the boat. What a joke! There I was, hanging on for dear life, screaming bloody murder with my legs flying all over the place. Each evening, we took in a show on the Las Vegas Strip. In July of 1996, Neil was married in Jamaica. It did my heart good to know my brother was happy.

Rick's dad continued to come over almost daily. We encouraged him to move in with us, but he refused. The three of us traveled as often as we could. When Rick's girls came to visit, they helped their grandfather's loneliness by staying with him, so he could enjoy his grandchildren and great grandchildren. At 84, George started dating. At age 85, he married and moved back to Washington State.

In August 1997, we decided to leave Las Vegas because 1.5 million people were living there now, compared to 800,000 when we came. We purchased 2.5 acres of land about 60 miles northwest of Las Vegas, in a rural town called Pahrump, a peaceful place with hardly any traffic. The town had an urgent care clinic, but no hospital; only plans to build one. There we had our dream house built that we had been designing for years. We felt God had planned this too; our escrow closed on January 9, 1998, which would have been my mother's birthday. We were also excited to find a very small church in Pahrump that was wheelchair accessible. We got to know everybody and made some long, lasting friendships.

Shortly after being married 30 years, Rick's left knee gave out completely. He had to have more surgery, a total knee replacement. Three months later the implant fell apart. Rick had to have the surgery redone. Rick went through months of therapy before he could use his knee again. We continued to go to God in prayer. We thanked God for providing us the strength to care for each other, but we were getting weary. By this time, I had 29 surgeries and Rick had 16.

In 2001, my son David applied for a job at a company called Paratransit Services, a private, nonprofit, company headquartered in Bremerton, Washington. This company provided transportation for the disabled! I was thrilled! David would definitely be an asset to Paratransit Services. He knew, first hand from me, the many challenges of disabled travelers.

During our years in Pahrump, I also heard from many of my friends from high school and the Wheelacade telling me their spouses had passed away. My best girlfriend in high school, Karen, lost her husband to lung cancer. My girlfriend, Marjorie, who led me to the Lord, lost her husband from asbestos poisoning of the lungs. How these women handled their losses I will never know. I felt blessed I still had my husband. My biggest fear was, "What would I do if Rick died and I was the one left behind?" I prayed every night, "God, please do not take Rick from me." Then one day, my son, Neil, called to let me know that Chuck had died. The last time I had talked to Chuck, he told me his diabetes was getting worse and he no longer had legs due to multiple amputations. Chuck was ready to be with Jesus. Chuck was in the hospital four of his final five years. I was grateful that Chuck did not die alone. His wife, a nurse, was with him until the end.

The longer we lived in Pahrump, population of 30,000, the more we noticed that many businesses did not comply with the laws set down by the Americans with Disability Act (ADA). After praying, Rick and I decided to check every business and compile a list of the laws that each was violating. We gave the list to the Sheriff's office and the Town Board. Some businesses were very appreciative; some could care less. At least we tried.

Between being involved with friends and church activities, we continued to travel. I felt blessed to have my wheelchair accessible van with my own portable potty. This was a dream come true. Rick always joked saying, "Have porta-potty, will travel." I did not have to worry if a public bathroom was wheelchair accessible anymore. I did not have to clean public toilets either. For many years, I had carried surgical gloves and disinfectant in my purse to clean the "rim" of the toilet, before "transferring" onto it. I could not sit on the "seat" because most seats wobbled when I pulled my pants either up or down. During one of our travels, I also had a tire come off my wheelchair and had trouble finding a repair shop. That was enough for me. Ever since that happened, we have always carried a spare wheelchair.

Over the next few years, Rick and I had more medical problems. The clinic closed its doors and Pahrump still did not have a hospital. This meant we had to travel to Las Vegas for almost all of our medical needs. In 2004, Flight for Life flew Rick to Las Vegas. His doctor diagnosed, incorrectly, that he was having a heart attack. I was scared to death! Driving to Las Vegas took over an hour. Three years previously, I had torn my right shoulder again and could not drive long distances. David came to my rescue and flew down from Washington State to drive me to and from the hospital until Rick came home.

In January of 2005, it was my turn. I had to spend ten days in the hospital in Las Vegas. I had double viral pneumonia. I almost died! Confined to a wheelchair was hard enough. Now I went home with two large oxygen tanks with 55 feet of tubing. We placed the tanks in our entry hall. Locating them here allowed me to stay attached to the oxygen and still be able to maneuver in my wheelchair throughout the house.

As soon as I no longer needed to use oxygen, Rick and I had a serious talk. We realized over the last ten months, we had made over 100 trips to Las Vegas for our medical care. More than anything, else, we needed medical care close by. Once again, we prayed. Right when we were praying, the phone rang. It was David. He called to tell us he was now President of Paratransit Services. We were so proud of him! During our conversation, we told David we had to move. David suggested we check out the Tri-Cities in Washington State. He said the area was high desert and got very little rain; winters were cold, including moderate snowfall.

After spending hours on the Internet, we contacted a realtor in the Tri-Cities. Once our realtor found some houses for us to look at, we called David to let him know we were heading north. He said he and his wife would come over on the weekend; they lived about four hours away. We made reservations, packed our suitcases, loaded our van, and off we went.

It was April. With spring in the air, everything was blooming. The colors were magnificent. Just before reaching the Tri-Cities, we were amazed at the outskirts, a combination of apple and cherry orchards and endless miles of farmland. We also saw acres of grapes growing on the vine. Wine was a commodity here.

On our first full day in the Tri-Cities, we drove all over the area. The Tri-Cities consisted of three small towns: Kennewick, Pasco, and Richland. The next day our search began. We were not having any luck until we drove to the last house on the realtor's list. As we approached the house, we noticed an open house sign out front. As I wheeled to the front door, I noticed there were no steps. After going inside, I noticed there were no steps anywhere and all the doorways were 36 inches wide. Rick and I were amazed at how accommodating this house was for my wheelchair and it was brand new. Caring for this home would be easier on me too; it was only 2,200 square feet, and we still had four bedrooms and two bathrooms. With Rick's bad knees, not having 2.5 acres to care for was a huge plus. That same day, we met with the builder and told him the things we needed done in the house to make it even more wheelchair accessible. The main problem was carpet. I needed the carpet taken up in all four bedrooms and replaced with tile to make it easier for me to push my manual wheelchair.

The following day, we met with the realtor and the builder. God worked out every detail, including a quick escrow, so we could purchase this house. Medical proximity was perfect. All the doctors and hospitals were within ten miles from our new house. Shopping was right down the street. We knew God was telling us this was where we belonged.

The next day David and his wife arrived. The first order of business was to show them the house we bought. They loved it! Then the four of us spent that weekend driving around taking in the sites. Three rivers run through the Tri-Cities: the Columbia, the Snake, and the Yakima. One afternoon we went to Columbia River Park to feed the ducks and geese. They ate bread right out of my hand. Sitting there, we watched people fish from the bank. I could see Rick drooling already. This would be the perfect place for him to fish and hunt. I wanted Rick, who had cared for me for so many years, to be able to do things that he only dreamed. All four of us had an enjoyable weekend. Rick and I looked forward to getting back to Pahrump so that we could contact a moving company, pack our things, put our house on the market, and move.

Before leaving Pahrump, we called and visited as many friends and family as time allowed. When the day came to move, we left our home in the capable hands of a realtor. Traveling north, we reminisced about our honeymoon. Almost 35 years ago, we had driven through Washington State on our way to Canada. Now we were heading back to Washington State to start a new adventure, in our brand new house, in a new town.

Upon arriving, we stayed in a motel, and waited for the moving company to deliver our belongings. It took three months to get the inside of our new home done, and the back yard landscaped, including fencing. Later that same year Rick had a shop built, so he could tinker. We felt blessed.

After residing in our new home for less than a year, all good things came to an end! Rick woke up one morning coughing up blood. I drove him to the emergency room. He had blood clots in his lungs and a clot in his left leg. The doctor thought this happened because he had shoulder surgery ten days prior. The doctor told me these blood clots were very serious; Rick could die! Rick had to stay in the hospital. As I left the hospital and entered our van, I thanked God our home was only six miles away. I could feel my body start to shake. I tried to calm down, but I could not. I cried all the way home. When I arrived home, there was a message on our answering machine from my boys; it was Mother's Day. I cried even more. This had been a horrible day, and it was not over yet. That evening I cried out to God saying, "There is no way You would bring Rick and me all the way up here and then take him from me." I hung onto God with everything I had!

It was during Rick's hospital stay, I realized I could not use the bathroom in his hospital room or any bathroom on the third floor. I had to take the elevator to the first floor and wheel through a maze of hallways to reach a wheelchair accessible bathroom. It was as if I did not have the right to pee! Not being able to use the bathroom stressed me even more.

After Rick came home, I wrote a letter to the CEO at the hospital about the bathroom situation. He wrote back and set up a meeting for me to meet with the construction engineer. At that meeting, I told him clearly, that every floor should have at least one wheelchair accessible bathroom for visitors to use. I also told him that in a hospital setting I could not understand why bathrooms in patients' rooms were not wheelchair accessible. What great people they were to work with. They promised me that every floor in the hospital would soon have accessible bathrooms. To see they cared and appreciated my input meant a lot to me. Over the years, I had learned to stand up for my rights and the rights of other disabled persons. I was no longer that sheepish woman who put on that happy face and said nothing. I had learned to fight with the best of them!

We finally found a church home under the leadership of Pastor David Parker called Central United Protestant Church. When we first drove into the parking lot, we noticed many wheelchair parking spaces and parking spaces marked for seniors only. We felt this church really cared about its people. When we went inside the church to see if I could use the bathrooms, none worked. Just when we were ready to leave, God sent me an angel. A custodian came by and asked if he could be of assistance. I told him the bathrooms would not work for me. He asked for my input. Within a short time, I could use all but one bathroom. We also joined a Life Group at church called Young at Heart. Every member welcomed us warmly and each has become an inspiration in our lives.

Once Rick was feeling better, he started fishing and hunting again. We traveled all over Washington State, Oregon, Idaho and even went back to Canada. We were also able to see David and his family more often. Because of our physical limitations, we had to set a limit of driving to a town that was no more than eight hours away. Then we could unload the van, stay for as long as we wanted, and explore. Even though it is hard to admit, we could not do what we used to do.

The following year, in April of 2008, Rick's father, a survivor of Pearl Harbor, died at the age of 96. We were sad, but knew he lived a long, full life. We were so thankful that family and friends had gathered with us one year previously to celebrate Dad's 95th birthday.

Four months later, Rick had back surgery for four compressed vertebrae. This would be our 50th surgery! We were not happy campers. I often told Rick, "I'm the gimp in this family and you're falling apart." We both had a good laugh; at least we still had a sense of humor. After surgery, Rick could not bend, lift, or twist for three months. We were so thankful we were living close to medical facilities. I could no longer drive because the torn rotator cuff in my right arm had gotten worse. Caring for Rick was getting harder too. Our church family and neighbors rallied around us like nothing we had ever seen before. After three months of being house bound, we were finally able to return to church.

Four days later, it was my turn again! While driving to our Young at Heart Life Group, I moved my left arm slightly, and excruciating pain shot through my arm. Rick took me directly to the emergency room. After doing an MRI, the surgeon said that my rotator cuff tore; it looked like shredded paper and was inoperable. I could not believe this had happened. Now it was up to God to make my shoulder well enough so I would be able to care for my husband, our home, and myself. I could not use my legs; now I had two torn shoulders. My life was changing even more now that I had to use an electric wheelchair full-time.

The following day I fell apart emotionally. "How am I going to manage with two torn shoulders?" I thought. I did not want to be a burden to my husband. I could not pray; Rick had to pray for both of us. Once Rick was through praying, I felt more peaceful. I knew that somehow, with God's help, I would get through this. Every day, Rick helped me in every way possible. He also took my arm and moved it up, down, and sideways to keep my shoulder from freezing. When my neighbor returned from vacation and heard what had happened, she came right over. After a short visit she said, "You have been through so much ever since I met you. I have never, ever, seen anybody with so much faith and deter-mination as you have!"

To be that kind of witness for my God made me feel good inside.

Two weeks later, Rick and I met with my shoulder surgeon. Once again, I was able to witness about the mighty power of God. Much to her surprise and delight, I had regained total use of my left shoulder. My doctor was shocked when I lifted both my arms up and over my head.

"See, God performed a miracle!" I said. "I have lost some strength in my shoulders, but I have total use of both my arms. I'm now able to take care of myself, wash, iron, cook, and clean again."

"God must have performed a miracle!" She said. "You are my only patient that can move both your arms up and over your head with two torn rotator cuffs. I have never witnessed this in all my years of practice."

"God knew I needed my arms. I feel so blessed."

Once again, with God's help I was victorious. St. Augustine said, "Flee unto God on the wings of faith." I thought to myself, "I am trying, God!"

33

A SPECIAL CHILD

"For in Him we live, and move, and have our being; as certain also of your own poets have said, For we are also his offspring." Acts 17:28. Many years ago, I came across a lesson called "Welcoming a Special Child." The devotion went like this, "Whosoever shall receive one of such children in My name, receiveth Me." Mark 9:37 – 'Although caring for a handicapped child poses many problems and can be very demanding, parents should welcome the little one into their home with thanksgiving. God richly rewards those who accept such a challenge with grace and devotion.'" [17] The following poem, "Heaven's Very Special Child," written by Edna Massimilla has great meaning to me too.

> A meeting was held quite far from earth;
> It's time again for another birth.
> Said the angels to the Lord above,
> "This special child will need much love.
> He may not run or laugh or play;
> His thoughts may seem quite far away.
> In many ways he won't adapt,
> And he'll be known as handicapped.
> So let's be careful where he's sent;
> We want his life to be content.
> Please, Lord, find the parents who
> Will do a special job for You.
> They will not realize right away

The leading role they're asked to play;
But with this child sent from above
Comes stronger faith and richer love.
And soon they'll know the privilege given
In caring for their gift from heaven;
Their precious charge, so meek and mild,
Is heaven's very special child." [18]

My parents not only welcomed me into their home, they made many sacrifices on my behalf. They always stood by me through every challenge I faced. God knew my parents were strong. God knew my parents would provide me with the necessary love and support I needed while growing up and in the years that followed. As I struggled to find out who I was and what God planned for my life, my parents were always there cheering me on. I knew beyond any doubt, that God provided me with the best parents in the world. I felt honored to call them Mother and Daddy. I knew they would always be there for me and they were.

God not only controls who our parents are, but He also selects our life partner. God has a special person all picked out for those of us who are disabled. I had to learn this lesson the hard way. When I married so young, and married multiple times, God was not a part of my life. When I messed up, God was patient and kept waiting for me to come back to Him. It would not be until years later that I realized God sent Rick to me. Rick would be with me, "for better or worse, for richer for poorer, in sickness and in health, to love and to cherish, until death do us part." In order to live with a handicapped person, with all of our daily challenges and mood swings, it takes a special person to be able to deal with all that. When I think of my husband, Rick, I think of that special person. When I think of all the things that Rick has had to endure, I wonder how he has been able to handle everything with such grace.

Rick and I just celebrated our 39th wedding anniversary. For 39 years, Rick has gone through my heartaches and my frustrations. He has shared my tears and my fears. He has shared my joy. He has been there through my many surgeries. That alone took a lot of patience on his part. Rick constantly reminds me that I have been there for him during his surgeries too. Without Rick, I would have never been able to see what I have seen in our travels. Facing challenges every day has become a way of life. Facing challenges outside my home has taught me patience. Facing challenges when we have traveled has taught me "where there is a will, there is a way." Throughout our married life, Rick has shown me that love never complains. I feel honored and lucky to have such a wonderful and devoted husband.

I have also learned many lessons being Rick's wife. Through Rick's unconditional love, he taught me to love myself more and quit beating myself up. For years, I would push my feelings aside. I would not ask for help. Rick said, "When we push aside our feelings, especially around others, we are indirectly hurting ourselves." What a true and profound statement that is. For literally years, I lived by the Scripture that says, in part, "I can do all things through Christ." In my mind, asking for help went against that Scripture. Oh, how wrong I was. Rick used to ask me why it was so hard for me to ask for help. I felt asking for help showed weakness; I did not want to appear weak to anyone. I was denying myself what I needed and denying Rick and others the opportunity to help me. As the years have passed and my disability has worsened, I have started asking for help more readily.

This past year, when Rick had back surgery, I had to ask for help. Neighbors and friends from church drove me back and forth to the hospital. They also would go grocery shopping whenever I needed them to. Our neighbors helped me get our home ready for Rick's return. Because Rick could not bend, lift, or twist they helped me install a bed cane to assist him getting in and out of bed. They also installed a toilet riser in one of our bathrooms. The more I learned to ask people for help, the more I could see the joy on their faces.

Every day Rick and I continue to thank God for our blessings. All four of our children are still happily married and doing well in their chosen professions. David and his wife continue to live in Washington State, as does David's stepson and his family. Neil and his wife moved to New Mexico last year; their children remain in Las Vegas. Rick's girls, their husbands and families are still residing in California. Out of our seven grandchildren and step-grandchildren, all are adults now, except for one; two are married and have families of their own. Miles separate us, but they are close in our hearts. We are hoping that as their work schedules lighten, they can come to see us more often. Even though it is hard to admit, it is getting harder for us to travel with our physical limitations. All 50 surgeries have finally taken a toll on both of us.

I am grateful for my twin brother, Neil. He had planned to stay at the University of Pittsburgh until he was 65, but decided to retire early. He and his wife are currently residing in Florida. Even though miles continue to separate us, I will always have a special place in my heart for my "Big Protector."

In Chapter 12 of II Corinthians, Paul writes about a thorn in the flesh. I have felt like Paul many times. It seemed over the years that whenever I tried my best, my best was not good enough. Many that did not understand my disability looked down on me. There were those that judged me, not knowing the full extent of what I went through. I thought that I felt the same way as Paul did in the Scripture, because the Scripture states, "And he said unto me, My grace is sufficient for thee; for my strength is made perfect in weakness. Most gladly, therefore, will I rather glory in my infirmities, that the power of Christ may rest upon me. Therefore, I take pleasure in infirmities, in reproaches, in necessities, in persecutions, in distresses for Christ's sake; for when I am weak, then am I strong." II Corinthians 12:9-10. I was not alone. Centuries ago, Paul felt just like I do today. When I am weak, I am strong because God is right there by my side.

From conception to the present day, God was and is always there. God took many years to mold me into what He wanted me to be. I am still a work in progress. God healed my many hurts. God taught me how to accept my life and make the most of it. God healed my sorrow when I felt rejected. God healed me when I lost family members. Every time I had to deal with my disability in an unexpected way and tears would fall from my eyes, I knew God was teaching me something new. God taught me to accept my shortcomings and not beat myself up. God taught me that it was okay for me not to be happy all the time. I learned to put less pressure on myself. By doing that, I had less chance of failing. "I waited patiently for the Lord, and he inclined unto me, and heard my cry. He brought me up also out of a horrible pit, out of the miry clay, and set my feet upon a rock, and established my goings." Psalm 40: 1-2.

I will continue to learn life's lessons until my time is up and I will be with my Lord and Savior, Jesus Christ in heaven. "Whom do I have to thank?" I ask. The answer is God. Simply said in Scripture it states, "Being confident of this very thing, that he who hath begun a good work in you will perform it until the day of Jesus Christ." Philippians 1:6. I can say without any doubt, the harder my challenges were, the closer I was to God.

God made this promise to every believer. It states, "And God shall wipe away all tears from their eyes; and there shall be no more death, neither sorrow, nor crying, neither shall there be any more pain, for the former things are passed away." Revelations 21:4. Oh, what a promise that is and I know it to be true because THROUGH IT ALL, HE WAS THERE. I am God's special child and I will some day be with my God forever in heaven. The Scripture says that Jesus will go and prepare a place. I, God's special child, will be face to face with my God. When I enter heaven's gate, I will leave this wheelchair behind and walk the streets of gold. Jesus Christ will put His arm around my shoulder and say, "Welcome home, my special child."

CONCLUSION

Thank you for taking this journey with me. I feel it is only fitting that I offer you the same opportunity that I was given years ago. Having a personal relationship with God the Father, God the Son, and God the Holy Spirit will prove to you daily the enabling power of God. I cannot imagine my life without His presence.

These guidelines are from the Four Spiritual Laws booklet that I gave my granddad mentioned in my book. The same booklet was in his hand when he passed away.

Campus Crusade for Christ International has distributed over 1.5 billion of these booklets. The process is very simple. It will only take you a minute of your time.

"Just as there are physical laws that govern the physical universe, so are there spiritual laws, which govern your relationship with God."

LAW 1
GOD **LOVES** YOU, AND OFFERS A WONDERFUL **PLAN** FOR YOUR LIFE.
God's Love
"God so loved the world, that He gave His one and only Son, that whoever believes in Him shall not perish, but have eternal life" (John 3:16, NIV).
God's Plan
[Christ speaking] "I came that they might have life, and might have it abundantly" [that it might be full and meaningful] (John 10:10).

"Why is it that most people are not experiencing that abundant life?"

Because...

LAW 2
MAN IS **SINFUL** AND **SEPARATED** FROM GOD. THEREFORE, HE CANNOT KNOW AND EXPERIENCE GOD'S LOVE AND PLAN FOR HIS LIFE.

Man Is Sinful
"All have sinned and fall short of the glory of God" (Romans 3:23).

"Man was created to have fellowship with God; but, because of his own stubborn self-will, he chose to go his own independent way and fellowship with God was broken This self-will, characterized by an attitude of active rebellion or passive indifference, is an evidence of what the Bible calls sin."

Man Is Separated
"The wages of sin is death" [spiritual separation from God] (Romans 6:23).

LAW 3
JESUS CHRIST IS GOD'S **ONLY** PROVISION FOR MAN'S SIN. THROUGH HIM, YOU CAN KNOW AND EXPERIENCE GOD'S LOVE AND PLAN FOR YOUR LIFE.

He Died In Our Place
"But God demonstrates His own love toward us, in that while we were yet sinners, Christ died for us" (Romans 5:8).

He Rose from the Dead
"Christ died for our sins ... He was buried ... He was raised on the third day, according to the Scriptures ... He appeared to Peter, then to the twelve.
After that He appeared to more than five hundred ..." (I Corinthians 15:3-6).

He is the Only Way to God
"Jesus said to him, 'I am the way, and the truth, and the life; no one comes to the Father, but through Me'" (John 14:6).

It is not enough just to know these three laws ...

Law 4
WE MUST INDIVIDUALLY **RECEIVE** JESUS CHRIST AS SAVIOR AND LORD; THEN WE CAN KNOW AND EXPERIENCE GOD'S LOVE AND PLAN FOR OUR LIVES.

We Must Receive Christ

"As many as received Him, to them He gave the right to become children of God, even to those who believe in His name" (John 1:12).

We Receive Christ Through Faith

"For by grace you have been saved through faith; and that not of yourselves, it is the gift of God; not as result of works that no one should boast" (Ephesians 2:8,9).

When We Receive Christ, We Experience a New Birth (Read John 3:1-8.)

We Receive Christ Through Personal Invitation

[Christ speaking] "Behold, I stand at the door and knock; if any one hears My voice and opens the door, I will come in to him" (Revelation 3:20).

Receiving Christ involves turning to God from self (repentance) and trusting Christ to come into our lives to forgive our sins and to make us the kind of people He wants us to be. Just to agree intellectually that Jesus Christ is the Son of God and that He died on the cross for our sins is not enough. Nor is it enough to have an emotional experience. We receive Jesus Christ by faith, as an act of the will.

The following explains how you can receive Christ:

You Can Receive Christ Right Now by Faith Through Prayer

(Prayer is talking with God)

God knows your heart and is not so concerned with your words as He is with the attitude of your heart. The following is a suggested prayer:

"Lord Jesus, I need You. Thank You for dying on the cross for my sins. I open the door of my life and receive You as my Savior and Lord. Thank You for forgiving my sins and giving me eternal life. Take control of the throne of my life. Make me the kind of person You want me to be."

Does this prayer express the desire of your heart?
If it does, I invite you to pray this prayer right now, and Christ will come into you life, as He promised." [19]

If you have prayed this prayer, I strongly urge you to surround yourself with other Christians. Find a church in your area and join in with others as you live your new life with Christ. You will be amazed at what He can do for you.

Blessings, Sharon Libby

END NOTES

CHAPTER 1 — A LIFE CHANGING EXPERIENCE

1. Summary from THE ILLUSTRATED COLUMBIA ENCYCLOPEDIA, Published and distributed by Rockwell House Publisher's Inc. by arrangement with Columbia University Press, NY and London. Edited by: Wm. Bridgewater and Seymour Kurtz, Library of Congress Catalog Card Number: 63-20205 – "Poliomyelitis" — 4948.

2. Victor Cohn, SISTER KENNY — THE WOMAN WHO CHALLENGED THE DOCTORS, © Copyright 1975. Printed in the USA @ Napco Graphics Arts, Inc. New Berlin, Wisconsin, 124-125. Used by permission.

3. Ibid., 125.

4. Ibid., 5.

5. Ibid., 42.

CHAPTER 4 — FINDING MY NICHE

6. Richard Carter, BREAKTHROUGH — THE SAGA OF JONAS SALK, © Copyright 1965. Simultaneously published in the U.S. and Canada by Trident Press. Distributed by Affiliated Publishers, a Division Pocket books, Inc., 1. Used by permission.

CHAPTER 27 — FACING LIFE'S CHALLENGES

7. Alfred Katz and Knute Martin, A HANDBOOK OF SERVICES FOR THE HANDICAPPED, © Copyright 1982. Greenwood Press, Westport, CN. A Division of Congressional Information Services, 155. Used by permission.

8. Ibid., 39.

CHAPTER 28 — COMING TO TERMS WITH LIFE

9. Joyce Landorf, "I've Been Thinking..." POWER FOR LIVING, Scripture Press Publications, © Copyright April 22, 1979. Power/Line Papers, Glen Ellyn, IL. Used by permission.

CHAPTER 29 — ACCEPTING GOD'S PLAN

10. Colleen Townsend Evans, A NEW JOY, © Copyright 1973. Fleming H. Revell Co., Old Tappan, NJ, 124. Used by permission.

11. Diane Lindquist, Staff Writer, "Polio: Disease thought dead has two lives." THE SAN DIEGO UNION, Printed: Monday, January 16, 1984. Used by permission.

CHAPTER 30 — AN ATTITUDE ADJUSTMENT

12. Edith Marks and Adele Lewis, JOB HUNTING FOR THE DISABLED, Reprinted with permission of Barron's Educational Series, Inc. © Copyright 1983, vii.

13. Ibid., vii.

14. Dr. John Maxwell, YOUR ATTITUDE: KEY TO SUCCESS, © Copyright 1984. Here's Life Publishers, San Bernardino, CA, 55. Used with permission.

15. Ibid., 70.

16. Ibid., 71.

CHAPTER 33 — A SPECIAL CHILD

17. Henry G. Bosch, "Welcoming a Special Child," OUR DAILY BREAD, © Copyright 1985 by Radio Bible Class, Grand Rapids, MI. Used by permission.

18. Edna Massimilla, "Heaven's Very Special Child," POEMS FOR THE HANDICAPPED, © Copyright 1956. Printed with permission, Hatboro, PA 19040.

CONCLUSION

19. From Have You Heard of the Four Spiritual Laws? Written by Bill Bright © Copyright 1965-2007 Campus Crusade for Christ, Inc. and Bright Media Foundation, Inc. All rights reserved. Used by permission. For more information and complete text, please visit: http://www.ccci.org. and/or http://www.campuscrusade.com/four_laws_online.htm.

APPENDIX: SCRIPTURE REFERENCES

CHAPTER 2 — ANOTHER STEP FURTHER

I Corinthians 13:13 — "And now abideth faith, hope, love, these three; but the greatest of these is love."

CHAPTER 4 — FINDING MY NICHE

Hebrews 11:1 — "Now faith is the substance of things hoped for, the evidence of things not seen."

John 3:16 — "For God so loved the world, that He gave His only begotten Son, that whosoever believeth in Him should not perish, but have everlasting life."

Proverbs 22:6 — "Train up a child in the way he should go and, when he is old he will not depart from it."

Psalms 23:4 — "Yea, though I walk through the valley of the shadow of death, I will fear no evil; For Thou art with me; Thy rod and Thy staff they comfort me."

Romans 8:28 — "And we know that all things work together for good to them that love God, to them who are the called according to His purpose."

CHAPTER 7 — SINKING DEEPER

Matthew 11:28-30 — "Come unto me, all ye that labor and are heavy laden, and I will give you rest. Take my yoke upon you, and learn of me; for I am meek and lowly in heart, and ye shall find rest unto your souls. For my yoke is easy, and my burden is light."

CHAPTER 8 — A CHILD IS BORN

Mark 9:23 — "Jesus said unto him, If thou canst believe, all things are possible to him that believeth."

Matthew 19:26 — "But Jesus beheld them, and said unto them, With men this is impossible, but with God all things are possible."

CHAPTER 10 — PEACE AT LAST

Psalms 40:13-14 — "Be pleased, O Lord, to deliver me; O Lord, make haste to help me. Let them be ashamed and confounded together who seek after my soul to destroy it; let them be driven backward and be put to shame who wish me evil."

John 14:27 — "...Let not your heart be troubled, neither let it be afraid."

John 14:27 — "Peace I leave with you, my peace I give unto you; not as the world giveth, give I unto you. Let not your heart be troubled, neither let it be afraid."

CHAPTER 12 — SMOOTH SAILING FOR A WHILE

Psalms 37:4 — "Delight thyself also in the Lord, and he shall give thee the desires of thine heart."

CHAPTER 13 — ADJUSTMENTS GALORE

Psalms 55:22 — "Cast thy burden upon the Lord, and He shall sustain thee; he shall never suffer the righteous to be moved."

CHAPTER 18 — DOWNWARD SPIRAL

I Peter 5:7 — "Casting all your care upon him; for he careth for you."

Psalms 27:7 — "Hear, O Lord, when I cry with my voice; have mercy also upon me, and answer me."

Psalms 30:10 — "Hear, O Lord, and have mercy upon me; Lord, be thou my helper."

CHAPTER 19 — FRIENDS FOREVER

Psalms 34:4 — "I sought the Lord, and He heard me, and delivered me from all my fears."

Psalms 27:1 — "The Lord is my light and my salvation; whom shall I fear? The Lord is the strength of my life; of whom shall I be afraid?"

CHAPTER 20 — ON THE ROAD TO RECOVERY

Philippians 4:4 — "Rejoice in the Lord always; and again I say, Rejoice."

Philippians 4:6-7 — "Be anxious for nothing, but in everything, by prayer and supplication with thanksgiving, for your requests be made known unto God. And the peace of God, which passeth all understanding, shall keep your hearts and minds through Christ Jesus."

CHAPTER 22 — THINGS ARE COMING TOGETHER

II Corinthians 4:8-9 — "We are troubled on every side, yet not distressed; we are perplexed, but not in despair; Persecuted, but not forsaken; cast down, but not destroyed;"

Philippians 3:13-14 — "Brethren, I count not myself to have apprehended; but this one thing I do, forgetting those things which are behind, and reaching forth unto those things which are before, I press toward the mark for the prize of the high calling of God in Christ Jesus."

CHAPTER 23 — SOME NEW CHALLENGES TO FACE

I Thessalonians 5:16-18 — "Rejoice evermore. Pray without ceasing. In everything give thanks; for this is the will of God in Christ Jesus concerning you."

Philippians 4:8 — "Finally, brethren, whatever things are true, whatever things are honest, whatever things are just, whatever things are pure, whatever things are lovely, whatever things are of good report; if there be any virtue, and if there be any praise, think on these things."

Philippians 4:13 — "I can do all things through Christ, who strenghtheneth me."

CHAPTER 24 — MANY CHANGES ON THE HORIZON

John 14:27 — "Peace I leave with you, my peace I give unto you; not as the world giveth, give I unto you. Let not your heart be troubled neither let it be afraid."

Matthew 6:34 — "Be, therefore, not anxious about tomorrow; for tomorrow will be anxious for the things of itself. Sufficient unto the day is its own evil."

Matthew 11:28 — "Come unto me, all ye that labor and are heavy laden, and I will give you rest."

Matthew 7:12 — "Therefore, all things whatever ye would that men should do to you, do ye even so to them; for this is the law and the prophets."

CHAPTER 26 — TESTING MY ENDURANCE

Hebrews 13:5-6 — "Let your manner of life be without covetousness, and be content with such things as ye have; for he hath said, I will never leave thee, nor forsake thee. So that we may boldly say, The Lord is my helper, and I will not fear what man shall do unto me."

I Peter 5:6-9 — "Humble yourselves, therefore, under the mighty hand of God, that he may exalt you in due time, Casting all your care upon him; for he careth for you. Be sober, be vigilant, because your adversary, the devil, like a roaring lion walketh about, seeking whom he may devour; Whom resist steadfast in the faith, knowing that the same afflictions are accomplished in your brethren that are in the world."

Galatians 6:2 — "Bear ye one another's burdens, and so fulfill the law of Christ."

Psalms 55:22 — "Cast thy burden upon the Lord, and he shall sustain thee; he shall never suffer the righteous to be moved."

Proverbs 3:5-6 — "Trust in the Lord with all thine heart, and lean not unto thine own understanding. In all thy ways acknowledge him, and he shall direct thy path."

II Corinthians 12:9 — "And he said unto me, My grace is sufficient for thee; for my strength is made perfect in weakness. Most gladly, therefore, will I rather glory in my infirmities, that the power of Christ may rest upon me."

Luke 18:27 — "And he said, The things which are impossible with men are possible with God."

Galatians 5:5 — "For we through the Spirit wait for the hope of righteousness by faith."

CHAPTER 27 — FACING LIFE'S CHALLENGES

II Timothy 1:7 — "For God hath not given us the spirit of fear, but of power, and of love, and of a sound mind."

Matthew 22:37-38 — "Jesus said unto him, Thou shalt love the Lord, thy God, with all thy heart, and with all thy soul, and with all thy mind. This is the first and great commandment."

Romans 8:6 — "For to be carnally minded is death, but to be spiritually minded is life and peace."

Colossians 3:2 — "Set your affection on things above, not on things on the earth."

CHAPTER 29 — ACCEPTING GOD'S PLAN

Proverbs 22:6 — "Train up a child in the way he should go and, when he is old, he will not depart from it."

Psalms 7:1 — "O Lord my God, in thee do I put my trust..."

Psalms 107:13 — "Then they cried unto the Lord in their trouble, and he saved them out of their distresses."

Roman 5:3-5 — "And not only so, but we glory in tribulations also, knowing that tribulation worketh patience; And patience, experience; and experience, hope; and hope maketh not ashamed because the love of God is shed abroad in our hearts by the Holy Spirit who is given unto us."

CHAPTER 30 — AN ATTITUDE ADJUSTMENT

Isaiah 40:30-31 — "Even the youths shall faint and be weary, and the young men shall utterly fall, But they that wait upon the Lord shall renew their strength; they shall mount up with wings like eagles; they shall run, and not be weary; and they shall walk, and not faint."

Matthew 25:21 — "His lord said unto him, Well done, thou good and faithful servant; thou hast been faithful over a few things, I will make thee ruler over many things. Enter thou into the joy of thy lord."

Psalms 51:10 — "Create in me a clean heart, O God, and renew a right spirit within me."

CHAPTER 31 — THE EXPECTED HAPPENS

Jeremiah 29:11 — "For I know the thoughts that I think toward you, saith the Lord, thoughts of peace, and not of evil, to give you an expected end."

CHAPTER 33 — A SPECIAL CHILD

Acts 17:28 — "For in Him we live, and move, and have our being; as certain also of your own poets have said, For we are also his offspring."

Mark 9:37 — "Whosoever shall receive one of such children in my name, receiveth me..."

II Corinthians 12:9-10 — "And he said unto me, My grace is sufficient for thee; for my strength is made perfect in weakness. Most gladly, therefore, will I rather glory in my infirmities, that the power of Christ may rest upon me. Therefore, I take pleasure in infirmities, in reproaches, in necessities, in persecutions, in distresses for Christ's sake; for when I am weak, then am I strong."

Psalm 40:1-2 — "I waited patiently for the Lord, and he inclined unto me, and heard my cry. He brought me up also out of an horrible pit, out of the miry clay, and set my feet upon a rock, and established my goings."

Philippians 1:6 — "Being confident of this very thing, that he who hath begun a good work in you will perform it until the day of Jesus Christ."

Revelations 21:4 — "And God shall wipe away all tears from their eyes; and there shall be no more death, neither sorrow, nor crying, neither shall there be any more pain, for the former things are passed away."

LaVergne, TN USA
11 December 2009
166747LV00003B/3/P